THE **COLLABORATIVE WORK SYSTEMS** SERIES

Building collaborative capacity in the world of work

BEYOND TEAMS

"The ability to innovate. . . comes from a skill that is underdeveloped in most companies: collaboration.

Knowing how to collaborate helps a company to create and transfer knowledge. Knowledge creation and utilization, in turn, lead to innovation.

Companies that understand this long-linked process, and make the appropriate investments needed to establish and maintain it, will be the big winners in the 21st Century global economy."

Raymond Miles, Charles Snow, and Grant Miles

THE **COLLABORATIVE WORK SYSTEMS** SERIES

CENTER FOR THE STUDY OF WORK TEAMS

BEYOND TEAMS

BUILDING THE COLLABORATIVE ORGANIZATION

Michael M. Beyerlein • Sue Freedman

Craig McGee • Linda Moran

JOSSEY-BASS/PFEIFFER
A Wiley Imprint
www.pfeiffer.com

Published by Jossey-Bass/Pfeiffer
A Wiley Imprint
989 Market Street, San Francisco, CA 94103-1741   www.pfeiffer.com

We at Jossey-Bass strive to use the most environmentally sensitive paper stocks available to us. Our publications are printed on acid-free recycled stock whenever possible, and our paper always meets or exceeds minimum GPO and EPA requirements.

Jossey-Bass also publishes its books in a variety of electronic formats. Some content that appears in print may not be available in electronic books.

ISBN: 0-7879-6373-9

Library of Congress Cataloging-in-Publication Data
Beyerlein, Michael M.
Beyond teams: building the collaborative organization / Michael M.
Beyerlein, Sue Freedman, Craig McGee, Linda Moran.
    p. cm.—(The collaborative work systems series)
Includes bibliographical references and index.
  ISBN 0-7879-6373-9 (alk. paper)
  1. Business networks. 2. Strategic alliances (Business) 3. Teams in
the workplace. 4. Cooperativeness. 5. Group decision making. I.
Freedman, Sue. II. McGee, Craig. III. Title. IV. Series.
  HD69.S8 B49 2002
  658.4'02—dc21
2002007171

Acquiring Editor: Josh Blatter
Director of Development: Kathleen Dolan Davies
Developmental Editor: Samya Sattar
Editor: Rebecca Taff

Senior Production Editor: Dawn Kilgore
Manufacturing Supervisor: Becky Carreño
Interior and Cover Design: Bruce Lundquist

Printing   10 9 8 7 6 5 4 3 2 1

DEDICATION

I dedicate this work to my Mother, to my wife, Sue, and to my
daughter, Marisa, the three most important influences in my life.
Michael Beyerlein

In memory of my father, Doug Powers, who collaborated
with everyone he encountered, and enjoyed it immensely.
Sue Freedman

I dedicate this work to all the leaders, practitioners, and change agents
who are trying to create more collaborative organizations. You are the
ones who are making the difference and will continue to do so.
Craig McGee

To my parents, who were the first ones to
teach me that collaboration was an art.
Linda Moran

CONTENTS

Preface for the Collaborative Work Systems Series xiii

Acknowledgments xvii

Preface xix

Prologue: A Scenario 1

PART 1 **PRINCIPLES AND PERSPECTIVES**

Chapter 1 Building the Collaborative Organization 11

Collaborative Work Systems as a Solution 13

Collaborative Competencies 14

Collaborative Capacity 15

The Collaborative Organization 17

Collaborative Culture 20

Collaborative Capital 21

Collaboration and Teams 23

The Payoff from the Collaborative Organization 25

Conclusion 30

Chapter 2   The Ten Principles of Collaborative Organizations 33

1. Focus Collaboration on Achieving Business Results 34
2. Align Organizational Support Systems to Promote Ownership 36
3. Articulate and Enforce "a Few Strict Rules" 39
4. Exploit the Rhythm of Convergence and Divergence 40
5. Manage Complex Tradeoffs on a Timely Basis 42
6. Create Higher Standards for Discussions, Dialogue, and Information Sharing 43
7. Foster Personal Accountability 45
8. Align Authority, Information, and Decision Making 46
9. Treat Collaboration as a Disciplined Process 48
10. Design and Promote Flexible Organizations 50

PART 2   APPLYING THE PRINCIPLES

Chapter 3   Collaboration in Manufacturing Settings 59

Definition of Manufacturing 60

Trends Affecting How We Work 61

Common Ways of Organizing 64

Challenges with Respect to Collaboration 65

When to Collaborate 67

How the Guiding Principles Apply 67

Implications for Executives 90

Chapter 4   Collaboration in New Product Development Settings 95

Definition of New Product Development 95

Historical Context 96

Trends Affecting New Product Development 97

Common Ways of Organizing 98

Challenges with Respect to Collaboration 99

When to Collaborate 100

How the Guiding Principles Apply 101

Implications for Executives 120

Chapter 5 Collaboration in Service Settings 127

Definition of Collaboration in a Service Setting 127

Historical Context 128

Common Ways of Organizing 131

Challenges with Respect to Collaboration 132

How the Guiding Principles Apply 133

Implications for Executives 150

Chapter 6 Collaboration in Virtual Settings 153

Historical Context 154

Definition of Virtual Collaborative Organizations 155

Trends Affecting Virtual Collaborative Organizations 158

Common Ways of Organizing 160

Challenges with Respect to Collaboration 162

When to Collaborate 164

How the Guiding Principles Apply 166

Implications for Executives 188

PART 3 STRATEGIES FOR IMPLEMENTATION

Chapter 7 Moving Forward 195

Collaboration Diagnostic Tool: How to Move Forward 197

Principle 1. Focus Collaboration on Achieving Business Results 211

Principle 2. Align Organizational Support Systems to Promote Ownership 212

Principle 3. Articulate and Enforce "a Few Strict Rules" 214

Principle 4. Exploit the Rhythm of Convergence and Divergence 214

Principle 5. Manage Complex Tradeoffs on a Timely Basis 215

Principle 6. Create Higher Standards for Discussions, Dialogue, and Information Sharing 216

Principle 7. Foster Personal Accountability 216

Principle 8. Align Authority, Information, and Decision Making 217

Principle 9. Treat Collaboration as a Disciplined Process 218

Principle 10. Design and Promote Flexible Organizations 218

Conclusion 223

References 225

About the Series Editors 231

About the Authors 235

Index 239

PREFACE FOR THE COLLABORATIVE WORK SYSTEMS SERIES

IN LAUNCHING THIS SERIES, it is the editors' intention to create an ongoing, dynamic forum for sharing cutting-edge ideas and practices among researchers and those practitioners involved on a day-to-day basis with organizations that depend on collaborative work systems (CWS) for their success.

Proposed publications in the CWS series include books devoted to specific topics, workbooks to guide planning and competency development, fieldbooks that capture lessons learned in organizations experimenting with collaborative work systems, software for facilitating learning, training materials, and assessment instruments. The goal of the series is to produce four new products per year that will build a foundation for a perspective on collaboration as an essential means of achieving high levels of performance in and across organizations. Our vision for the series is to provide a means for leveraging collaborative work practices around the world in for-profit, government, and not-for-profit entities.

Collaborative work systems are those in which conscious efforts have been made to create strategies, policies, and structures as well as to institutionalize values, behaviors, and practices that promote cooperation among different parties in the organization in order to achieve desired business outcomes. While many organizations vocalize support for teamwork and collaboration, collaborative work systems are distinguished by intentional efforts to embed the organization with work processes and cultural mechanisms that enable and reinforce collaboration. New forms of organization continue to emerge with CWS as an essential facet. Team-based organizations and self-managing organizations represent types of collaborative systems. The computer revolution has made possible network, cellular, and spherical forms of organizing, which represent more transorganizational forms of collaboration.

Why the urgency? The challenges organizations face seem to be escalating rapidly. The number of global issues that impact an organization proliferate, including the terrorist threat, continued deforestation of ancient lands by debtor nations, wars, famine, disease, the accelerating splitting of nations' consciousness into the haves and the have-nots around the globe, which fuels hatreds—all aspects of interrelated political, social, economic, environmental challenges that will ultimately reduce quality of life on a worldwide scale if not addressed. These are the systemic, wicked problems that depend on many minds lodged in a common value set committed to improving human welfare in all settings. The business community must work with city, county, and state governments, with nation states, and with transnational organizations, such as the United Nations and the World Bank, to bring enough intellectual and financial capital to bear on the problems to do something about them—demanding collaborative initiatives at all levels.

Individuals working well together—this seems like a relatively simple proposition. Yet barriers abound in organizations that tend to inhibit collaboration at every turn. Social barriers are erected for a variety of reasons, including turf wars and mindsets that lead to hoarding of specialized knowledge rather than sharing. Fear of loss seems to be amplified during economic downturns as operating budgets are trimmed, fueling a multiplicity of negative personal scenarios, including loss of jobs, promotional opportunities, titles, and perks, which in turn can threaten self-esteem and professional identity. Barriers to establishing effective collaborative work systems can also reflect lack of cross-training, cultural norms and reward systems that reinforce individual performance, organizational political realities that reinforce competition for scarce resources among units, and differing technical languages that make communication challenging. However, despite these difficulties, some companies appear to overcome the significant barriers and benefit from the positive consequences of effective collaboration.

People in and around organizations have been experimenting with and learning about designing effective work processes for millennia. Researchers and practitioners have been capturing the lessons learned since the early part of the 20th Century. That process continues as we embark on the 21st Century. There will be much to document as changes in global business practices and new generation technologies enable more effective ways of organizing, operating, competing, innovating, and collaborating. Technical developments during the next quarter century will create unheralded challenges and opportunities in an increasingly interdependent world.

The move from muscle-based work to knowledge-based work has been so profound that some writers have called it the age of the knowledge economy. It demands new levels of collaborative expertise and a shift in focus to intangible forms of capital.

Knowledge grows through the development of organizational routines. Knowledge includes knowing what, but also knowing how and why. Each employee carries a somewhat different library of knowledge and a unique perspective on how to apply it—termed intellectual capital. The network of interaction among knowledge workers creates a rich environment where ideas can grow and blossom in stair-step fashion—termed social capital—and where there is widespread competency around teamwork at all levels of the organization in various forms—termed collaborative capital. This form of capital provides the foundation for leveraging what the other forms contribute, but it demands radically different ways of organizing work and involving employees in its design and practice.

In summary, collaborative work systems provide one of the key competency areas that organizations can focus on for building vitality and excellence, including competitive and collaborative advantage. On a daily basis, people come together to make decisions, solve problems, invent new products and services, build key relationships, and plan futures. The effectiveness of those gatherings and the effectiveness of the systems that emerge from them will depend greatly on the collaborative capacity that has been built in their organizations.

A high level of collaborative capacity will enable more effective work at the local and daily levels and at the global and long-term levels. We can solve our immediate problems more effectively, and we can cooperate more effectively to take on the emerging global issues that threaten us in the 21st Century when we have the skills, values, and processes for effective collaboration. This series of publications is intended as a catalyst in building that collaborative capacity at both local and global levels.

Michael M. Beyerlein, Ph.D.
Susan T. Beyerlein, Ph.D.
Center for the Study of Work Teams
University of North Texas

James Barker, Ph.D.
United States Air Force Academy

ACKNOWLEDGMENTS

THE CRAFTING OF THIS WORK relied on input from many people over many years. Each of the authors had mentors and colleagues and manifold learning opportunities that led to the effort to create this book. We can only thank them in general from this forum.

Direct contributions to the book came from friends, colleagues, and staff members who discussed, read, critiqued, and helped prepare parts of the manuscript. We would like to single out several of those people for special thanks.

Nancy Gorman from the Center for the Study of Work Teams contributed in myriad ways in manuscript preparation. She helped the authors link up across time zones, kept careful track of developments, proofread chapters, formatted chapters, and assembled the whole manuscript from the pieces the writing team created. The process and the quality of the book both benefited from Nancy's efforts.

Three reviewers, Kay Quam, Fran Rees, and Lorraine Ukens, provided very useful guidance in refining the presentation of the ideas in the book. In addition, Hugh Wilson and Jill Nemiro provided feedback on specific chapters. Our editors at Jossey-Bass/Pfeiffer made the project into a product. Josh Blatter conceived the idea for the series on Collaborative Work Systems for which this book is the flagship. Kathleen Davies and Samya Sattar provided guidance for both our process and our design.

Although our virtual team of four authors spent an intense twenty months preparing the content, the quality of presentation of the ideas depends heavily on the people mentioned above. We appreciate their support.

"HOW DO WE DEVELOP ORGANIZATIONS capable of thriving in a world of rapid, unpredictable change?" "How do we apply what we've learned about the magic and the limitations of teams and team-based organizations to today's increasingly dynamic environments?" These two questions were the basis for undertaking this book. As it evolved, we added a third question: "How do we create organizations that support collaboration in the multiple, varied forms, forums, and time frames that exist today?" This book is our answer to these three questions.

During our journey, we moved from thinking about effective teams and the systems that supported them to thinking about the context and culture required for "collaborative capacity." We searched for new ways to think about teaming that would address the complexity and unpredictability of today's work life and still enable people to reach the goals that successful teaming or successful collaboration affords. Our conclusion is that many, although clearly not all, of the behaviors, values, and discipline that once characterized effective teams have to be translated and embedded at the organizational level. In addition, we need shared principles and practices to create organizations capable of forming and re-forming their members and their external partners into a shifting collage of people engaged in productive collaborative activity. We call these organizations *collaborative* organizations.

This book was written for the many people within organizations who need to work collaboratively:

- For *executives* who want to understand how collaborative organizations can increase the quality and speed of collaborative decision making in their organizations;

- For the *supervisors and managers* who were told, "Get those people to collaborate" and found it doesn't happen just because it is mandated;

- For *human resource, learning and development, and organizational effectiveness practitioners* who want a guide to the practices that are essential for moving collaboration from pockets of the organization to broader organizational applications; and

- For *people* working in collaborative settings seeking to understand why sometimes it works, but other times it is too hard or the results too poor to justify the time to collaborate.

This book is divided into three parts. The Prologue profiles a case that represents a wide range of collaborative forums. Part 1, Principles and Perspectives, includes the first two chapters. Chapter 1 introduces concepts essential for a pyramid of collaborative excellence and articulates the benefits for organizations that build that excellence. Chapter 2 identifies and explains ten principles that are the foundational constructs of collaborative organizations. These principles represent a way of shaping the culture and context of the organization to foster efficient and effective collaboration action. All readers should read Part 1.

Part 2, Applying the Principles, presents a series of four chapters that explain how the principles apply in four different business settings: manufacturing, new product development, service, and virtual. Readers may read only the chapters that interest them and should certainly start with the chapter that interests them the most.

Part 3, Strategies for Implementation, provides strategies for assessing the collaborative capacity of an organization as well as specific suggestions for transforming an organization into a collaborative organization.

It is our hope that this book generates some real excitement about teaming and collaboration and their potential to provide competitive advantage in today's organizations. While most of these organizations use teams and collaboration extensively, the strategies typically used to manage and support them tend to reduce and often even eliminate the potential synergy they provide. This book is a search for the environments that encourage and support the exciting, rewarding, breakthrough synergy of successful collaborative efforts. We hope you will join us in that search.

Michael Beyerlein
Sue Freedman
Craig McGee
Linda Moran

W E BEGIN THIS BOOK with a brief scenario that most readers will recognize. Collaborative practices occur in many parts of the organization on a daily basis with varying degrees of success. Look for examples and for opportunities to work better together in the following vignette.

CURRENT REALITY: A SCENARIO

Monday 7:47 a.m. in Fenwick Inc.'s Nanotechnology Division Headquarters' Conference Room

Fred Penton, president of the Nanotechnology Division, smiles as he steps into the conference room. He is the first to arrive and might have five minutes of quiet before the others come in. He looks at the corporation's new logo hanging on the wall: a triangle of shifting rainbow colors with the three words "NANO," "BIO," and "CYBER." Combining nanotechnology, biotechnology, and cybertechnology had been a huge gamble, but the payoffs were starting to come—first with pairing two of the technologies together, and now from combining all three technologies in revolutionary ways.

The innovation of combining the three technologies was a bold move and created a temporary breathing space for Nanotech. The products had to roll out fast and be marketed effectively if market share was to be protected. Competitors were forming, such as the new partnership between Hewlett-Packard, Pfizer, and Nanomachine, Inc., that was announced in this morning's *Wall Street Journal*. Others would follow shortly.

"Good morning, Fred," Ben Calder calls. Ben is vice president for manufacturing at Nanotech. He prides himself on never being late for meetings and feels slightly irritated with Fred for arriving first. That feeling is quickly overwhelmed by the resurgence of frustration that he felt all weekend. The weekend had been difficult, fraught with equipment breakdowns and other production disruptions.

Over the next twenty minutes, the others arrive—Jean McKenna, vice president of sales; Dat Nguyen, chief financial officer; Bonnie Jenkins, human resources director; Pat Banthum, director of engineering; and Andy Fenwick, the general manager.

"Good morning, Ben. I hope you had a decent weekend for once," Andy commented. He had become concerned about the recent production difficulties with the new products. "No," said Ben as he pulled out the chair opposite Fred and sat down heavily. "The past couple of months I have had to come in for at least half a day every Saturday and Sunday to help Winston Settles, my shift manager, deal with production problems. I don't feel that he can handle some of the issues, and we are behind on shipping the new magnetophase units again. You know, I selected Winston myself and groomed him for the position when I thought I might move up, but maybe I made a mistake. He just doesn't seem to be acting accountably, and I'm having to get more and more involved in daily decisions again."

"Well, you know, Ben," said Andy, "the more you stay involved, the more difficult it is for Winston to find his own style. Even though Winston might do things differently, what you need to focus on is setting standards and goals and coaching him to achieve those goals.

It's a matter of providing support without solving the problems for him. I've found that this fosters personal accountability. That's what I do with each of you. I try not to become too involved in the details but hold you accountable for the results. Let's talk about it later."

8:15 a.m.

The meeting had been under way about fifteen minutes. The leaders of the division met every Monday morning from 8:00 to 12:00 A.M. Today, the primary agenda items were energy—where to find a dependable backup supply—a supplier contract, and a copy of HP's new version of the nano-bio diagnostic computer, which was a major competitor with Nanotechnology's own instrument.

After drifting off in thought about a test plan for a new product, Fred was brought back to the meeting when Ben raised his voice a few decibels. "I need clean, reliable power now. Brownouts don't just slow us down; they completely disrupt the production process. I can't wait for Pat to develop that fuel cell system. I need the backup power today. I think we all understand that this issue has both short-term and long-term components and involves some complex trade-offs. Why do we have trouble working together to come up with a solution that handles the short-term and the long-term together? Anybody? We all seem narrowly focused on our particular areas of responsibility." He looked around the room . . . no response.

Finally, Pat spoke up: "You know, Ben, I think you've got a point. We do tend to focus on our own departments. I think each of us tries to look out for the division overall, but its hard to keep that broad focus. We try to collaborate on most decisions, but there's always the tension between departments."

Fred nodded. Being fairly new at Fenwick, he had noticed the fragmentation among the different departments. The division was functionally organized, and the traditional business processes had created a silo mentality within the departments. He spoke up: "I think we all acknowledge that, but we haven't taken the time to sit down and discuss how we reach decisions and how to create a better dialogue around the really tough choices. But for the power supply issue, we'd better figure out a way to address it right now. Ben's right. Without a reliable production process, we'll lose the advantage we have with being first to market. Our customers will tolerate only so many delays."

Andy interrupted: "I think one approach involves partnering with FuelCell. They can provide us with the power we need, when we need it. Another option is to purchase our own backup generators."

"Wait a minute, Andy," Dat interrupted. "I follow energy companies on the market and thought that FuelCell only sold to utility companies. How are we going to buy anything from them?"

Fred jumped in again: "Listen, everybody. This issue affects us all—some of us now, but all of us later. For example, Andy's people will need to be involved in fitting the generators to our existing power grid. Dat will have to get his people to forecast costs and savings and possible profits from partnering with FuelCell. And so on. We could wander all over the place on this decision. I want to set up a process so we can work quickly and cover the information and options thoroughly. I'd like to start a task group so they can come back to the whole group with a recommendation. Does that make sense to you?" Nods from around the table encouraged Fred to go on.

"Okay, this is a little more complex than it seems. One of the key issues is that we think we can use our nanotechnology to help Fuel-Cell make smarter membranes for separating hydrogen from other gases and hence increase the cell's efficiency. We have to explore how our R&D people work with them to commercialize that technology. That means R&D, legal, and finance are involved first. Later, sales and marketing and manufacturing are involved. That's nearly everybody," emphasized Fred.

Ben spoke up: "I agree with the direction you're taking, Fred, but that's a lot of people. And historically, when we pull a task group together, we often get back something we don't agree with."

Fred nodded and asked: "Well, how should we deal with that?"

Dat spoke up: "You know when we've done that in the past, we haven't always been clear on our expectations. I think each of us has in mind what the answer is, and we expect the task group to come back with something that supports that. Some of my people on the task groups complain that they thought they had more decision-making authority than they actually did. And you know, part of that came from the fact that the group in this room had more information and we discussed how it affected different areas. So we understood some of the ramifications better, but didn't share that with the task groups. I think we need to do a better job of orienting task groups with everything we know—specially around the urgency of the issue, what we think our product/manufacturing strategy is, and so forth. Also, I think we need to build in more time for them to check in with us and bring us up-to-date. After all, we're all learning all the time and it's too easy to get off in different directions on something like this."

Andy stood up and walked around behind his chair, reflecting on the conversation. "You know," he began, "we haven't done a very good job of setting expectations in the past. And another point: we've always just assumed that the task group will come together and do their work. But I think we need to provide better structure and more discipline to the process. We just assume that people inherently know how to collaborate. What we should do, I think, if you all agree, is to establish a process by which this group collaborates. We can set up processes for us to clearly provide guidance, share information, test assumptions, and so on. And one thing is especially important: we need to become more disciplined about who is involved at what phase of the process. Collaboration is nice, but if we aren't disciplined around it, we'll have the wrong people involved at the wrong time, and it would become counterproductive."

Ben had been musing about the conversation. He now spoke up: "You know, I think you're right. Creating a task group is probably the right approach. And I'm sure they'll be working with us and other people informally. It's a complex problem; a number of people need to be involved." He paused and then continued: "I have just one other question: how are we involved with FuelCell? We certainly don't want to be sharing our technology with them. They might decide to use it for their own benefit."

Fred spoke up: "Ben, we have to think about our relationship with FuelCell a little differently. We have to think about them as a partner, not someone to fear. You're right that we will need to think through the legal arrangements and what information we share, but I think we need to approach this from the standpoint of a relationship of trust. We can learn a lot from them. And another point in favor of this collaboration is that no one else has our technology. It has a lot of potential for them, so they won't want to jeopardize the relationship. We don't know what our final relationship with them will be. It may be a joint venture, it may be co-marketing, it may be a virtual corporation, or it may just be an ongoing informal technology exchange. Regardless, it will be some sort of collaborative relationship, so we might as well set the groundwork now."

Fred continued: "You know, Ben, in R&D we have a lot of collaborations—with universities, contract research groups, and so on. Those have really panned out for us. And each of those is different. Some of the collaborations are just through virtual participation on electronic networks and listservs, where different researchers share information and pursue professional interests. Others have been virtual teams that we created around a particular technology."

Ben acquiesced:, "Okay, but let's make sure we cover ourselves on the legal front." Andy assured him that they would.

"Okay then," Fred said, "I'll take responsibility for pulling the task group together and getting them started. I'll come to each of you asking for your suggestions on who you want to participate and the process for them to follow. I'll work both with the team as a whole and with each of you individually to develop that process."

The group all nodded and Andy moved on to the next agenda topic.

The vignette represents a scenario many managers and leaders face daily in their organizations. These types of conversations take place frequently. They represent the types of struggles leaders face every day. The world is complex, changing rapidly in unknowable ways. The complexity in organizations today comes from increasingly complex technology, rapidly changing customer requirements, and more competition, both in sheer numbers of competitors and in their sophistication. While the scenario may not be exactly the one that you as a leader are involved in, the authors trust that you can recognize similarities with situations you are faced with.

The vignette illustrates the many facets of collaboration. Some collaboration is between individuals, like Winston and his manager, Ben. Other collaboration is among a group of leaders. Some projects require collaboration across functional areas. Other collaboration crosses organizational boundaries, as with Nano-technology and FuelCell. Collaboration occurs in many different settings . . . manufacturing, new product development, sales, and so on. And collaboration occurs for many different purposes and to accomplish different objectives.

The vignette illustrates some of the difficulties with collaborating effectively:

- Lack of personal accountability (as illustrated by the relationship between Winston and Ben) prevents people from trusting others and coaching them to perform to acceptable standards;

- Managing complex tradeoffs (as illustrated in the dialogue of the leadership team) requires people to bring conflicting perspectives to the table and integrate them effectively; and

- Misalignment of information, authority, and decision making (as illustrated by the discussion of the difficulties with task groups in the past) prevents people from making effective decisions.

This book provides insights about how to collaborate more effectively. Collaboration is inherent in many situations. While collaboration occurs all the time, the intent of this book is to provide basic principles for how to *improve* that inherent collaboration and, with some intentionality, improve the collaborative capability within organizations.

The vignette highlights some of the principles of effective collaboration presented in this book:

- Foster personal accountability;
- Manage complex tradeoffs on a timely basis; and
- Align authority, information, and decision making.

These and other principles are further explained and illustrated in the chapters in this book.

The book is organized into three parts. Part 1 consists of chapters 1 and 2. In this part of the book, we establish a common framework for effective collaborative work systems. The scenario presented above provides a common point of reference for the reader, illustrating some of the challenges leadership faces in establishing more effective collaboration. Chapter 1 introduces concepts essential for a pyramid of collaborative excellence; it also identifies some benefits to the organizations that foster collaboration. Chapter 2 presents the guiding principles that are the foundational constructs of effective collaboration. These principles apply across multiple settings and are present at both an organizational level and at an individual level, where collaboration is the way the work is accomplished. Most readers would benefit from reading Part 1, as it provides a comprehensive understanding of the major constructs of the book.

Part 2 is all about application. Readers may choose to read the chapter on the setting most similar to their current workplace. For example, people who collaborate on new product development may want to read that chapter next. Others may want to understand the application of the guiding principles in greater detail, so they may want to read several chapters on multiple contexts.

For those wanting to select a chapter, here is a brief guide. Chapter 3 is a discussion of the guiding principles in manufacturing settings. Chapter 4 gives an illustration of how the principles apply in new product development organizations. Chapter 5 is focused on settings where services are provided, rather than tangible products, and Chapter 6 was written for those using virtual teams.

Last, Part 3 consists of Chapter 7 only, which provides some guidance for assessing your current collaborative capacity and for moving forward.

"The trick is to create a design that allows a community to learn from itself, to come up with its own solutions to its problems. And then have the restraint not to try to impose those solutions on every other community in the name of efficiency."

Richard Pacale, April 2001 (Fast Company)

"Perspective is worth fifty IQ points."

Gary Hamel

"Ideas are the competitive currency of our times. Collaboration is how companies learn to consciously choose which ideas are worth acting on and which are not."

McGehee (2001, p. 52)

PART 1

PRINCIPLES AND PERSPECTIVES

CHAPTER 1

Building the Collaborative Organization

T HERE ARE NEW AND INCREASING DEMANDS on today's organizations. Connectivity, uncertainty, and speed combine to make work environments more complex and more demanding. Connectivity or "the death of distance" (Cairncross, 1997) means that organizations (and all of their current and potential competitors) has instant access to customers, to colleagues, and to highly sophisticated information about their performance. Uncertainty means that organizations are required to create increasingly sophisticated products, delivered to increasingly demanding customers, across continually re-forming boundaries. In addition, managers must stay alert for the technological changes that will make products obsolete, services substandard, or prices noncompetitive. Everyone now faces a speed requirement created by a dizzying rate of unpredictable, discontinuous change.

More is known about an organization's customers, employees, and competitors than ever before. Tools exist that do much of the routine, back-breaking, mind-numbing work required in the past. Highly sophisticated knowledge of what costs what, what makes money, and exactly where the best sources of profits lie drives focused decisions. On the other hand, global competition, fueled by disparate labor costs, creates intense and escalating competitive pressure on many organizations.

The accelerating rate of change for products and the increasing variety of products offered result in complex and changing requirements both for people and for systems. In addition, customers, suppliers, and technological innovations change at breathtaking speeds and require quick responses in order to protect relationships or competitive positions. Clearly, organizational life today is unpredictable and likely to become more so.

All of this puts new pressure on employees and on traditional ways of managing them. Organizations expect employees to have the skill, confidence, and commitment to use the plethora of tools and information available and to advocate for change when necessary. Structures are required that can deploy workers to meet shifting demands and priorities without the upset and delays historically associated with change. Managers expect workers to work together, often with changing collections of colleagues, to accomplish complex, demanding work. They expect their members to accomplish tasks that require a sophisticated understanding of the tradeoff decisions inherent in their businesses, tasks that require almost constant learning of new skills, and work that requires the trust, respect, and commonality of purpose necessary for cooperative effort. In short, the structure and people who make up today's organizations must be able to join together to accomplish complex, demanding work. New ways of thinking about how to structure and manage the people and the components of today's organization are required.

The designs used for organizations in the past cannot be used given the demands on today's, much less tomorrow's, organizations. A number of innovative designs have emerged in recent years to address these new demands, including: flexible organization; high performance work organization; new design plants, self-managing organization; virtual organization; reengineered corporation; and ambidextrous organization. John Child and Rita Gunther McGrath (2001) identified four common characteristics across these types of organizations: interdependence, disembodiment, velocity, and power. The new forms have been designed to overcome the formality and rigidity of hierarchical, bureaucratic organizational structures and to enable more creative, emergent, and spontaneous responses to problems and opportunities. Cross-functional integration, flattened hierarchy, and empowerment are essential. Such design changes increase the adaptability of the organization, but only when accompanied by management changes, including a shift in perspective about front-line workers and the ways they can add value.

Collaborative Work Systems as a Solution

Consciously designed and nurtured collaborative work systems (CWS) provide a key foundation for achieving competitive advantage. Organizations that actively leverage the talent of their people through knowledge sharing, mutual support, and co-creation outperform organizations that depend on talent alone.

Collaboration means working together. Effective collaborative means working together efficiently and effectively. This is not a new requirement for business success, but it has become a critical success factor that applies to all the relationships that create a business, including those with customers, business allies, suppliers, divisions, departments, functions, projects, specialties, vertical levels, and employees.

Many experiments have been tried to solve the problem of organizing work in ways that are good for the business; some of those experiments have included ways to make the workplace a better fit for human beings. A win/win solution where the company and its members benefit from the way work gets done has the best chance of enduring in changing times. (At least a win/not lose must replace the old version of win/use.)

A traditional, bureaucratic organization based on command-and-control hierarchy is designed with firm horizontal and vertical boundaries and the dominant practice of "repeat" rather than "create." As a result, the design is often too rigid, too simplistic, and too impoverished to adapt to a more complex world. The old organizational structure is too rigid to adapt quickly to changing environmental conditions; it is too simplistic to match the complexity of the environment; it is too impoverished through suppression of human talent and collaborative synergies to create a rich variety of responses to the challenges of the 21st Century environment. Although pure bureaucracies are now less common, the assumptions that underlie them continue to have strong influence on managers.

Why do we expect the collaborative organization to outperform a traditional bureaucracy? Because the collaborative organization capitalizes on the abilities of the members of the organization more effectively and leverages the synergies that occur in networks of people. Collaborative organizations are characterized by intentional efforts to create structures, cultures, forums, and practices that reinforce collaboration. Designing the strategies, structures, processes, and culture enables improved flow of information and other resources across boundaries.

One such example of a collaborative organization is a team-based organization (TBO), where a team of interdependent contributors is the basic unit of work and a series of hierarchical teams reaccomplishes the lateral coordination necessary to integrate the work of their teams and the rest of the organization acts as support. Within a TBO, many forms of teams are utilized, temporary and permanent, functional and cross-functional, local and distributed. This wide array of team forms shows that collaborative work is being organized in creative ways to fit the situation. Leaders and change leaders in collaborative organizations are continually seeking ways to make their organizations more effective, adaptive, and relevant.

Work is becoming more complex, so individuals and isolated groups are not as effective as teams, who have the synergy essential to achieving performance goals. Employee learning and growth, sharing of information, responsibility, partnering, commitment, and so forth are promoted by the collaborative organization environment. Traditional organizations tend to keep decision making, information, rewards, and power at the top. As a result, the minds and hearts of the lower level employees are seldom engaged. Katz and Kahn (1978) referred to this as "partial inclusion"; others simply say, "Check your brain at the door," meaning "We only want that part of you that can do the simple and repetitive job we have designed." In a rapidly changing, fiercely competitive, global business environment, limited use and development of employees results in a "dumbing down" of the organization and competitive advantage is lost. The CWS environment requires significant changes, but the result is a workforce that thinks and cares—leading to a culture of commitment.

Collaborative Competencies

Organizations can be partitioned several ways—horizontal and vertical linkage, inside and outside the organization, within and across disciplines, and between people. The goal of the collaborative organization is to remove inappropriate barriers among these groups and individuals and to create opportunities to work seamlessly. Unfortunately, it seems that barrier building is more common and more natural than productive collaborative exchanges. An assessment of most people and most organizations would provide a low score on collaborative abilities. Creating the knowledge, skills, attitudes, culture, and support systems necessary to create the collaborative organization produces impressive results, including:

- People collaborate more seamlessly, that is, fewer hiccups occur;
- People adapt more quickly to changes in products and services, changes in customer requirements, changes in work processes, and changes in the competitive environment;
- Nonproductive competition between people and systems drops off and is replaced by a preference for cooperation;
- The team becomes the more common unit of responsibility;
- Ideas and information are not dropped into the chasms between silos; and
- The organization functions as a more intelligent system because information and knowledge are shared more quickly and completely.

Collaborative Capacity

Effective collaboration in work situations represents a way of achieving competitive advantage in the marketplace. Effective collaboration represents a key facet of organizing. It contributes to customer satisfaction in myriad ways, including responsiveness to customer needs, quality of products and services, cost management, innovation, and speed. The collaborative processes in a highly collaborative organization consist of dynamic, interwoven, and disciplined exchanges of knowledge and information, participative decision making, and co-created solutions to emerging problems. Companies like Hewlett-Packard and Intel have created some of the infrastructure that enables effective collaboration across boundaries. Pioneering companies, such as W.L. Gore & Associates, Inc., provide examples of fully implemented collaborative designs. The two questions here are

1. What creates the foundation for achieving effective collaboration in all parts of the organization?
2. What additional practices could companies like HP and Intel design that would take them to the next level of collaborative capacity?

Collaborative practices apply to multiple levels of the organization: vision or mission level, business level, organizational level, interrelationships between level in the organizational chart, and so forth. Collaborative capability is built at each of these levels. In addition, there are breakdowns that can occur in terms of who one collaborates with, both laterally and vertically.

Knowing, learning, creating, and relating are the most important processes in the organization. They make intelligent and inventive decision making and effective follow-up possible. Every organization has facets that promote or inhibit these processes. For example, in an organization with a strictly enforced chain of command, relating is often legislated in ways that prevent important information from reaching high-level decision makers. Both formal design features and informal cultural influences impact the ability to use the collaborative potential of the organization. Other constraints, such as limited time, information, tools, experience, and so on also have an impact. The ideal CWS would be based on values, structures, and practices that make effective collaboration possible on every appropriate occasion. Many organizations are taking steps to move in this direction. However, most conceptualize the goal in limited ways.

The most common structural change to improve effective use of collaboration is the introduction of work teams. Typically, based on analysis that identifies interdependent processes, a boundary is defined around a group of workers and changes in responsibility, identity, and training are imposed. The team designation creates a pocket of collaborative practice that focuses team member effort and attention and supports collaborative relationships and processes. Well-designed and supported teams provide:

- A useful mix of expertise,
- An opportunity to increase commitment through involving employees in decision making,
- Leveraging of resources through identification of interdependencies,
- Pooled energy through commitment to the team or common purpose, and
- Possible synergies in decision making.

Work teams represent a leap forward in collaborative potential for many organizations. The problem is that most teams fail primarily because they exist in what can be termed a hostile environment—an environment that neither demands nor sanctions collaboration.

The team-based organization (TBO) has emerged as a solution by providing an environment within which a variety of teams can flourish. The TBO is characterized by:

- Teams as the basic unit of work and accountability,

- Teams leading teams,

- A variety of team types (temporary versus permanent, production versus research, and so forth),

- Alignment of support systems with team needs, and

- A culture promoting collaboration and accountability.

A culture that promotes collaboration includes adequate attention to the informal aspects of collaboration. The transformation from a traditional organizational structure is slow and challenging. Everything must change. For example, the selection system must identify people with a tolerance for change and ambiguity, a preference for teaming, and an ability to learn. As the transformation progresses, however, collaborative capacity is built.

Every organization depends on collaboration. By definition, people organize in order to accomplish tasks that cannot be accomplished as isolated individuals. The collaborative organization does not *require* formal teams or a TBO, but collaborative potential is often enhanced by the use of those structural devices. Teamwork is possible without work teams. Southwest Airlines, Johnsonville Sausage, Semco of Brazil, Asea Brown Boveri, and the W.L. Gore Company are examples of this. High levels of collaboration are possible because of the sense of community, enjoyment at work, continuous learning, and the creation of a sense of meaning on a daily basis (Kets De Vries & Balazs, 1999).

As collaborative capacity increases, its value as a source of competitive advantage increases. Competitive advantage lies in the facets of an organization that are not easily replicated. A new computer system only provides advantage until competitors buy and install one. The talent of a single individual can be hired away. But the collaborative network of relationships within an organization or across its boundaries with customers, suppliers, and partners cannot be bought, copied, or stolen; it must be created from scratch in competing organizations. Hence, collaborative capability remains a key source of competitive advantage.

The Collaborative Organization

Thousands of researchers and millions of business people have been inventing new and better ways to organize work for many years. Over that period an advanced social technology of work design has emerged. An accumulation of lessons learned from research and practice has informed more effective practice. New forms of organizing have been invented and tested, and the process continues.

The collaborative organization is designed for effective coordination, shared decision making, and decision implementation. The emphasis is on a collaborative approach, because that provides an opportunity to utilize multiple perspectives and generate synergies and commitment. The collaboration occurs across both vertical and horizontal boundaries, so flow of information, people, coordination, and materials escape the constraints of silos. The collaboration rests on a culture of shared responsibility, authority, and accountability for results.

Table 1.1 illustrates three levels of collaborative work systems: work teams, team-based organizations, and the collaborative organization. Each level aims at increasing the organization's capacity to serve its customers, employees, and owners with an increase in investment and results moving from left to right. Each design advocates changes intended in order to

1. Increase employee ownership of, and involvement in, the organization and the accomplishment of its goals;

2. Make decision-making processes more public and more disciplined;

3. Decrease the influence of position power and increase the influence of expertise in decision making;

4. Increase the organization's capacity to identify and respond to relevant changes in its environment;

5. Promote learning and the sharing of learning across the organization; and

6. Increase both the ability and propensity of members to collaborate within and across levels of the organization.

There are, however, significant differences in the ways that traditional teams, team-based organizations, and collaborative organizations approach similar goals. Much of this difference in approach is driven by the kind of work for which the models were derived. Traditional teams were created and initially implemented in manufacturing settings. The model created teams that were relatively stable, intact, and composed of members with similar status and expertise. Team-based organizations were designed primarily for organizations responsible for abstract and highly interdependent work, usually in the development arena. Members in these organizations were often on multiple teams, and coordination was critical. The concept of collaborative organizations represents an attempt to create a context and culture that embodies the values and behaviors common to the other two, but that recognizes the dynamic nature of today's environment and the need for collaboration in multiple arenas.

Table 1.1. Comparison of Three Levels of Collaborative Work Systems

	Traditional Teams	Team-Based Organizations	Collaborative Organizations
Characteristics of the Work	Concrete interdependencies that can be broken down into smaller (team size) units	Abstract work that requires significant levels of planning and decision making; significant interdependencies across teams and at business unit levels	Fluid set of interdependencies that may exist inside and outside the organization; moving target; varying levels of complexity
Primary Focus of Collaboration	Team	Project	Varies
Organizational Type	Traditional	Matrix	Varies
Purpose of Redesign	Cohesion, commitment, better use of expertise at all levels of the organization	Coordination, resource management, responsiveness, better use of expertise	Responsiveness, coordination, entrepreneurship
Primary Intervention Point	Relationship	System	Culture/Context
Framework for Decision Making	Consensus within self-managing teams; star model; teams and managers negotiate over goals, schedules, and so on	Consensus and voting within teams; hierarchical and lateral set of governing and coordinating systems; teams managing teams; expertise/accountability primary source of influence	Varies; decisions made at all levels of the organization; clear and communicated set of priorities and tradeoff criteria; highly disciplined decision making; expertise, accountability, and relationship sources of influence
Collaborative Units	Co-located, management created, intact teams	Manager-created project teams; problem-solving teams; coordination teams and management teams; management-appointed team leaders	Individual, team, and organization units of accountability; multiple sets of temporary and semi-permanent teams and organizations; manager-created and spontaneously created teams and partnerships

Collaborative Culture

The term that summarizes all of the informal aspects of the organization is *culture.* In recent years, researchers have identified several levels of culture within the organization. *Nested* cultures are subcultures within a larger cultural system, such as teams where members have agreed to do things in a ways that are not in alignment with the organizational patterns around them. *Cross* cultures are those that link people across boundaries, such as the loyalty engineers and other professionals feel for their profession and the bonds it creates within and outside the organization. With so many subcultures influencing behavior in the organization, members experience conflict, and misalignment is common.

Culture may range from the type where the assumptions, beliefs, and values of the members support authoritarian and submissive behaviors across all levels of the organization to one where there is mutual trust and respect and a strong sense of equality. The latter characterizes the collaborative work system. A collaborative culture includes:

- Trust and respect in everyday interactions;
- Egalitarian attitudes among members at all ranks;
- Power based on expertise and accountability;
- Shared leadership where all members take initiative;
- Valuing of diverse perspectives;
- Commitment to the success of other members, rather than just one's own;
- Valuing of truth and truth telling;
- Commitment to continuous improvement of the whole organization;
- Active learning; and
- Personal responsibility.

The impact of these cultural facets depends on a strong and consistent consensus about the values and on their practice by leaders. Delpizzo (1999) calls it the "organizational software" required for enterprise success. The facets of culture determine both the nature and the style of the organizational routines that drive the effectiveness of communication, cooperation, and collaboration within an organization.

Most organizations demonstrate some of the above cultural facets, although they may occur in pockets rather than across the board. Work teams may represent such pockets embedded in traditional environments. As such, they are at risk; the dominant culture is likely to act like a corporate immune system, applying pressure for them to re-conform (Pinchot, 1985). A well-developed team-based organization is likely to have most of these facets in place, with the proviso that continuous development is underway, but a collaborative organization depends on these facets. One of the best examples of such a design is the W.L. Gore company, described below.

W.L. GORE, INC.: A COLLABORATIVE ORGANIZATION

A world-class collaborative organization is a rare thing. Most organizations are somewhere on a continuum from command-and-control to a highly developed collaborative organization. W.L. Gore anchors the right end of that continuum as an outstanding example of a fully developed collaborative organization. The company operates in a way intended to enable the full potential of each member.

At W.L. Gore, practices are based on commitment, empowerment, and innovation. Culture is based on risk taking, personal responsibility, trust, and collaboration. There are no formal teams, but teaming occurs as appropriate. For example, core groups ranging from three to eighteen members work across the boundaries of disciplines, plants, and countries (Pacanowsky, 1995).

Other examples of businesses that have many similar characteristics to a collaborative organization include Lockheed Martin's Government Electronic Systems, Syncrude Canada's Mine Mobile Maintenance Division, and Sequa Chemicals (Purser & Cabana, 1998), and Oticon in Denmark (LaBarre, 1996). Each of these organizations has relied on collaborative work systems to achieve business results.

Collaborative Capital

We are introducing the new term of *collaborative capital* (CC) as a process and relationship system representing a key asset of the organization. Collaborative capital resembles the established term "intellectual capital" (IC). Intellectual

capital captures the idea that intelligence/knowledge have an implicitly recognized value for an organization. The products and services that the intellectual capital produces have explicitly recognized value. Intellectual capital
represents one key capability of the organization—the ability to produce, capture, and synthesize information into knowledge that *can be used* to produce
some product or service. Sometimes that service may simply be the sharing of
information or knowledge, as in consultation.

Simply put, IC represents what we know and how well we use it; CC represents who we know and how well we work together; and financial capital
represents the current score in the marketplace of how well we meet our customers' and stakeholders' needs. (The terms "social capital" and "relationship
capital" represent the social network part of collaborative capital and not the
disciplined processes of effective collaboration.)

The foundation level of collaborative capital consists of the ability to collaborate at the lowest level of peers within the organization and simultaneously
have that group collaborate with the highest level members. The highest level
of collaborative capital is generated by a corporation with the ability to collaborate effectively (fast, good decisions that also build long-term relationships)
at all levels and with current and potential customers around the world. This
process completes a key communication and feedback loop with significant
ramifications for the way a business operates.

Collaborative capital includes both the process of collaboration and the relationships to make that collaboration work. It represents an interweaving of the
social network, work processes, and organizational structure, which include
the formal and the informal communication in the organization. Collaborative
capital rests on a foundation of competencies, structures, and culture that
enables collaborative practices. The external relationship part of the organization is already considered an asset, priced into the sale of all businesses. For
example, the customer base of a company is a significant asset based on established relationships. Researchers are working on ways to capture the internal
facets of collaborative capital; examples include Kennedy's index (2001) for
team return on investment.

Some measures of collaborative capital can be formalized, just as some collaborative practices can be formalized. However, an intuitive assessment for the
effectiveness of the organization's collaborative work systems can be picked
up by walking around, looking, and listening, that is, managing by eavesdrop-
ping. The approach represents a holistic assessment based on tacit knowledge

acquired from years of learning from experience. It should not be discounted but rather used as a way to validate the quantitative assessment of performance.

The beginning point is recognizing that collaborative practice and process builds a new asset for the organization: collaborative capital. At one site where required overtime led to the operators working from 7 a.m. to 10 p.m. for three weeks before having a day off, the operations manager said, "It was the resilience created by the teaming initiative that got us through this tough time." Measurement of CC remains challenging in such situations, but its value is increasingly recognized.

Collaboration and Teams

Teams are perhaps the most studied, if not the most prevalent, form of business collaboration and much of what is discussed in this book relates to the design, management, and work processes of successful teams. It is important to remember that teams are simply the forum for the collaborative processes, and not the process itself. Teams can be effective or ineffective at collaboration, both within the team and between the team and other individuals and teams inside and outside of the organization.

If teams represent the most recognized form of collaboration, team-based organizations (TBOs) represent one of the most advanced current forms of a Collaborative Work Systems (CWS). A TBO capitalizes on the competitive advantage of collaboration that grew out of socio-technical systems work, where the need to jointly optimize the social and technical facets of the organization was recognized as the key to performance (Beyerlein, 2000). The building block of the TBO is the team: teams are the unit of accountability and teams lead teams. This is a radical shift away from the individual focus of most organizations. It provides the opportunity to create synergies within work groups and across boundaries and so to leverage human resources.

Today teams are central for businesses to accomplish their work goals and manage the complexity of their work. Since there are many misunderstandings about teams, the following definition will be used in this book:

> "Teams are defined as a group of individuals who work together to produce products or deliver services for which they are held mutually accountable" (Mohrman, Cohen, & Mohrman, 1995, p. 2).

Mohrman, Cohen, and Mohrman distinguish teams from a team-based organization. They say that team-based organizations are "Organizations in which teams are the core performing units" (p. 6). Many of the early examples of teams in organizations described the installation of teams in pockets of the organization, instead of redesigning the work and the systems to support teams as the foundation for accomplishing the work. Team-based organizations may also have multiple types of teams, and the teams may be an alternative to the multiple layers of organizational structure. However, team-based organizations usually develop after years of successful implementation of teams.

Throughout the 1970s and 1980s, more businesses experimented with teams, many with amazing success, including manufacturing sites such as Corning Glass and Saturn and service companies such as Aid Association for Lutherans and Shenandoah Insurance. In the 1990s, businesses moved beyond experimenting with teams to implementing them on a large scale to achieve their strategic goals. While many organizations struggled with their performances some American businesses realized that their members were not being used as effectively as they could be. These organizations were team-based, since they used teams to complete their core business (Mohrman, Cohen, & Mohrman, 1995).

These team-based organizations flattened their structures and redistributed decision-making responsibility to better align with the expertise and perspective of their members. Organizations that utilized teams well had impressive results, according to Fisher (1999):

- The TRW Company, Canada LTD, in Tillsonburg, Ontario, a plant that manufactures automotive steering components, increased total sales per employee by 179 percent in five years;

- The Borg-Warner Automotive plant in Frankfort, IL, which makes automatic transmission bands, reduced its work in progress by 73 percent in five years;

- The Baxter HealthCare Corporation in Mountain Home, AR, which makes disposable medical products, improved their first-pass yield 71 percent over five years to 99.4 percent;

- The Dana Corporation in Hopkinsville, KY, reduced their order-to-shipment lead time by 67 percent in five years;

- The Quaker Oats Company in Danville, IL, had production employees who reduced the plant's product-development cycle time by 75 percent in five years; and

- The Halliburton Energy Services Duncan Plant, which produces equipment for the oil industry, reduced their manufacturing cycle times from 103.7 days to 28.5 days and improved their on-time delivery rate from 64 percent to 94 percent in five years.

As organizations published their success stories, others moved to copy the practices and planned to implement teams, among other strategies. One study (Tudor & Trumble, 1996) reported that one in five companies planned to implement teams in the near future as part of their strategy to meet the new expectations in the marketplace. Another survey reported that the number of project teams had exceeded the number of production teams.

Teams changed the standard by which work was being completed across the United States. However, in the late 1990s a shift occurred from the use of formal teams toward more temporary and project-based forms of collaboration (Lawler, Mohrman, & Benson, 2001). Now collaborative organizations are beginning to raise that standard. They represent an intentional and disciplined utilization of the synergies of working effectively together in many ways under many circumstances.

The Payoff from the Collaborative Organization

Collaborative work has been around since the beginning of civilization. The leveraging of individual resources provides a synergy that exceeds individual effort. Recently, managers have rediscovered the benefits of effective collaboration. We will describe three types of benefits, illustrating the "business case" for collaboration. These types of benefits include: general qualitative benefits, benefits reported by specific work sites, and broader benefits to the overall corporate "bottom line." As researchers and practitioners over the last twenty years, we have identified a number of benefits that managers of high-performing CWS report themselves. These are summarized below.

Qualitative Benefits

One of the greatest benefits of the collaborative organization is the generation of greater commitment among members. Members take greater personal ownership for their work. They require less direct supervision. They self-initiate to solve problems, improve processes, and work with customers to ensure that their needs are met.

Collaborative organizations tend to be more flexible and better able to adapt to changing business conditions. One of the key features of the collaborative organization is that members develop a greater set of skills and competencies. They are able to better cover for absences, training, vacations, and business trips of other members. Similarly, members can be shifted around as demands change. If business conditions change, a different balance of skills and abilities may be required. With more multi-skilling, the collaborative organization can easily adjust to the changing requirements.

Collaborative organizations develop the skills of employees better. They focus on helping people develop those skills they are interested in and those that will benefit the organization. Often people are used in more strategic ways. When managers are freed up from the day-to-day supervision of people, their roles are redefined in many more value-adding ways. Some examples include: exploring new technologies or processes; working more closely with customers to ensure their needs are met; and problem solving on complex, recalcitrant issues.

And last, the collaborative organization creates flatter, more flexible organizations. Levels of management are stripped out. With fewer layers, communication with the top levels improves. It is easier for the leaders of the collaborative organization to communicate problems they are facing and to ask for resources needed to resolve these problems. Members of the collaborative organization have better access to senior leaders, who can provide them more immediate, accurate, and unfiltered information about the business environment and related business strategies. Alignment improves the thinking of senior leaders and front-line operators. Everyone is pulling in the same direction and understands what is going on. Staffing costs are also reduced.

Benefits Reported by Collaborative Organizations

A number of company sites report dramatic improvements as a result of implementing collaboration. For example, Monsanto introduced formalized collaboration into their Greenwood, SC, nylon fibers plant using self-directed work teams. The role of the traditional supervisor was redefined into that of team leader, providing greater autonomy to teams. Monsanto reported a 50 percent productivity increase over a five-year period (*Chemical Processing*, 1990).

Shenandoah Life Insurance redesigned their back office processing area. They broke down traditional functional work areas and replaced them with multifunctional work cells. They were able to process 50 percent more applications with 10 percent fewer people (Hoerr, Polluck, & Whitestone, 1986).

Celestica, a $3 billion chip manufacturer, completed a comprehensive redesign into a CWS at their Toronto facility. They created a customer-focused CWS comprised of customer accounts manager; manufacturing, process, and quality process engineering; and supply chain to address needs of individual customers. This resulted in a 100 percent productivity increase, thereby leading to an increase in manufacturing capacity without additional labor or equipment. The manufacturing cycle time was reduced eight-fold, and quality (defects/unit) improved by a factor of two (Dyck & Halpern, 1999).

Pratt and Whitney instituted a team-based lean manufacturing system and pay-for-skill/gain-sharing plan at a seventeen-year-old aircraft engine components manufacturing plant in Maine. They broadened job descriptions so that inspectors did repair as well as inspection. The gain-sharing plan generated a first-year payout of $1,633 per employee. Overall operating costs fell 20 percent. Defect rates dropped 30 percent. A three-tier pay-for-skills system enabled the CWS to be automatic, conscious, and creative (*Wall Street Journal*, 1996).

Broader Benefits to the Overall Corporate "Bottom Line"

Other organizations report even more dramatic financial results, resulting in dramatic improvements to overall business metrics. Kravetz (1988) conducted a study looking at the differences in financial performance of companies with traditional management practices versus "progressive" management practices. Progressive management practices included collaboration-based organization structures, team-based reward systems, and extensive training. When tracking the financial results of Fortune 500 companies over a five-year period, he found:

	Progressive	Traditional
Profit growth	10.8%	2.6%
Sales growth	17.5%	10.7%
Earnings growth	6.2%	-3.9%
Dividend growth	13.4%	9.2%

Lawler and his colleagues completed a series of surveys measuring the financial impact of team-related practices (Lawler, Mohrman, & Benson, 2001).

In their most recent survey of a broad range of Fortune 1000 companies, they found that team-related practices were associated with the following:

- 66 percent higher return on sales,
- 20 percent higher return on assets,
- 20 percent higher return on investments,
- 14 percent higher return on equity,
- 1,700 percent higher return to investors, and
- 257 percent higher market-to-book ratio.

Barry Macy has spent over ten years studying the leverage that arises from change efforts in industry. In a study of more than two hundred companies examining sixty major change initiatives and calculating the behavioral and financial outcomes for each, Macy concluded that collaborative-based organizing comes out on top (Macy & Izumi, 1993) and that collaboration in various forms has more positive impact than any other approach to reorganization.

Other researchers and practitioners have found similar results. The body of evidence is now clear. Collaborative-based organizations significantly improve overall business performance by any number of measures used.

Leveraging the Most out of the Collaborative Organization

Leverage means multiplying effort. Archimedes said about 2,500 years ago: "Give me a place to stand and I can move the earth." He meant that he needed a platform from which he could apply a lever that could move anything. The inertia in organizations resisting change may seem to have a mass the same as the earth's. But finding platforms to work from that enable change under such conditions is a treasure hunt worth the investment of time and money. Collaborative-based organizing stands out as one of the few proven platforms.

A lot of organizational processes are essential to growth and stability in volatile markets. The processes include: learning, inventing, redesigning, communicating, leveraging, organizing, motivating, locating, linking, serving, leading, training, conversing, debating, assessing, and adapting. Organizational strategy, structure, policy, and practice are designed with the goal of making those processes work effectively and in concert. The continued existence of the organization depends on it. In spite of the impression given by Wall Street, organizing for sustainability is a marathon, not a sprint, in most ways.

The processes are executed by people. Some have been automated, but the outputs from those subsystems are handled by people. The decisions to use those automated systems are made by people, and the systems are overseen by people. People do the learning, the deciding, and the relating. Even in the case of a highly automated plant, people engineered the site, managed the site, and created the markets for the site's outputs. When the business world was simpler (pre-1973), it was possible to do a lot of that work as an individual. Since then, it has increasingly required collaboration with team members who have diverse backgrounds.

Organization—Learning Dialogue, Knowledge Sharing

Intelligence comes into play when appropriate information from the environment is utilized in making decisions about what actions to execute. Business intelligence is a people process. Individuals from the executive suite to the shop floor can demonstrate it and sometimes do so in impressive ways, from the executive suite to the shop floor. Using collaboration leverages the intelligence of individuals. This is most evident in creative problem solving, where complexity and uncertainty reign. That territory used to belong to executives, scientists, and engineers, but now it belongs to everyone associated with an organization. Routine used to be the dominant organizer, but changing environments require frequent nonroutine responses, which means that intelligence is a key to organizational sustainability. In other words, collaboration between people, and especially across organizational boundaries, makes the organization smarter.

Collaboration and Community

An atmosphere that encourages and enables collaboration begins to look a lot like a community. Ogdin (www.it-consultancy.com/extern/sws/community.html) differentiates community from other kinds of organization with the following characteristics of success:

- *Boundary and Exclusivity:* some definition of who is a member and who is not;

- *Purpose:* some reason for the community to exist beyond just "having community":

- *Rules:* some limits on community member behavior, with a threat of ejection for misbehavior;

- *Commitment to Others' Welfare:* some essential caring by each member for others in the same community, or at least some responsibility of individual members toward the community; and

- *Self-Determination:* the freedom to decide for oneself how to operate and whom to admit to team membership.

Community represents the informal part of the organization. Collaboration occurs in both formal and informal processes and environments. The leveraging of collaboration is optimized when the processes cross boundaries: formal and informal, project to project, level to level, company to customer, company to supplier. A network of collaborative processes across all of these kinds of boundaries produces excellence.

Conclusion

Disciplined practice of key principles builds core competencies that, in turn, create capital in various forms that can be transformed into each other. Ask yourself three questions:

1. What are the assets that add value to the organization and create competitive advantage? Your answer may look like this:

   - Finance (cash, property, investments, etc.)
   - Leadership
   - Market share
   - Customer relationship
   - Intellectual (knowledge/learning/intelligence)
   - Organizing (for example, flat, fast, flexible)
   - Time (a key resource)
   - Relationship (for example, social network)
   - Technology

Intelligent use of these assets is a key to achieving market share.

2. What are the core competencies that are robust (they contribute to development of all of the types of capital)? Your answer may look like this:

   - Collaborating
   - Executing well

- Changing
- Creating/innovating
- Learning
- Relating (based on emerging definition of customer service)
- Organizing
- Assessing
- Scanning
- Communicating
- Adapting
- Preserving (what do we keep stable?)

These are all written as gerunds to indicate that they are processes that form the skeleton of a dynamic system. These processes can be executed well or poorly. Collaborative approaches grease the wheels of the execution to move toward world-class levels of performance.

3. What are the principles and disciplined practices that build the core competencies? (This is the topic of the next chapter, where the ten key principles for creating collaborative excellence are described in detail. Disciplined practice is considered prerequisite for capitalizing on these.)

The problems managers face range from: (1) *simple, linear* situations, where problem definition is easy (tame problems) and an algorithm can be plugged in to determine a solution, to (2) *ill-defined* situations, where the problem is not clear from the beginning so it is not clear what the solution should be, to (3) *wicked* problems, where stating the problem *is* the problem. Wicked problems are complex with interdependent facets (Pacanowsky, 1995).

With "wicked" problems, when a solution is applied to one facet, other parts of the problem change. The most salient facets receive the most attention, but a new facet revolves into awareness after a partial solution impacts the whole. To make matters worse, the context of the problem requires that the solution be context-specific. The solution must be invented over time. Organizational transformation for solving the problems of competition and of collaboration are wicked problems. Multiple perspectives must be integrated in a dance of change as incremental and revolutionary changes are introduced into the situation.

There is a tendency in organizations to ignore wicked problems, which cause cognitive strain, and to take a purely incremental approach to the facet of the day, hoping for the best. In wresting with wicked problems, heuristic guidelines replace algorithms, continuous creation replaces simple reinvention, collaborative thinking replaces unilateral decision making, and a framework of principles and values replaces a menu of standard responses. New solutions are created jointly over time within the framework.

To compete in the business environment of the 21st Century, organizations must be designed to engage the minds and hearts of their members and create effective relationships across all boundaries. The hardware and software technologies have been tried often in the past twenty years, but they have often failed to create more effective organizations. The development of collaborative work systems has been emerging as an essential piece of the puzzle. As the competitive landscape shifts, those who are quickest to adopt the advanced social technology of collaborative design are likely to be the winners. The collaborative organization enables the optimal development of the intellectual and social capital that increases the financial capital for an organization.

The next chapter presents ten principles that represent the foundation for effective collaborative processes and the generation of collaborative capital. An organization creates its collaborative advantage by operationalizing those principles through disciplined processes and consistent practices.

CHAPTER 2

The Ten Principles of Collaborative Organizations

CREATING COLLABORATIVE ORGANIZATIONS is a long-term process. Most organizations have pockets of excellent collaboration found in specific internal teams, with specific customer groups, or even within large project endeavors. Few, however, can boast of excellent collaboration across the dynamic cadre of relationships that form their world of work. We propose that, when you undertake such an endeavor, you look at the overall capacity of your organization to engage in efficient and productive collaboration and take steps to improve that capacity.

This focus represents a departure, or perhaps a next step, from some of the more traditional discussions about teams and teaming. The principles presented here are designed for application at the organizational level. Because teams and projects form and re-form today at record speed, it is extremely important that the organization possess the characteristics that once defined the time-focused, high-performing team. This chapter is about the characteristics of such an organization.

The following discussion represents a "how to" for ensuring that your organization has the capacity and commitment to collaborate efficiently and effectively across levels, teams, projects, functions, and organizational boundaries. It is also about effective collaboration with external partners—customers, vendors, business partners, and government and other nonprofit agencies.

Ten principles that support building the collaborative organization are described below—characteristics that enable the organization to collaborate efficiently and effectively across the myriad collaborative tasks required in today's business environments. The ten principles are

1. Focus collaboration on achieving business results.

2. Align organizational support systems to promote ownership.

3. Articulate and enforce "a few strict rules."

4. Exploit the rhythm of convergence and divergence.

5. Manage complex tradeoffs on a timely basis.

6. Create higher standards for discussions, dialogue, and information sharing.

7. Foster personal accountability.

8. Align authority, information, and decision making.

9. Treat collaboration as a disciplined process.

10. Design and promote flexible organizations.

Table 2.1 on page 52 provides a summary of the information about each principle.

1. Focus Collaboration on Achieving Business Results

To suggest that collaboration be focused on business results seems to restate the obvious. It is hard to imagine non-business reasons for creating or sanctioning formal collaborative activities. This principle, however, goes beyond wanting people to talk about work and beyond wanting them to focus on specific business-related outcomes. It is also about providing a common context, fueled by education and communication that ensures that all members of the organization understand and are committed to the specific business goals and strategies of the organization. This kind of focus on business results empowers participants in formal and informal collaborative activities to act in the best interest of the organization.

Organizations with a focus on achieving business results include members who:

- Understand the central purpose of their business, including responsibilities to customers, investors, and other stakeholders;

- Recognize the competitive nature of their business and the source of their current and potential competitive advantages;

- Recognize who their customers/clients are and the importance of anticipating changing customer/client requirements;

- Understand their role and responsibilities in relationship to the performance goals of each of the organization's units and subunits; and

- Make decisions consistent with both long-term and short-term business requirements.

Importance

To focus collaboration on business results provides a context and the motivation for working together. It provides all organization members with a common purpose, a sense of membership in a larger endeavor, and a set of shared assumptions. Such a focus also provides the motivation for members to ignore, or work through, personality or values differences.

The vast majority of organization members want very much to accomplish good and meaningful work. They want to be proud of who they work for and proud of the work they do. Thus, members must have a sophisticated understanding of the overall goals of the organization. They have to be able to explain those goals to others and to understand how the goals apply to the many choices about work they make every day. They also must understand the relationship of those goals to their individual and collective responsibilities and to the responsibilities of those with whom they must collaborate (Lawler, 1986).

✓ When It Is Working

When collaboration is focused on business results, participants begin with a common understanding of what they need to talk about, how they must prioritize their time, and the tradeoffs that have to be made. To paraphrase Steven

Covey, they begin with some common ideas of "the end in mind." Collaboration takes place with a broader understanding of the need to balance the needs of the participants, the needs of the immediate task, and the requirements and goals of the larger organization. This focus helps deter the creation of solutions that don't serve the goals and objectives of the larger organization. More importantly, perhaps, it sets the stage for the revisions and compromises when, in spite of the best-laid plans, teams generate non-compatible solutions.

✗ When It Is Not Working

Collaborative efforts that lack a focus on business results are common. They happen most often in organizations without the educational, communication, and direction-setting processes that help members understand and embrace business goals and priorities. Symptoms typical of such organizations include:

- Discussions that appear to be without direction or appear to be directed toward different goals;

- Continuing or recurring disagreements among participants from different departments, organizations, teams, or functional groups;

- Decisions or actions that serve the goals or priorities of the specific collaborative unit and fail to serve the larger entity; and

- Decisions or recommendations that are frequently ignored or overturned by upper management.

2. Align Organizational Support Systems to Promote Ownership

Ownership, in this context, refers to the personal commitment of organization members to the business and its outcomes. People rarely engage in the complex, frustrating, and risky activities that characterize successful collaboration without personal, often passionate commitment. Support systems are the organization's most direct way of fostering such commitment. These support systems include:

- Leadership systems (who is allowed or expected to lead; what the criteria are for awarding leadership; how leadership relates to accountability, expertise, and commitment; what style of leadership is valued);

- Information and communications systems (what is communicated to different people and by what means; what information is available to which people at what point in time);

- Performance management systems (what behaviors are important; how the organization monitors individual and collective action in relationship to these behaviors; and how it rewards, both formally and informally, desired behaviors);

- Learning system (the organization's attitudes about and processes it uses to train and learn from its members; the processes for assimilating; information and perspectives available from the outside world; and the criteria and the processes for decision making); and

- Organization and design system (process and criteria used to create reporting, learning, and task-specific units and the relationships between those units).

In collaborative organizations, these support systems are consciously designed and actively managed to support collaborative activity.

Importance

Effective collaboration vests organization members with the responsibility for critical, time-sensitive decisions. Unless members are fully informed about and committed to the organization, vesting decision-making responsibility with them can be dangerous. Support systems that educate, involve, and reward appropriately are prerequisites for outstanding collaborative capacity. Furthermore, these support systems must be consciously designed to ensure that they align with one another and the overall goal of effective collaboration.

✓ When It Is Working

When the support systems are aligned correctly, organization members are encouraged and rewarded for acting in ways that are consistent with the organization's goals. Descriptions of how each support system functions in a collaborative organization are given below.

Leadership System. Leadership roles and responsibilities in collaborative organizations are diverse. Leaders serve as managers, teachers, coaches, and coordinators. Leadership is expected and accepted from members at all levels of the organization, depending on the requirements of the situation. Expertise and commitment are as important as formal leadership status in determining who serves as the leader in a given situation.

Information and Communication System. Collaborative organizations depend on a constant and efficient flow of information and ideas. They require sophisticated information technology (IT) systems, accompanied by a culture that both models and encourages open communication. Collaborative organization members also need access to their customers or information about their customers, as well as access to other key stakeholder information and perspectives.

Performance Management System. The performance management system includes the system for directing, and redirecting, the behavior of employees toward the achievement of organizational goals. In collaborative organizations, these systems provide direction and rewards at the individual, team, and organizational level.

Learning System. Collaborative organizations have sophisticated formal and informal learning systems. There is a high value placed on continuous learning. Well-designed training and development programs and well-established processes for pooling information about lessons learned, problems solved, and trends anticipated are a part of this system. The organization pools its collective data-gathering and information-processing skills to improve its processes and to anticipate the future challenges and opportunities.

Organization and Design System. Collaborative organizations, and the collaborative units within those organizations, are designed to reflect the changing nature of work. Typically, they are composed of a combination of temporary and semi-permanent teams, each created based on the requirements of the task, the level of interdependency involved in the work, and the expertise required. In addition to these formal collaboration mechanisms, members are encouraged to engage in the collaborative activities necessary to meet their collective responsibilities.

✗ When It Is Not Working

Organizations with non-aligned support systems send mixed messages. It is hard for members to know when to compete and when to cooperate. Members are unsure about where to spend their time and energy and what rewards to expect if they expend extra effort. Confusion exists about what is important—

collaboration or individual performance. People talk about "not walking the talk" because the actions they see as most supportive of the organization don't appear to be recognized or rewarded.

3. Articulate and Enforce "a Few Strict Rules"

"A few strict rules" refers to a set of guiding principles that govern decision making within the organization. These rules define the overall values and competitive approach of the organization and allow organization members a great deal of leeway to accomplish goals. These rules or principles provide a consistent direction for the organization and ensure the cohesion necessary for productive collaborative effort. These rules may include:

- The relative weight of cost versus performance in product design decisions;
- The relative importance of a specific customer or set of customers;
- The overall ethical principals of the organization;
- The relative weight of quality versus speed in service delivery; and
- When and how the organization responds to change.

Both the formal and the informal leaders of collaborative organizations enforce adherence to these "rules." The organization maintains the necessary cohesion and coordination to meet its objectives by consistently applying these guidelines. Within these parameters, however, individuals and teams are encouraged to use innovative, even experimental, approaches to accomplish their goals and the goals of the organization.

Importance

Organizations today operate in complex, highly dynamic environments. Success is often dependent on the ability of all members to collect and respond effectively to complex, shifting information from a variety of sources. The decisions, however, need to be made within a consistent context that assures that the organization maintains its commitment to its customer, its principles, and its competitive position. The ideal system represents an optimum balance between a highly structured environment that limits the ability of its members to adapt to changing requirements and a chaotic environment that provides little consistent direction for its members.

✓ When It Is Working

The "strict rules" allow teams to function comfortably within the boundaries of their responsibilities. They allow teams to deal with other teams with the assurance that those teams are functioning under the same set of rules. The "few" rules allow these groups to respond to the dynamic nature of the business with flexibility and creativity. In addition, organization members recognize what is valued within the organization and what is not tolerated and behave accordingly. They can articulate what the boundaries are in very clear, concise terms.

✗ When It Is Not Working

When an organization has too many rules, organizations spend way too much time waiting for permission or trying to manage upward. When an organization has too few rules, tasks are not completed, false starts are common, and individual and small group goals take precedence over the goals of the organization. Members appear unsure about how much energy to devote to a particular set of tasks or goals because what they are expected to do is constantly changing. In addition, the lack of rules creates a lack of clarity about what is important to and valued by the organization.

4. Exploit the Rhythm of Convergence and Divergence

Divergence and convergence are core processes for all collaborative activity. Without these processes, collaboration, in any real sense, simply does not take place. *Divergence* is the process by which collaboration participants surface the different perspectives that need to be considered. *Convergence* is the process members use to reach agreement.

Importance

We learn the processes of divergence and convergence as children, although no one ever labeled them for us. As soon as we noticed that playing with someone else was fun, we learned to raise different perspectives (divergence) about what, where, and how to play. We surfaced and processed the various alternatives and made a decision to play at one or more of the alternatives (convergence). We learned that power plays a role in the decision-making process (if you want to play with your older brother, you play what he wants to play), as do the availability of tools (you have to have a ball to play ball); the limits of the environment (you can't play baseball without a yard or field); the role identity of the players (boys don't do tea parties); and the dictates of upper management (you aren't allowed to play in the mud). With all of this complexity, almost all of us were able to manage the divergence and convergence processes successfully. We played with other kids.

The beauty of our early efforts at collaboration is that we had a common goal with our collaborative partners (to have fun), and we had a shared set of assumptions (we believed fun was relatively easy to achieve and involved action of some kind). We were not likely to get bogged down in the process of continuous divergence (we wanted to play; we didn't want to talk about playing), and we were able to test out our decision empirically (we played our choice, determined it was fun, and changed it when it wasn't). We diverged and converged in an acceptable rhythm with little or no thought as to the relative balance of time spent in each activity.

As collaboration becomes more complex, and the time lapse between decision making and empirical testing becomes greater, managing the divergence and convergence processes becomes much more challenging (and much less fun). However, it is this management, which takes place at an organizational, team, and individual level, that results in all significant collaborative achievements. Inadequate rigor in either process produces poor results and frustrated participants.

✓ When It Is Working

When convergence and divergence are managed effectively, there is a recognizable rhythm to the process. This rhythm exists in the organization as a whole and for the individuals and teams engaged in collaborative work. There is an overall sense of balance between the time and attention given to surfacing the various perspectives or divergent forces and the time and rigor spent working through those alternatives. Decisions are seen as informed, if not always correct, and subject to testing and revision when necessary.

When this principle works well, complex collaborative activities take place in cycles, forming a series of "iterative processes that produce a product that is agreed upon by all parties" (Mohrman, Cohen, & Mohrman, 1995). These cycles use tools and strategies to ensure adequate divergent activities, including surfacing individual member perspectives, comparing data from multiple sources, generating a number of options and scenarios, concretizing abstractions, and involving all pertinent perspectives in decisions. Tools and processes are also used to manage the convergence process, including agreeing on decision-making perspectives (values, goals, tasks, tradeoff criteria), analyzing data using previously agreed on approaches, using criteria to sort through options, making plans as explicit as possible, and clarifying decision-making responsibility (Mohrman, Cohen, & Mohrman, 1995).

✗ When It Is Not Working

When the convergence and divergence rhythms are not managed well, an organization or team suffers from limited vision or inadequate completion—or simply an incorrect pacing of these two activities. Organizations and teams who fail to exploit divergence will overlook information or perspectives critical to their success. Organizations and teams who manage convergence poorly don't make decisions fast enough or well.

5. Manage Complex Tradeoffs on a Timely Basis

The term *tradeoffs* refers to those decisions that involve weighing the relative costs and benefits of two or more interrelated, but to some extent conflicting, criteria. Because of the increasing complexity of products, processes, technology, and markets, complex tradeoff decisions are now required at all levels of many organizations. These decisions typically require specific skills, specialized expertise, detailed and timely information, and the ability to review and process the implications of a variety of alternatives quickly and accurately.

Importance

Many collaborative systems exist to make and execute complex tradeoff decisions. Often collaborative work involves almost instant integration of complex and/or dynamic information to make costly decisions with long-term implications. The quality and speed with which the team can make these decisions is a major determinant of organizational success.

✓ **When It Is Working**

A collaborative unit that makes and executes the correct tradeoff decisions is a highly disciplined team. The members of these groups have a clear, shared understanding of the criteria on which to make the decisions, a defined process for collecting and reviewing relevant information, and a respect for the differing expertise of various members. They also have a keen appreciation of the need for speed in making these decisions. Finally, the organization provides clear escalation paths for the team so that decisions for which they lack the necessary information or perspective can be passed up or over quickly and effectively.

✗ **When It Is Not Working**

Collaborative units that cannot make effective tradeoff decisions either fail to make decisions or make poor decisions. Typically, these groups lack clarity about, or agreement on, the complex set of criteria (the tradeoffs) necessary to make an informed decision or the information to apply those criteria in an informed manner. An example is a manufacturing management team that decided to accelerate production at the request of a key customer. Soon after they made the commitment to the customer, they discovered that meeting that request would require double shifts, a cost increase that eliminated most of the profit from the product. In addition, the double shift resulted in mandatory overtime, causing several key employees to leave, which ultimately resulted in an even longer production time. Because the team was not aware of, or at least did not consider, all the tradeoffs involved, they undertook a course of action that turned out to be in direct conflict with their intended goal.

6. Create Higher Standards for Discussions, Dialogue, and Information Sharing

"We are confused at a higher level about more important things." This statement, made about a self-managing work team at Texas Instruments in the early 1990s, summarizes this principle perfectly. Creating higher standards for discussions, dialogue, and the sharing of information continually raises the level and complexity at which collaborative participants are able to consider alternatives and contribute to the organization's success.

Importance

In raising the standards for discussions, dialogue, and information sharing, the organization builds its capacity to manage the increasing complexity characterizing business today. It also builds the capacity and commitment of each member to contribute to the collaborative processes. The result is an organization—and organization members—that can cope more effectively and more creatively with an increasingly unpredictable world.

✓ When It Is Working

When the bar is raised for discussions, dialogue, and information sharing, organizations experience a multitude of positive results, including:

- Members and teams who have easy access to well-organized information;
- Members and teams who know who the "experts" are and can easily call on them for advice and counsel;
- Members and teams who are able to integrate what they've learned and apply it to new situations;
- Members at all levels of the organization who are excited about what they are learning and creating; and
- Members at all levels of the organization who ask questions and provide stories and illustrations that expand the ability of the participants to see a problem or opportunity from a variety of perspectives.

✗ When It Is Not Working

When the organization does not actively engage in "raising the bar" on discussions, dialogues, and information sharing, collaborative capacity is seriously limited. Examples of those limitations include:

- Members and teams who develop emotional attachments to their own (limited) perspectives;
- Members and teams who are uninformed or unnecessarily delayed because of a lack of access to information;
- Detailed, time-consuming discussions about the wrong issues;
- Managers/leaders who are not helping to educate members and teams about the bigger issues;
- An absence of breakthrough thinking; and
- Too much information, too little knowledge.

7. Foster Personal Accountability

Personal accountability is both a requirement for, and the result of, successful collaborative work. Organization members who feel personally accountable believe their success is directly tied both to meeting their commitments to their colleagues and to the success of the organization. Members and teams are often personally and passionately committed to what they do, how well they do it, and the outcomes that result.

Importance

Collaboration is necessary when the correct decision or course of action is not known or when the decision requires the active commitment of a number of people to make it work. The participants have to work through a series of activities that define a correct decision or course of action. It is hard to envision a situation where this process could work if the participants do not feel personally responsible for the results.

Effective collaboration requires that each individual fulfill his or her role effectively, provide some value-adding contribution, and feel personally responsible for both the process used and the results of the collaborative effort. Members with a strong sense of personal responsibility need little or no supervision related to motivation or commitment. They identify what needs to be done and initiate actions to accomplish those tasks. They perform work that is of high quality and they meet their commitments to their colleagues and to the work itself.

✓ When It Is Working

When members accept personal responsibility, they are passionate about the organization and their individual and team responsibilities as a part of it. As a result, we are likely to see members and teams who do the following:

- Argue frequently, question authority often, and complain loudly about any barriers to meeting their team or project goals;
- Subjugate personal agendas for the collective whole;
- Take on tasks outside of their normal scope and volunteer to help their colleagues;
- Deliver on their commitments and accept responsibility for their mistakes;
- Organize and manage their own work; and
- Are led by managers who are free from the task of "motivating employees."

✗ When It Is Not Working

When members cannot see the relationship between the effort they put into the organization and their own well-being, then their priorities are not likely to align with the goals of the organization. Examples of how this misalignment can be seen include:

- Members and/or teams are more concerned about their own careers than about the well-being of the organization;
- Members talk often about the "personal agendas" of others;
- Members and teams focus on a single organizational metric;
- Members and teams spend much of their time blaming other teams or individuals;
- Few people initiate ideas and actions;
- Members do more to keep things from happening than to make things happen; and
- Little action is aimed at making things easier or better.

8. Align Authority, Information, and Decision Making

The earlier example of collaborating over what to play is a perfect example of aligning authority, information, and decision making. As teams of children deciding what to play, we had the information necessary to make good decisions, the skill necessary to process that information, and the authority to implement a decision. We were highly committed to the outcome and well aware that the process had to have enough buy-in so that all members would actively support the decision. We could also assess the results and make corrections as necessary. Collaboration is most efficient and effective when it has these characteristics.

Importance

Frequently, organizations demonstrate a "pick two" mentality when assigning tasks to teams. For example, management teams often assign implementation planning for a new program to the team that will ultimately have to implement the program. They also mistakenly assume that the team will have the information and perspective to make a decision congruent with larger organizational goals. That is, they "pick two" by aligning decision making and authority and fail to ensure the necessary alignment of information. Of course, aligning all three is a difficult task and one that deserves a great deal of management attention.

The benefits of decisions that are aligned with information and authority include:

- Decisions are made quickly;
- Decisions are implemented by people committed to the success of the implementation;
- Participants have the information to participate fully in the decision-making process; and
- Organization members experience a sense of control and accountability about the work they do.

✓ When It Is Working

Organizations and teams who have aligned decision making with authority and information are characterized by:

- Members with the skills to make the decisions, including business, administrative, and communications skills;
- Information available through multiple media, that is, the information paradigm has shifted from a need-to-know basis to a desire to share openly and directly with members;
- Members responsible for completing the work who have as much discretion as possible in deciding how the work gets done;
- Information flowing across levels in a fluid and dynamic manner;
- Teams that understand clearly when they are acting in an advisory capacity and when they are or will be directly accountable for implementation as well; and
- Members who understand which decisions they can and should make and which decisions require collaboration with others.

✗ When It Is Not Working

No complex organization achieves consistent alignment between information, authority, and decision making for all collaborative units at all times. However, organizations that are consistently out of alignment suffer some very consistent consequences. These include:

- Decisions and plans have to be reworked because those responsible for implementation were not included in the process;

- Decisions are made carelessly because those making the decisions were not ultimately accountable for the results;

- Low morale and high turnover are present because people feel they have little or no control over their work or the results of it; and

- Sub-optimization is present at a variety of levels because decision makers lack the perspectives and information to optimize processes or results.

9. Treat Collaboration as a Disciplined Process

Organizations that treat collaboration as a disciplined process recognize the cost, the risks, and the potential benefits. These organizations approach the process as they would any other business process—striving to define the processes and tools that are most effective and ensuring that those processes are replicated wherever appropriate. Such organizations also work to identify and improve those collaborative processes that have the most significant effects on either their short-term or long-term bottom line.

Treating collaboration as a disciplined process requires attention to the design and execution of collaborative activity. It doesn't mean that one process or way of work is followed for all collaborative work, but it does mean that the process is always conscious. In addition, such organizations and teams are as concerned about the processes used (including the information considered) in collaboration as they are about the results. As a result, upper management is much more able to rely on the decisions and recommendations of subordinate collaborative units. In addition, those same units are more able to provide decisions and rationales in a form that communicates to and is supportive of the goals and objectives of upper management and other collaborative units.

Importance

Disciplined collaborative processes enable organizations to make faster, better decisions (Mohrman, Cohen, & Mohrman, 1995; Pasmore, 1994). The research on decision making clearly points to disciplined processes, not time spent in decision making, as the most important contributor to good decisions. In addition, treating collaboration as a disciplined process results in the use of common tools and practices that allow members to convene, process information, make decisions, and report findings seamlessly across the organization.

✓ When It Is Working

Organizations that treat collaboration as a disciplined process are able to manage multiple, interrelated collaborative efforts in a timely fashion. They are able to do this because a great deal of thought has gone into designing the groups or teams doing the collaborating, both in terms of who is involved and in terms of the relationships among the teams. Also carefully managed are the mission and objectives of the teams; the information, processes and tools used; and the ways in which relevant information is distributed to and among the teams. Typically, in organizations using disciplined processes you will see:

- An almost religious commitment to agendas and minutes;
- Clear escalation paths so that collaborative groups that are "stuck" on a decision are able to appeal to a higher and/or better-informed authority quickly and easily;
- IT systems that provide common databases, easy access to needed information, and sophisticated communication tools;
- Members and teams skilled in the use of a number of systematic decision-making processes;
- Meetings that start and end on time; and
- Decisions that are rarely overturned either by upper management or by the team itself.

✗ When It Is Not Working

A number of things can happen when collaboration is not treated as a disciplined process. Examples include, but are in no way limited to these:

- Haphazard attention to agendas, timing, minutes, and other communication responsibilities;
- Decisions that are overturned frequently, with few attempts to explain the reasoning to those who made the original decision;
- Management that spends more time evaluating the results of collaborative decisions than evaluating the processes used to make those decisions;

- Progress that is not tracked or managed systematically; and

- Problems or delays in one collaborative unit that have direct consequences for other units not identified or addressed until the consequences
  are both major and costly.

10. Design and Promote Flexible Organizations

"How will we know who to kill?" This was the question many executives asked
when team-based organizational systems were first suggested. The executives
really didn't want to kill anyone (usually), but they did believe it was critical
to identify, and unequivocally express their concern to, those individuals who
did not meet their responsibilities. The executives were concerned about
accountability. While their motivations may have been mixed, their concerns
were legitimate. An organization depends on its members to meet certain
responsibilities and needs ways to provide sanctions when they do not.

The issue of accountability is one of the main reasons we have hierarchical
organizations with clear, often singular, reporting relationships. It's just easier in
clearly boxed, strictly hierarchical organizations to know who should decide,
who is accountable for results, and how rewards and sanctions should be delivered. The problem is that the business world no longer seems to fit this model.
Projects, task forces, and so forth are constantly created to manage the complexity of work today. Few challenges fit into one organizational entity. The power of
team and the power of collaboration are required simply to address what are now
everyday issues. Creating a successful organization requires a level of flexibility
that is not serviced by traditional boundaries or traditional roles.

Flexible organizations are able to form and re-form multiple types of collaborative projects and teams to accomplish increasingly dynamic work
requirements. They represent a different way of thinking about organizations.

Traditional organizations sought to create very clear reporting relationships,
the ideal being a single boss for each employee. Organizations dealing with
more dynamic and complex demands evolved into a matrix system, with people reporting to one person for immediate work requirements and another person for some level of functional responsibility. Woven within each of these types
of organizational structures are teams created to accomplish a variety of purposes. For many organizations, these teams or projects have become so pervasive that they represent the major way work is being done.

Flexible organizations are different in that they accept the dynamic nature of business and react with organizational structures—and the accompanying culture and support systems to allow a new level of fluidity. These organizations deliberately loosened the traditional boundaries between managers and subordinates and foster and reward leadership at all levels of the organization. These organizations have members who are able to work collaboratively within the organization and with customers, vendors, and temporary external partners. They have an increasing number of members who can collaborate with members of very different countries and cultures. The flexible organization is, in many ways, the only effective response to a global environment.

Importance

One advantage of flexible organizations is their ability to respond to shifts in business conditions. They are capable of adapting more quickly to shifting product features, technology trends, customer preferences, and competitive pressures. They shift personnel quickly into business units where they are needed. These organizations decentralize decision making so that more decisions can be made at levels closer to where the problems and opportunities arise (Galbraith, 2001).

✓ When It Is Working

Flexible organizations are characterized by people comfortable with broader roles, as opposed to well-defined jobs. These organizations actively sanction work across department and other boundaries. The management team functions more often as a team and works to resolve complex questions at higher levels so that subordinates are empowered to "do whatever it takes to get the job done." Organization members feel free to communicate laterally and vertically with others in the organization.

✗ When It Is Not Working

When organizations are not flexible, people are often more aligned with their bosses or areas of expertise than with the work at hand. Members are often unwilling—or unable—to create the shared understanding necessary to work effectively in teams with people from differing backgrounds and perspectives. A lack of organizational flexibility can also lead to these problems:

- Decision making is too slow or too out of touch because it is concentrated in the upper levels of the organization or within other units that do not have the necessary perspective or expertise;

- Projects, teams, and/or individuals lack the resources necessary to do their jobs;

- Projects, teams, or individuals have limited commitment to collaborative activity that is not under the direct supervision of their immediate managers;

- Reorganizations are frequent;

- The organization has an inability to anticipate or adapt well to change.

The ten principles described above work interactively to create a collaborative organization. They are summarized in Table 2.1. Organizations most able to thrive in today's environment work toward improvement in each of the ten areas in concert. Indeed, adherence to the principles leads to the creation of collaborative capacity at the organization level.

Table 2.1. The Ten Principles for Building Collaborative Organizations

Principle	Importance	When It Is Working	When It Is Not Working
1. Focus Collaboration on Achieving Business Results	Creates a common purpose and context for decision making	Agreement on priorities; deliberations always include business results/concerns (both long- and short-term); groups or teams subjugate to needs of overall business unit or organization	Conflict between team or small group results and larger organization goals; frequent, nonproductive disagreements; relationship goals overshadow results goals
2. Align Organizational Support Systems to Promote Ownership	Fosters commitment to and understanding of the overall goals of the organization	Members are informed and committed; members experience little conflict between their personal goals and the goals of the organization	Poor and/or slow decision making; confusion over what is valued or important; members unwilling to make commitments of extra time or effort

Table 2.1. The Ten Principles for Building Collaborative Organizations, Cont'd

Principle	Importance	When It Is Working	When It Is Not Working
3. Articulate and Enforce "a Few Strict Rules"	Creates the necessary cohesion to foster goal-directed cooperative effort while maintaining the flexibility to respond to changing demands and opportunities	Individuals and teams have a shared understanding of what is valued in terms of behavior and outcomes in the organization; individuals and teams are able to operate productively across boundaries and make decisions consistent with the goals and strategies of the organization	In organizations with too many rules, members are unable and unwilling to act without permission, fail to respond to new opportunities and demands, and spend almost all of their time managing upward; in organizations with too few rules, small group and individual goals dominate; there is a sense that "no one is in charge"
4. Exploit the Rhythm of Divergence and Convergence	Provides the necessary balance between generating new and exciting ideas and the discipline necessary to do the job	The organization is able to create new, shared ideas and to meet commitments to customers, shareholders, and employees; members recognize when it is important to concentrate on "thinking outside the box" and when it is time to make a decision, complete the product, or deliver the service	With too much divergence, decisions are made and remade, products are not finished on time, organization goals are not met; with too much convergence, new or creative ideas are limited, members move to a decision too quickly with little exploration of new ideas, different perspectives, or information from external sources
5. Manage Complex Tradeoffs on a Timely Basis	Provides the information and disciplined processes for making the complex decisions in new situations	Members of decision-making groups have a shared understanding of the criteria to use in making tradeoff decisions; members are aware of the various weightings senior management has selected for tradeoff in specific situations	Bad decisions are made; no decisions are made; available expertise is ignored when making decisions; teams cannot articulate the issues or decision-making criteria used

Table 2.1. The Ten Principles for Building Collaborative Organizations, Cont'd

Principle	Importance	When It Is Working	When It Is Not Working
6. Create Higher Standards for Discussion, Dialogue, and Information Sharing	Raising the standards for discussions and dialogue ensures that more information is considered and more potential consequences anticipated in each example of collaboration	People have the information they need when they need it in formats they can use; discussions indicate a level of understanding and sophistication that ensures that the right issues are being considered	Decisions are made without consideration of the most important issues or the most valuable information; the same decisions are made again and again; decisions are made that sub-optimize the goals of the total organization
7. Foster Personal Accountability	Effective collaboration requires that each individual fulfill his or her role effectively and provide some value-adding contribution	Members need little or no supervision in the traditional sense; members identify what needs to be done and initiate actions to accomplish those things; members perform work that is of high quality and meets their commitments to their colleagues and to the organization	People wait for direction before acting, place blame, and do not acknowledge their responsibility when a mistake is made; members look to satisfy their individual objectives versus overall business objectives
8. Align Authority, Information, and Decision Making	Collaborative decision making is most effective when the team has the information necessary to make good decisions and the authority and accountability to implement those decisions	People are willing and able to make effective decisions in a timely manner and to be held accountable for those decisions; people who have the information and authority actually make the decisions.	Decisions are made at one level in the organization and then have to be remade as more information is discovered; people are not accountable for the decisions they make
9. Treat Collaboration as a Disciplined Process	Ensures that the correct information is considered, the deliberations are focused and balanced, and the decisions are workable	Team members can explain how they make decisions; common forms exist for summarizing and reporting collaborative activities; there is a sense of order and discipline in collaborative activities	Decisions are made without considerations of all relevant points of view; people with power exert more influence than their information or accountability warrants; collaborative activities are characterized by chaos

Table 2.1. The Ten Principles for Building Collaborative Organizations, Cont'd

Principle	Importance	When It Is Working	When It Is Not Working
10. Design and Promote Flexible Organizations	Foster multiple grouping across members to meet the changing requirements of the organization to do the work	People are able to work productively with members at layers and all functional groups within organization; groups form and re-form seamlessly to do the work	The organization is constantly being redesigned; collaborative activities that involve people with different managers are nonproductive; new groups take a long time to reach productive activity

The following four chapters, Section 2, explain how the principles can be applied in different settings: manufacturing, new product development, service, and virtual settings. There is no need to read these chapters in order. We recommend starting with the chapter that is most consistent with your experience.

The final section of the book covers strategies for building a collaborative organization.

"If we cannot visualize why we have to get off the 19th Century hierarchy train and into the self-organizing information exchange, we will be unable to fully muster the commitment, constant learning, and intense interaction necessary for mutual growth and development into the 21st Century and beyond."

Rosabeth Moss Kanter

"Most people are performing at low levels because of personal or organizational disintegration. They possess much more intelligence, talent, and creativity than their present jobs require or even allow."

Stephen Covey, 1999

PART 2

APPLYING THE PRINCIPLES

CHAPTER 3

Collaboration in Manufacturing Settings

THE WORLD OF MANUFACTURING has been changing radically and at an increasing pace. Every aspect of that world is in flux, including customer behavior, global competition, organizational form, employee types, and so on. The traditional form of organizing around hierarchical command and control that made manufacturing so successful in the early 20th Century is like an eggshell that is bursting open from the pressure to adapt to the many rapid changes. That means new challenges frequently arise for manufacturing. Responding to those challenges will take every ounce of intelligence in the organization, which means that collaborative practices are essential to leverage the principle that "all of us are smarter than any of us."

Tracking the invention of new forms of manufacturing organization through the 20th Century shows a sequence that includes functional, divisional, matrix, network, and cellular structures (Miles & Snow, 1994). The new forms evolved at single work sites and spread through companies and industries. For example, the Texas Instruments (TI) experiments in employee involvement at their Dennison, Texas, plant moved from the suggestion box to quality circles to cell teams to self-directed teams to integrated product teams, and then they began to influence other TI plants. The success of this experiment then contributed to the spread of such design ideas across the industry and from industry to industry as the competitive advantage of this new idea became obvious. Much of that advantage emerged through control of cost and quality. More recently, advantage has become obvious around speed, innovation, and collaboration.

Increasingly, manufacturing is managed through a complex set of collaborative relationships, including alliances, joint ventures, supply-chain partnerships, marketing agreements, and various kinds of work teams. For example, high-tech manufacturers have outsourced parts production to companies such as Flextronics, where the partnership is implicit in the supply chain (Marks, 2002). These relationships only work when there is a common understanding of the objectives, policies, and strategies, some skill at teamwork, and a willingness to cooperate in keeping the arrangement flexible. Organizations' boundaries have become more open, so resources from outside can be accessed, including outsourced functions. Successful coordination across boundaries requires extra attention to collaborative practices where understanding and keeping commitments lead to trust between partners. But many attempts to create advantage through unity fail, such as the 90 percent of mergers that fall short of financial expectations.

Definition of Manufacturing

All organizations are composed of people who use tools to do work producing products and/or services for customers. The SEC identifies 140 different industries under the heading of "manufacturing," ranging from food to airplanes to computer chips. The companies vary by such factors as process versus batch production, customized design versus standardized products, simple versus complex products, geographic location, and education level required for frontline workers.

"Manufacturing" is typically thought of as the production of a tangible product from physical materials. The product may take one second or one year to build; it may be tiny or huge, simple or complex, identical each time or tailored and unique. Other production would probably be classified as "craft work." The production work requires raw materials, information, money, people, energy, and intangibles such as direction, standards, and customers.

Trends Affecting How We Work

Manufacturing organizations are characterized by employees from several generations with increasing education, work that requires more skill, work that must be coordinated and integrated across complex products and projects quickly, customers who want tailored products with high quality delivered quickly and cheaply, increases in global competition, and rapid changes in technology. This challenging situation means that the old solutions to the problem of organizing are not adequate. New ways of organizing are being developed continually. Some of those experiments are small and some large. Some work well and some do not. Each experiment is a risk taken because of perceived trends in the business environment, such as globalization, mass customization, and supply chain management.

Globalization

A few decades ago, most organizations supplied local customers and benefited from having a small territory to themselves. Multinationals were the only global traders. The multinationals that dominated their industries had few global competitors. Japan's emergence as a serious competitor in automobile and electronics manufacturing in the 1970s marked a change. Now competition in those industries and others comes from a number of countries, some of them having become industrialized in only a few decades. In addition, small companies can now achieve effective global distribution through use of Internet communications, shipping through FedEx and UPS, small outlet shops, or partners.

Although cheap labor continues to drive the spread of manufacturing facilities to second- and third-tier economies, the spread of technology and information and the initiative of people in those countries where very low standards of living were the norm has created opportunities and a critical mass. The economy is now a global economy; competition is now global. Core competencies have shifted from physical facilities, to financial assets, to technological and informational, toward the design of organizations and involvement of people. To keep the price of a product competitive in an industrialized nation, all of these factors must be well-tuned. Perhaps when the collaboration between different components of the company is so well developed, geographic, cultural, and skill barriers add more cost than cheap labor adds value.

A Changing Workforce

The average age in the United States and in most Western European countries is climbing. That means the proportion of the population that provides the workforce is shrinking. Other countries in the world, such as Mexico, present different demographic profiles with much younger average ages. This fact, plus the ever-increasing amount of education required for technical work, will make it more difficult to hire qualified workers in manufacturing in the future. The competition for new hires and for retention of current employees will escalate.

Spread of Democracy and the Market Economy

Serious competition is emerging from sources around the globe for a number of reasons, but one of the key drivers is the shift toward democratic government and a willingness to invest in a market economy. The lessons learned from Russia's disastrous attempt to shift from a socialist to a market economy are aiding some other countries in executing a smoother transition. As a result, there is an opening of markets, but also a liberating of people and ideas that leads to new competition.

Explosion of New Technologies

New tools appear every day. Some of the tools consist of new hardware or evolution of existing equipment, such as handheld computers for tracking parts movement or shipping. Other perhaps more important tools consist of new software packages that enable equipment and information to operate in more coordinated ways and result in less mind-numbing work by employees.

Mass Customization

When manufacturers who are used to producing for the mass market decide there are many mass markets of smaller size, they start customizing products for smaller and smaller groups of consumers—down to the ultimate consumer. Build to order (BTO) is a way of tailoring products to customer needs. Simple products, like Burger King's Whopper (with or without mayo) are not too challenging. Dell showed that it could also be done for computers, but larger products like cars and trucks may be a bit more challenging. Yet Daimler-Chrysler AG is customizing products with its Dodge Dakota. Built-to-order is an ambitious approach to customer satisfaction, challenging every facet of the manufacturing process. It demands a reconfiguring of the partnerships that typically make up a contemporary manufacturing line. The increase in options leads to an increase in variety. The customer is more satisfied, because "one size does not fit all." But manufacturing processes must change radically.

More Risk, Less Security

Margins have shrunk for most businesses. Although, for several decades about 95 percent of new businesses have failed in their first five years, a larger number of major businesses seem to be failing lately. The risk is increasing, yet the risk takers are the ones who lead the race. Terrorist activities throughout the world add another element of risk, increasing overhead with processes and procedures for security that slow down work and delivery, costing money and time and cutting into narrow margins. In the late 1990s, unemployment in the United States was at record lows, so many technical workers immigrated to the United States to fill jobs. Germany and other European nations had similar problems at both technical and labor levels.

By late 2001, however, the global recession had reversed the trend, and unemployment was climbing. Layoffs in the millions cut overhead to enable companies to survive, impacting many families and towns, particularly when entire plants that small towns depended on were closed. The risk became palpable and shared by many.

Supply Chain Management

In the late 1980s, the flow of parts and products from suppliers to manufacturers to customers was recognized as a continuous stream that had to be managed for competitive advantage. The relationships between links in the chain must be attended to, in addition to the quality of the goods and information. Companies that cull the weak suppliers, set standards for suppliers who remain, and build collaborative relationships with them are leading their industries in performance. A great deal of waste and error can occur in each handoff as a part or piece of information moves across boundaries from one company in the chain to the next. Elimination of waste and misunderstanding reduces overhead, similar to the way lean manufacturing eliminates the same problems within a plant.

Leadership

The nature of leadership has shifted from an administrative emphasis to a management emphasis to a leadership emphasis. Ways of leading that were adequate when competition was less than global and the pace of change was subdued are not adequate for the 21st Century business environment. Leadership and affluence in the future will increasingly depend on foresight, continuous innovation, and rapid response capabilities. The most important factors determining the future success of most U.S. manufacturing sectors will be the willingness and capability of corporate managers (Quinn, 1983):

- To make long-term strategic investments, and
- To innovate continuously in both organizational and technological domains.

Many U.S. managers adopted the limited niche, price skimming, elitist strategies they once disparaged in European companies. Enron's rapid decline in the fall of 2001 represents this kind of management perspective. Rather than using the full potential of scale economies to take advantage of emerging world markets, some U.S. managers concentrated on a series of highly segmented domestic product niches. Some mistakenly focused on luxury rather than on quality within their segments and overlooked the logic of the experience curve. Others defended existing investments far too long, rather than adopting more attractive new product lines or processes.

But leadership among managers is only part of the trend. Empowerment of employees has shifted leadership responsibilities down to the shop floor. When a team member sees a problem, he or she takes the initiative. For example, at Toyota, line workers stop the line when an error is detected. At Eastman Chemical, they call a meeting on the spot to work out a problem. The spread of leadership responsibilities and capabilities means more minds are working on the problems of performance.

Common Ways of Organizing

A variety of ways of organizing manufacturing organizations have been developed over the years. In general, organizations have become flatter, more flexible structures with an increased need for coordination. Decision making has become decentralized, and more cross-functional design has emerged.

Different types of designs are required for different products. For example, producing computers may be more flexible than producing boxes of cereal or batches of paint. Within those workflow designs, some collaboration has always taken place, even when the support systems have focused on individual performance.

The evolution of collaborative systems has paralleled the increasing involvement of employees in decision making. From suggestion box to quality control circle to task force to work team, new and more collaborative tools emerged over the latter half of the 20th Century. As work teams spread, variations in design emerged, including those with high levels of autonomy, those involving members from multiple disciplines, and those linked electronically. Manufacturing is complex and diverse enough to incorporate all of these types and more.

A more recent shift has been to move up a level in collaborative organizing to systems that integrate teams. These systems have been referred to as "high performance work organizations," "high performance work systems," "self-managing organizations," "team-based organizations," and so on. The names represent a combination of changes in organizing work that include fine-tuning of processes, a shared understanding of the business goals, involvement and empowerment of employees, and collaboration across boundaries. Companies that are advanced examples of this trend in design have won awards for their achievements and customers for their products.

Challenges with Respect to Collaboration

Manufacturing managers have sought better ways to organize in order to make better use of resources. The resource focus was physical assets in the 19th and early 20th Centuries, then people, and now intangibles like intellectual and social assets. Collaboration in manufacturing is ubiquitous. It occurs both formally and informally throughout the organization. The challenge is to recognize when it adds value and then to act on that opportunity.

Because most people grew up in bureaucratic, paternalistic, and small-sized systems, they do not naturally have the ability to recognize the collaborative opportunities around them. Personal and organizational history create blindness and inertia to capitalize on collaborative opportunities.

Within manufacturing, the first challenge to address is that of narrow mental models for organizing. People cannot easily envision possibilities they have not experienced, for example, if one has never worked on a great team, one's standards and expectations for collaborative payoffs from a team are low. One underestimates the potential so motivation is diminished to build collaborative competencies. Benchmarking, scenario planning, and vision work all help with this problem.

There is a tendency to discount the importance of the social side of the organization. Partly, managers take it for granted; partly, they consider it a nuisance rather than an opportunity; and partly, they see it as something to "do to" employees rather than a way to participate and partner with them in change work.

A corollary of the above two challenges is failing to spot opportunities for collaboration. The boundaries in organizations are usually so firm and fixed in members' minds that they fail to recognize opportunities for linking across them. For example, a team may see itself as an isolated island, or a top management group may see the vertical levels below it as gaps that are not to be crossed, or technical employees may rely on their language to create power and control over critical information.

People work to meet their needs. The needs may be simple, such as a paycheck, more long-term, such as a promotion, or intangible, such as making a contribution to society. Whatever the goals, the reward and recognition system within the organization influences when people will collaborate to achieve their goals and when they will work in isolation. In a competitive environment, striving for a promotion may produce great fragmentation problems in upper management, including hoarding of resources, undermining of colleagues, and simplistic understanding of decision requirements.

The valuing of cross-functional collaboration became obvious with the emergence of matrix designs in the 1960s, but multidisciplinary efforts that include finance, accounting, HR, marketing, and so forth emerged more slowly. The failure to see the opportunities created costs in many ways, including products that could not sell or sales that didn't match the product features.

With the computer revolution, a bias emerged toward technical solutions to work problems. The computer and related technology were viewed as a panacea. Huge investments were made in technology, but payoffs were significantly below expectations (Keil & Mixon, 1994/1995). The common theme was the failure to integrate the technical changes with appropriate social changes, what Emery and Trist (1969) labeled sociotechnical systems issues. The technical bias still dominates most management thinking.

When to Collaborate

The opportunities to collaborate in manufacturing are prolific. They are both formal and informal. They can be identified and supported or inhibited. The question is: When does it pay to collaborate? The short answer to that is

- When one person does not have all the expertise required for a decision, and

- When more than one person needs to be committed to the decision for effective implementation.

Collaboration fails to pay off under three circumstances: (1) when people decide inappropriately to come together for work; (2) when people fail to work well when together; and (3) when the wrong people come together. If either expertise or commitment is required, people need to get together around a decision and be involved in the process. Meetings are held for a number of reasons— some require collaborative processes and some do not. Some of them should not even be held.

If the process of meeting, formally or informally, is distorted, contaminated, subverted, unskilled, abbreviated, and so on, the coming together is not enough to achieve collaborative exchanges. A number of factors play a role in whether the time spent together is well-spent or not. Consequently, a number of opportunities for benefiting from collaboration may be lost. The losses occur around all organizational processes, but are minimized when principles of effective collaboration are in place.

How the Guiding Principles Apply

The Ten Principles of Collaborative Organizations described in the prior chapter are presented below within the context of manufacturing. Each principle is explained as it relates to manufacturing; then a discussion follows dealing with the signs of successful and unsuccessful practice. Table 3.1 on page 92 provides a summary of this information. Key questions that the guiding principles are designed to answer include:

- What would you do if you wanted to increase the effectiveness of collaboration?

- What if you wanted to exploit the real advantages of collaboration?

1. Focus Collaboration on Achieving Business Results

"Business results" is a commonly used phrase that represents the performance of the business unit, a phrase used to refer to any size unit but most commonly quantified at the company or corporate level. As with many such phrases, it is used for many purposes and with many meanings in conversation, but the consequences can be quite clear.

The key problem with understanding the *meaning* of the term "business results" is lack of specification of the level of the business unit; the key problem with utilizing the term is lack of alignment across business levels. In this book, we refer to "business results" as a concept that applies to all levels of collaboration—from the value derived by creating a new joint venture between companies to the value derived from effective dialogue at "the water cooler" (learning and creativity generated by informal conversations in social settings). Business results from collaboration require focusing attention on the goal of performance improvement. That is not uncommon, but a shared understanding by all members of the organization of which business results are important, how to measure them, and how to communicate about them seems to be uncommon. Such universal understanding of business results is essential for creating world class operations.

✓ When It Is Working

There is a lot of collaborative activity in every work site—informally, if not formally. People are jointly discussing, solving problems, and making decisions all the time. Leaders deliberately and systematically develop and support collaborative activity. As a result, they fail to build one of the key resources in the company—the collective ability of the organization to solve problems.

Business results use customer response as the pivot point and business processes involve customer input. Teams interface directly with customers, acquiring data on what is important to that customer for prioritizing service and making decisions.

All members have common understanding of the "who, what, why, where, when, and how" of measurement. Metrics are chosen for integrating the different parts of the organization. For example, metrics represent sets of teams, instead of individual teams. Managers encourage collaboration across department lines, discipline lines, project lines, and production lines and shifts to avoid suboptimization.

✗ When It Is Not Working

There are a number of signs that indicate that the focus on business results has been lost. For example, line workers cannot describe the organization's mission, vision, goals, and strategies. There is a tendency to take for granted that "everyone probably knows this stuff" or to believe "if I know it, everybody does" or "they don't need to know this stuff—after all, they're not managers." Front-line workers fail to take the initiative to think about business results because of a learned helplessness, that is, they have been punished for offering suggestions in the past, so they have given up, they lack information, or they haven't had the training needed to think in strategic ways. There is a management fear that "if production workers start making decisions, I will be out of a job." The ability to focus on business results is blocked or undermined by private limits and concerns.

Decisions are made that undermine collaborative practices, create silos, or ignore business results. For example, competition is intentionally encouraged between teams or between shifts, leading to hoarding of information, hiding of tools, undoing the work of the prior shift, and so forth. Zaleznick (1992) gives the following example: "The chief executive of this company encourages competition and rivalry among peers, ultimately rewarding the one who comes out on top with increased responsibility. These hybrid arrangements produce some unintended consequences that can be disastrous. There is no easy way to limit rivalry. Instead, it permeates all levels of the operation and opens the way for the formation of cliques in an atmosphere of intrigue." This CEO may think he understands competitive advantage, but clearly he does not understand collaborative advantage or the importance of having every member of the organization focusing activity and thought on business results for the whole organization.

2. Align Organizational Support Systems to Promote Ownership

Support systems compose part of the organizational infrastructure that facilitates carrying out the processes necessary to do the work; to manage, control, coordinate, and improve it; and to manage and involve the people who are doing it. Support systems can promote performance or inhibit it. As the organization has evolved over time, the design of each support system will have changed, but the fit between the support system and the performance goals of the organization may not have been reexamined. Fit must be established anew after each major organizational change, and with continuous change being the common theme these days, that means continuous assessment of fit. It is essential that support systems align with the units that actually perform the work.

A lot of behavior is created by environment; the stimulus for a behavior, and therefore for performance, often comes from outside the individual employee, rather than independently from within the person. The reward and recognition system is a commonly cited example. However, other aspects of the employee's environment also prompt certain behaviors, such as tools, information, and trust. Changing the environment through reengineering of the support systems can enhance performance. The goal should be having employees who say, "I have a voice, I am heard, and I care that I am heard," "I can feel that I am making a contribution and it is appreciated, so I am committed to this work," and "I have the tools and support I need to do a job I can be proud of."

Teams and groups of teams are embedded in an infrastructure that either promotes or inhibits their performance. Like most polarities, one can argue that this is not "black or white." But it is so important that here we argue that the infrastructure MUST be aligned with the needs of collaborative groups, like teams, or performance will be inhibited. Often the support systems in the infrastructure are the last thing to change, so maximum benefits from collaboration and teaming are slower to develop. For example, a team cannot make good decisions without having access to appropriate information. Several key support systems are identified below with suggestions about critical practices (adapted from Hall, 1998).

Leadership System. There is a tendency to define the term "leadership system" in narrow terms. One vice president defined it as "senior executives." However, leadership is demonstrated when any member of the organization takes initiative, articulates a vision or goal, pushes back, suggests a solution or decision, or restates a question. So executives, senior managers, middle managers, front-line managers, and team members can all contribute. The combined contribution determines the strength of the leadership system; this is not a zero sum game—the leadership pie can grow with involvement. Research shows the following as key mechanisms of leadership:

- Expecting work groups to succeed (somewhat like the self-fulfilling prophecy);
- Providing resources that enable the groups;

- Anticipating needs of teammates and direct reports and removing hurdles to performance;

- Supporting the expression of leadership behaviors at all levels of the organization; and

- Being open to multiple perspectives.

Information and Communication System. The flow of information and ideas represents the circulatory system in an organization. The same kinds of problems can occur—hardening of the arteries representing reduced flexibility, anemic information, and blockages. The IT/IS system can facilitate flow or impede it. The organization's culture can do the same. Collaborative activity is stifled when flow is not supported, so it becomes more difficult to make informed decisions and take intelligent, discretionary action in the pursuit of business goals. Mechanisms that aid in communication include:

- Easing collection, organization, storage, and access of key information that enhances performance, such as best practices;

- Establishing a knowledge management system;

- Modeling of open sharing by top managers;

- Providing opportunities for contact between those who do the work and their customers, externally and internally; and

- Focusing on *the interface between technology and people,* rather than either exclusively.

Performance Management System. Support systems are intended to enable high levels of performance and to create conditions that increase commitment to business results. For example, performance management systems include rewards and recognition, measurement, development, and feedback processes that can be systematized and become dependable subsystems. In most organizations the reward and recognition subsystems are focused on individual performance. Focusing them on team performance is a step in the right direction, but it doesn't go far enough. Teams can become silos and optimize their own behavior at the cost of the performance of the larger organization. For example, teams can compete for resources rather than cooperate and thus reduce the performance of all involved. Gain sharing is typically done at the business unit level, so all individuals, teams, and levels must cooperate to achieve rewards that are shared; it represents a site-based program, rather than a team-based program, and the line-of-sight to unit goals is clearly communicated to guide and align the performance of all members. Pay for performance may not foster collaboration, but a "broad-banding" of compensation may and also enable people to be more responsive to the customers.

Learning System. The pervasiveness of change in manufacturing mandates that learning be continuous by all members. The learning system includes both formal and informal components. Most organizations focus on formal training and development. However, the informal may be more critical to success. For example, consider the value of skilled and knowledgeable employees sharing their knowledge in a timely fashion with newer employees or employees in other parts of the organization. Knowledge sharing and transfer depend on a number of conditions. The first is willingness to share. That attitude emerges from an organization where the win-win perspective dominates, where it is clear that contributing to the intelligence of the larger system benefits one's own situation. Thus, educating each other is a practice that must be modeled at all levels, rewarded through joint compensation and valued by all.

Organization and Team Design System. Team design is the most important factor in determining individual team performance (Hall, 1998; Wageman, 1997). The design of the team includes decisions about who is on the team, how many members are on the team, how interdependent their work is, and how much self-management is practiced. As important as team design may be for the individual team, an organization consists of many teams and many other forms of work groups—formal and informal, temporary and permanent, functional and cross-functional. The design of the organization can enhance or stifle the ability of people to work together effectively. Collaborative practices can be built into the design or contradicted by it. The traditional bureaucracy created rigid lines of interaction and strong boundaries around behavior that minimized opportunities for collaboration. The complex work of the 21st Century demands collaborative approaches, so flatter, looser structures that permit flexible organizing become essential.

✓ When It Is Working

When there is little or no gap between the support a team has and the support they believe they need, there is a great sense of potency or "can do" among the members. They feel empowered to take initiative and do so. They go after the information they need and get it and use it. This results in ideas for innovations in products, processes, and services flowing from the front lines. Team members feel recognized and rewarded for their work, so their commitment and investment of energy and ideas increases. They remain loyal to the company even during difficult times. The competencies of the group continue to grow, because the members have both the desire and the means for achieving new learning.

Leaders of support systems collaborate with one another to create an optimal performance environment for the work teams and groups rather than competing with each other. Members of support groups view line workers as customers and work to serve them. Upward feedback is welcomed for improving the support processes.

✗ When It Is Not Working

Work groups and work teams are the customers of the support systems. When those systems are not working, there is a lack of alignment with the needs of the teams. That shows as lower than expected levels of performance and frustration in the teams. For example, members feel they need information to make a decision or understand a problem but are unable to access it, because they don't have authorization or the information is not archived or computer terminals are not available to front-line workers.

When there is a misalignment of leadership styles with empowered groups or teams, the conflict results in lack of support that undermines both the performance and the morale of the members. When members have an idea or an opportunity for improving the work processes, they feel stymied by the blockages they run into in attempting to express or implement the idea. A sense of hopelessness grows and the "team initiative" loses credibility.

3. Articulate and Enforce "a Few Strict Rules"

This principle is about how you manage the company—identifying the things you *always* do. Rules should operationalize the principles you adhere to. Rules set criteria for decision making and for tradeoff decisions. Just as we identified ten principles for effective collaboration in Chapter 2, other principles need to be identified for managing quality and for customer relationships. Rules identified must be enforced so that all members of the organization behave in harmony around the rules. Brown and Eisenhardt (1998) wrote of rules: "Simple structures and extensive communication allow people to engage in more complicated and adaptive behaviors."

For example, there may be a rule that "We will have supervisors as a part of the team, but all teams design their own roles so the roles emerge to fit the circumstances; that way the teams remain adaptable." The rule sets a boundary for action without impeding creative problem solving within the boundary. Rules establish boundaries around behavior formally, just as norms do informally.

The main issues around a few strict rules are (1) limit the number to the essential (do away with 80 percent of the current rules and retain or create the vital few); (2) focus the rules on improving performance for everyone; (3) make the rules universal; and (4) make the rules clear and understandable by all. Then they will work well.

As with many things, there is a moderate level that is appropriate and that must fit the situation. Having too many rules complicates the organization unnecessarily and creates barriers to innovation and collaboration, whereas having too few rules creates a lack of coherence and alignment.

When designing your vital few rules, consider including the following:

1. Be very careful about the commitments you make and keep all of those you do make. Trust will erode rapidly for each time you fail to follow through on a commitment.[1]

2. Articulate these rules, for example: "This is who we are, and this is how we are going to do business."

3. Make the tacit rules of the culture explicit to minimize misunderstanding and maximize alignment.

4. Require permissions for exceptions to these few strict rules and establish a clear process for deciding exceptions that all will adhere to.

The "HP Way" established under the leadership of Hewlett and Packard was based on a few strict rules: (1) personal accountability; (2) personal respect; (3) lots of autonomy; (4) tolerance for learning from mistakes; (5) no tolerance for dropping the ball ("We didn't meet the goal, so we will not celebrate completing the project"); (6) decisions based on data; and (7) being on time at all levels of the organization—for example, executives felt as bad about being late to a meeting as anyone else in the organization did.

---

[1]For example, at Texas Instruments' defense plants in the 1980s and 1990s, it was clear that a manager could not get ahead who didn't live by keeping commitments, and the culture taught this to new managers. This was in contrast to companies where people agreed to everything and failed to discriminate between those requests or ideas that they had resources and energy for and those they did not.

As an example, consider the experience of customers when they asked for some small variation in a product. What did the employee focus on—the customer or the rules? Did the seller or server exercise a little discretion and provide what was needed—delighting the customer—or deny the request because of the "the rules." Customers are lost every day for "just following the rules" behavior. Customers feel frustrated being treated as just "a number" rather than as a valued customer for whom special efforts might be made. Front-line employees need discretion within the guidelines of the vital few rules for making those special efforts often and appropriately.

Order and control are necessary, but there needs to be a balance with variety and discretion that allows for tailored responses to environmental demands. The company that fails to focus on the customer loses customers. The company that fails to notice and adapt to changes in its business environment fails to survive. A balance is needed, which can be partly achieved by designating a few strict rules or principles of operation—strict in that they are not to be violated without special processes of approval and few in that there is some freedom of movement within the boundaries they set.

✓ When It Is Working

With everyone following the same set of strict rules, there is a sense of membership, and a coherence emerges for the organization. People do challenge the status quo. People are able to explain "how things work around here." It is obvious that values are shared across members of the organization. The innovation quotient for the organization is high.

✗ When It Is Not Working

With too many rules, people are not very curious about other possibilities. There is no understanding of the status quo. When rules and norms are not aligned, subterfuge and isolation emerge as the group creates its own island of identity within the larger system, following their norms, rather than the rules. If the boundaries are too tight, innovation and adaptability are stifled. If there are too many rules, the thinking becomes overly controlled and sterile—ideas for innovation come from only a few places in the organization.

4. Exploit the Rhythm of Convergence and Divergence

The strength of a company is at its maximum when the diversity or divergence of ideas is valued and the integration or convergence of those ideas is effective and timely. Convergence and divergence represent processes of sharing ideas that alternate in a rhythm that is like the two halves of a zipper fitting together.

The process of convergence/divergence is often suboptimal. For example, many people see meetings as a waste of time. That perception typically occurs because participants fail to use the tools of effective meeting management, such as agenda setting, action steps, facilitators, and so forth. But they are right that coming together can be nonproductive under some circumstances. Consider the old saying, "If you want to kill the motion, send it to committee." When is it worthwhile taking time to meet or even just to talk? When should we walk down the hall to talk face-to-face rather than send an email? When should we make a phone call to a remote site instead of an email? Questions like these should be answered from the framework of the convergence/divergence rhythm in collaborative process—the pattern of making divergent perspectives explicit and then folding them in on one another to create hybrid solutions that have the combined strengths of several single answers. Thus, knowledge can create value within our organizations to the extent it can move around, just like electricity.

Jazz is often used as a metaphor for this process, where musicians converge during part of a piece and take turns doing solo work during another part to build completely new musical experiences from old standards as their creative flow creates new opportunities and new musical ideas.

There are important patterns and guidelines for when and how people come together and break apart in a problem-solving or creative process. The rhythms of people converging and diverging around problems and issues are determined by three factors:

1. The formal scheduling requirements, such as periodic meetings;

2. The socially agreed on norms about when to regularly come together, such as coffee breaks or lunch; and

3. The specific events of a project or task, such as a crisis.

All three options are important and must be balanced with each other. The concerns of the manager here should be as follows:

• Recognize the role all three factors play;

• Remove barriers to formal, informal, and critical gatherings; and

- Find ways to utilize the interface between the three factors, such as allowing informal discussions to generate the agendas for formal meetings.

Formal meetings with agendas are not the only convergence tools. Informal meetings, including the little chats "around the water cooler," are very important opportunities. For example, at Xerox, field technicians often ate lunch together, not just for the social benefits, but because it gave them a chance to share their technical problems and the lessons learned from work in the field. It was an informal mechanism for knowledge transfer invented by the front-line workers. Collaborative practice relies on moving toward and with each other; that is what builds synergies.

✓ When It Is Working

When the rhythm is utilized as a tool for managing the process of thinking and discussion, time spent in effective discussion pays off in higher quality solutions and decisions and more commitment to the decisions. The rhythm of working together and working solo is understood and managed. Informal gatherings complement formal meetings. Formal meetings are timed and managed in ways that make them useful to all participants. Informal meetings occur frequently and easily cross horizontal and vertical boundaries. Meeting management tools are utilized, so follow-up occurs regularly. People come to meetings prepared for discussion. Trust and openness in meetings promotes sharing, so convergence of ideas is not hampered by information hording or fear. Willingness to leave certain things "unfinished" acknowledges that ambiguity has value. The convergence/divergence process is anchored by real deadlines, so the rhythm fits the situation.

✗ When It Is Not Working

When the rhythm of convergence and divergence fails to match the needs of the situation, opportunities for both convergence and for divergence are missed. Creativity and innovation seem rare and synergies seldom occur. A bias for action and discomfort with ambiguity and uncertainty lead to unilateral decision making or premature closure in meetings without the corrective advantage of consensus decision making. Hidden agendas subvert the process during meetings; already having "my answer" in mind prevents hearing what others have to offer. Lots of ideas and decisions from meetings go "plop!" or evaporate after the meeting breaks up. Follow-up is poor.

5. Manage Complex Tradeoffs on a Timely Basis

Few situations benefit from the use of black-and-white solutions or black-and-white decision making. Tradeoffs are often required to balance the pros and cons of the situation. Two kinds of tradeoff situations must be managed: established and emerging. In established situations, the tradeoffs are clear, so all members understand them; but in emerging situations, clarity is missing, so the tradeoffs are difficult to articulate.

There are processes for resolving tradeoffs, such as increasing core events, bringing in stakeholders, and doing system analyses, but principles drive the resolution, such as "cost is always the criteria." In the case of the Mars Deep Space Microprobes 2 that failed its mission on December 2, 1999, critics argue that a full system test should have been run, but there was only one prototype left and the team felt that it should not be destroyed in a full test, so, with a cost focus, they chose to do partial tests to allow for further work, that is, budget limits created the constraint. (Of course, the failure of the probes to transmit data after penetration of the soil at 400 KPH may have been due to hitting a rock.)

Investigators of the NASA Mars missions concluded that failures resulted from inadequate staffing and too little funding. Poor management allowed careless errors to sneak through: the Mars Climate Orbiter engineers failed to convert English units to metric, and the Mars Polar Lander likely crashed because of software bugs. The solution under a "faster, cheaper, better" philosophy is to eliminate or postpone some missions, since resources are not available for lowering risk with an ambitious program (Rhea, 2000).

Collaborative processes can enable open discussion and quick tradeoff decisions. The discipline of this process may include identifying all stakeholders and their needs and arranging appropriate participation in the decision-making process.

Tradeoff decisions must be made at appropriate levels. For example, a mechanical engineer's criteria probably include tradeoffs such as what works versus what does not work and how fast the prototypes can be developed versus how well they will hold up under different conditions. A line manager's criteria probably include tradeoffs such as safety versus economy and length of run versus time to tool up. These are quite different perspectives that cannot be coordinated intelligently without collaborative dialogue, which must begin with specifying the principles about how the tradeoff decision will be made. The principles must be made explicit and articulated at a high level.

The frame of reference for making tradeoff decisions is articulated at the management level by the top leaders, then communicated to operations, and finally passed down to the team. For example, at Pratt & Whitney, automating assembly saves a great deal of money and improves quality in manufacturing through standardization. They don't want to design parts that can't be installed by robots, but must have a process for deciding exceptions, since nonstandard parts will cost extra. Those exceptions represent tradeoffs between design and cost.

Management may have little information on some technical tradeoff decisions, but will probably have plenty of information around cost goals. So accountability must be tied to expertise and tradeoffs. The person with the information is expert, regardless of power.

Other tradeoffs include: (1) time versus quality, (2) speed versus risk, (3) product features versus budget, (4) short-term versus long-term, (5) speed versus safety, and (6) product improvement versus product development. In considering tradeoffs, if only two alternate solutions seem available, a serious effort should be made to generate a third solution that allows a move beyond the tradeoffs—that is, transcending them.

✓ When It Is Working

When tradeoff decisions are being handled with an effective collaborative process, decisions do not have to be made again. The decision process is more disciplined higher in the organization. Decisions are made quickly in a disciplined manner; information that is appropriate is included. Decisions are documented along with their rationale so that the decisions do not have to be re-made. Decisions are made in a way that leads to follow-up, including action steps, specifying who is responsible for what and setting deadlines. Multiple perspectives are valued and sought routinely.

✗ When It Is Not Working

When tradeoffs are handled poorly, either a bias toward action or a bias toward drawn-out information gathering shows. Some decisions are rushed, some are never made. A single point of view drives decisions. Unilateral decision making occurs frequently. Authority dominates expertise in the decision-making process. Long-term goals are sacrificed for the short-term. The wrong people participate in the process. Employees at all levels feel frustrated because of lack of input and perceived incompetence of decision makers.

6. Create Higher Standards for Discussions, Dialogue, and Information Sharing

Working well together depends on a shared understanding. Making sense is the beginning point for making intelligent decisions and coordinating with one another. Collaboration provides a key factor in the sense-making process. It provides inputs from multiple perspectives and generates shared meanings that enable coordinated action.

But too often, decisions are made unilaterally—by individuals or groups—without appropriate input or appropriate participation. Transforming the approach through collaboration means setting new standards for discussion, dialogue, and information sharing. Open, deliberate sharing of information and knowledge is a process that adds a great deal of value. However, these qualities do not emerge by accident. They must be pursued.

The first step in collaborative discussions is asking good questions. Questioning is a dominant strategy for making sense of a situation. First, a question defines a solution space. Imagine a jigsaw puzzle with one piece missing near the middle. The surrounding pieces (the knowns) define what is missing. Asking good questions accomplishes a similar objective: identifying what is known and what is not and thus defining what must become known. Asking the right question creates at least half of the answer.

Mohrman and Tenkasi (2000) say that the important work in knowledge work is done in conversation. Reynolds (1967) says, "Conversation is thinking in its natural state. Thinking is the conversation within us." The quality of conversation varies from monologue to dialogue. Monologue means one person speaks *at* another, not *with*. Dialogue is shared exploration toward greater understanding, connection, or possibility. Ray Stata (1994), former CEO of Analog Devices, wrote, "Our conversation skills coupled with our commitment of each other's success largely determine the quality of our relationships." In other words, collaboration depends on effective conversation. Guidelines for dialogue in its most basic form include:

- Talk about what's really important;
- Really listen to each other—see how thoroughly you can understand each other's views and experience;
- Listen for the other person's concerns—probe and dig to discover them;
- Say what's true for you without making each other wrong;

- See what you can learn together by exploring things together; and
- Avoid monopolizing the conversation—make sure everyone has a chance to speak.

Dialogue is shared exploration toward greater understanding, connection, or possibility. It represents the highest quality level for conversation and rests on a high level of engagement.

One characteristic of any system and any work system is its boundary. The boundary provides a set of conditions that determines what gets in and what stays out and what goes out. For example, at a meeting of the top management group (TMG), the door may be open to any member of the organization to sit in, or it may be closed to anyone who is not a formal member.

For example, one manufacturing steering team in aerospace with members representing a vertical slice of the plant, including top managers and union members from the shop floor, established a principle to enable dialogue between different levels and captured it with the phrase, "leave your hat at the door." There were still clear differences in what information a member brought to the meetings and what actions and decisions various members could implement outside the meetings. But in the meeting, a union member could openly share perceptions with the top managers of how the process of change was working, where it could be improved, and who, including managers, needed extra attention.

There are simple steps that can be used to build a complete circuit of communications. First, a manager should ask for input from groups impacted by the decision. Second, the manager can communicate: "This is what we decided to do and why." Third, he or she can push certain decisions all the way down (empowerment): "Which of these things do I NOT need to have done my way?" That is such a critical point that someone once suggested "tattoo it on your hand." Finally, the manager can ask the team to inform him or her of decisions and can listen when team members talk.

Employees create information to fill a vacuum. When management fails to share information, employees make their best guess and spread it around; sometimes they are wrong and problems ensue. When the information is incomplete, the grapevine adds to it; when the information is contradictory (the words contradict the actions of the managers), the employees select the part that makes most sense. When the information looks like a lie, employee respect for managers plummets. When the information is one-directional (top-down), employees tune out. Open and honest sharing of as much relevant information as possible leads to involvement and ownership by employees, especially if management encourages two-way flow of information (bottom-up, as well as top-down).

✓ When It Is Working

Conversation more frequently moves beyond transactional exchange of information to the transformational, which builds high quality relationships. There is better sharing of mental models, assumptions, expertise, wisdom, tricks of the trade, and tacit knowledge, so misinformation is reduced and coordination improved. Depth and breadth of knowledge that is shared is recognized as more important than before. Mistakes are shared and discussed, not buried under the carpet. The right data is brought to the table. The knowledge bases are accessed and maintained on a routine basis. People actively seek out different perspectives to test ideas and base actions on those differing views and values. Conversations engage people's diversity creatively to generate greater shared understanding. Discussions cross horizontal and vertical lines about what impacts a function's contribution to the larger goals. Methods of checking and resolving conflicting information are in place. Conflict focuses on issues, rather than on people. Lower level employees are involved in higher level meetings, even if it is just to sit in. There is dialogue about the reality of tradeoffs and about how business gets done.

✗ When It Is Not Working

Conversations cannot seem to move beyond conflict (concern about this happening often prevents convergence when it is needed). Conversations often feel oppressive, boring, or depressing. This might happen because participants are trying to avoid conflict, intimacy, or surprises, or it might just be habit. (Common examples are extreme politeness, tightly controlled meetings, and alienated marriages.) The style of communication is "telling" rather than discussing (for example, at one plant, trainers had no input when a manager was making up the schedule for delivering training).

Decisions are made behind closed doors; there is a limited flow of new information into the process while a decision is being made; and there is limited communication of the decision or at least its rationale out to the rest of the site after the decision is made. Tight boundaries limit the flow. They encourage isolated islands of work and so make it easy to ignore alignment with the rest of the organization and the welfare of the organization as a whole. Functional loyalty interferes with loyalty to the larger organization. People feel in the dark much of the time—at all levels of the organization. There seems to be a lot of misinformation.

7. Foster Personal Accountability

In effective collaborative organizations, people take personal responsibility for their work. Consider this contrast: at a first level of responsibility, when a machine operator sees a problem, he or she can write a work order and ship it to maintenance and forget about it until the maintenance engineer notifies him or her that the machine is ready to run; at a second level of responsibility, he or she can track the order and be ready to start up as soon as the okay is given; or at the third level, as with total preventive maintenance teams, the operator can work collaboratively with peers and with maintenance personnel until the machine is repaired and cleaned up and ready to run—with the maintenance engineer pointing out things to operators while working on the repair process. Which of these scenarios is likely to result in the least down time over a year? The one where people take responsibility. For example, in Sweden, there is a steel mill where all employees have the same job title: "responsible person."

Stata (1994), when he was CEO of Analog Devices, frequently spoke about the connection between conversation and commitment, emphasizing the point that the quality of conversation led to the quality of commitment and that led to jumps in productivity. Thinking of organizations and business processes as networks of conversations, it was clear to Stata that the performance of the company was determined by its competence in making and fulfilling commitments to internal and external customers.

Stata differentiated between *accountability*, what you have promised or committed to do, and *responsibility*, your way of being toward the success of others. Accountability tends to be imposed from outside the person, but responsibility is imposed on oneself because of concern for the success of others. The distinction is similar to the difference between the "letter of the law" and the "spirit of the law." Personal responsibility involves expectations of oneself. It underlies good organizational citizenship, because it reflects commitment to values.

Chartering a team is one mechanism for generating personal responsibility that is in alignment with the values and mission of the team and hence the organization. The chartering process typically provides an opportunity for personal statements to be made and processed by the group as the members work toward a shared set of norms to guide their behavior. Norms might include honoring each other, keeping commitments, and working to help one another succeed and excel. This may be most difficult and most important with the top management group.

Responsible people take commitments seriously. They say "no" to a request whenever they have doubts about keeping the commitment. Keeping commitments is important. Breaking them rapidly destroys trust, so not making them casually is a way of protecting and building trust. Those keeping commitments will be perceived as dependable, and others will work to respond in kind.

Some employees have the inner strength to act responsibly under any circumstances. But most people do a better job when the barriers to contribution are not too high. Employees must be enabled. If employees are not clear about the business logic, they are liable to do the wrong thing, even with the best of intentions. For example, if the technical staff is not educated about business goals, they may drift off into work that does not connect to the larger strategy. An empowered organization incorporates a learning organization where people learn about the business, customer needs, and what creates profits, as well as learning from their mistakes.

Fear of accountability comes from not being prepared to live with the consequences of a decision or an action. The fear often results in a failure to turn errors into learning opportunities through reviewing the action taken, identifying the lessons, and making appropriate changes. Mistakes must not be punished; they must be studied, so learning occurs.

Personal responsibility can include taking on more authority—even pushing the edge, as when advanced teams request more autonomy and responsibility. Enlightened self-interest recognizes that contributing to the success of the larger enterprise ultimately pays off for oneself.

✓ When It Is Working

The path between performance and rewards is clear. The organization rewards personal responsibility and has negative consequences for the opposite. Personal interests are aligned with business goals, so people want to do what needs to be done to make the system effective; it's a win/win situation. There are few hidden agendas, and those that exist are challenged. Unions support the collaboration because they feel it is a more effective way to accomplish the work. People initiate actions without being asked or directed (good citizenship behavior). People deliver on their commitments. Performance indicators are focused on an individual level, as well as on team and organizational levels.

✗ When It Is Not Working

People continually ask, "What are the expectations?" Ambiguity about roles and lack of information reduce opportunities to act responsibly. Like any group of people, top teams can fall into destructive practices—for instance, the public humiliation of team members. Such behavior creates fear and defensiveness and can intensify problems by isolating and scapegoating individual team members. Because the top team's conduct is mimicked lower down in the organization, this kind of behavior may be mimicked by lower level teams. Few efforts are made by the company to align with employees' needs, such as daycare centers, affirmative action, and signs of respect for differences. Commitments are made quickly and frequently. Commitments are often broken. Self-interest competes with the interests of the larger organization. Hidden agendas and political maneuvering frequently subvert the larger processes. WIIFM? ("What's in it for me?") is a frequent response to requests.

8. Align Authority, Information, and Decision Making

"Who decides what" needs to be an active choice—thinking about that should be a common activity not only of managers but also of other members in the organization. Any group empowered with a decision *should ask* this *before* making a decision.

A team may want authority but not accountability. For example, at one time, the managers at Texas Instruments had to do "barrier removal" but did not like to. Managers said to the teams: "Do not bring me problems; bring me solutions." Too often that is reversed in practice. Aligning authority and responsibility also includes protecting teams from decisions they are not prepared to handle. As one manager said, "It's called delegating, not picking a scapegoat in advance."

For example, a team responsible for hiring of new members requires a lot of preparation, including training on legal issues, diversity issues, and selection processes such as interviewing. Effective decision making requires both information and authority; one without the other leads to poor performance.

Empowerment means pushing information, rewards, and decision making down to the lowest levels of the organization (Lawler, 1988). However, it is not an opportunity for a manager to push down decisions he or she does not want to make. And it is also not just pushing decisions up—reverse delegation. The team needs to take responsibility when the scope of a decision is aligned with their resources. It includes setting the context for success and accountability—clarifying the expectations and the consequences.

Sometimes different voices should be listened to and sometimes not. Who makes what decisions and with what input is pivotal in deciding when to collaborate and how. The rules for such decisions should be carefully determined and made public.

✔ When It Is Working

People with the expertise make the decisions, rather than just people higher in the hierarchy. There is clarity about which people have the expert information, what the limits of the decision making are, and how to obtain other related information. There is clarity about the principles under which to make the decisions (for example, the technical person makes the decision on the technical dimensions). Expectations are clear about meetings before they start. Information is easily accessible. Decisions are communicated promptly with the rationale.

✘ When It Is Not Working

Misalignment of authority, information, and decision making shows in the large number of poor decisions, unimplemented decisions, and unmade decisions. There is confusion about who should be involved in the decision making and about who is responsible. People avoid making decisions. There is excessive delegating both upward and downward. Placing blame on others to protect oneself is widespread.

9. Treat Collaboration as a Disciplined Process

A disciplined process represents a key principle, the need to deliberately and actively practice the other nine principles presented here. Disciplined process applies to other areas as well, such as quality and customer service. It also indicates a need to consider facets of collaborative systems, such as culture, processes, practices, and structure, as a foundation for building social and intellectual capital in the organization. Effective collaborative work systems cannot be created and sustained unless members are disciplined about appropriate principles. A disciplined approach to the practice of the other nine principles is the basis for building a collaborative organization.

Disciplined processes are utilized in a number of ways in manufacturing; some of them contribute to increasing the value of collaboration. For example, responsibility charts are one tool for treating collaboration as a disciplined process. Kaizen, which involves standardizing before you innovate, introduces rigor that leads to efficiency. Process management depends on disciplined design (Hammer, 2002). "Disciplined" means the process must be practiced across the whole organization and so standardized.

Other examples include the processes for effective meeting management. For example, taking notes in meetings enables others to share, to write down what was decided and stick to it at the next meeting, that is, only change it by conscious decision. Use "Who, What, and When Action Charts" to capture this information and share it.

For example, start and run meetings the same way each time. Do check-ins, even polling, to gain public acknowledgement of commitment to decisions. Making commitment public increases the likelihood of follow-up outside the meeting. Without follow-up or execution of action steps, the potential value of a meeting remains unrealized and the meeting becomes a waste of resources.

Hewlett-Packard has done good work on dynamic teams with fluctuating membership (1996). They standardize to empower the people, force people to behave in certain ways to empower them, and use new rules of order to impact the quality of the process. Disciplined processes like these are not achieved overnight; they evolve toward higher levels of maturity over time when attention and resources are focused on them.

✓ When It Is Working

Roles are defined clearly. The schedules include milestones. Choice of communication medium is thoughtful. People are clear on deliverables. People are clear on who should be involved. There is agreement on the disciplined process. A disciplined process is used to identify the stakeholders for a project or initiative. The process is explicitly adopted and practiced across the whole organization.

✗ When It Is Not Working

Quality of products or services are hit or miss and cannot be delivered in a dependable manner. Parts of the organization are left behind in the attempt to transform the rest. Processes are not aligned with the organizational strategy. Variation in practice is excessive. Processes are limited to low-level, small-scale activities rather than crossing the whole organization.

10. Design and Promote Flexible Organizations

The term "re-invention" implies that change only has to happen once. Fifteen years ago, that seemed to make sense. Today, continuous change is essential and the pace of that change is rapid. Fifteen years ago, some industries might have had fairly stable environments. Today, with deregulation, global competition, and rapid technological change, nearly all companies must cope with turbulent environments. Continuous change has become a requirement for business survival, and collaborative approaches to it improve the process and benefit from the process. To create that flexibility:

- Create shared understanding around problems, issues, and opportunities;
- Design work group boundaries for responsiveness to the environment, especially to customers;
- Create flexible structures;
- Educate people to be change savvy (sophisticated);
- Co-locate people and use technology to facilitate collaboration and thereby coordinate change;
- Embrace loose collaborative structures in place of rigid ones; and
- Plan for a continually accelerating rate of change.

One method for designing flexible organizations involves large group meetings, such as search conferences, open space, and future search (Holman & Devane, 1999). The meetings are participatory strategic planning activities. Emery's Participative Design Workshop (PDW) uses high involvement where teams redesign themselves, including goals, metrics, and so forth. Continuous redesign is kicked off by this process. Design from the first session is not a big leap, but the change to a mental model of having a sense of control over their own design is an important and empowering change for the participating teams. For example, Storage Tech's redesign work in manufacturing ran participative design workshops. The consultant came back in six months and said, "This is not what we agreed to in the PDW." The customer said, "Yeah, we have continued to redesign ourselves to better meet business needs."

The lowest level in the organization is most adaptive (Baskin, 2001). Adaptability is the ability to make changes in a timely fashion to perceived changes in the environment. Hence, organizational responsiveness is facilitated as frontline workers engage with customers and suppliers. Empowerment creates conditions for discretion and thereby for local adjustments.

In the new model of organizations, boundaries are much less rigid. Now there are different bases for identity in the organization, so suboptimization may be avoided more easily and a more fluid organization may be created.

For example, a crayon manufacturing company went from having a line for each color to a more flexible manufacturing design when a new customer wanted "ethnic crayons." The palette changed to make it possible to produce on demand. Company representatives had a good information exchange with customers. Employees had good knowledge of what was needed and were able to make the adjustments.

An adaptive organization changes constantly; it is more akin to continuous quality improvement. As environmental change accelerates, we must increase attention to it and create appropriate responses. We must educate managers to understand the environment and match the internal variety or diversity to the turbulence. As turbulence increases, we must increase employee involvement in problem solving and innovation and minimize the number of rules and the amount of management control. When employees take some control the payoffs include reduced stress, increased commitment and ownership, and increased quality of problem solving and innovative ideas.

✓ When It Is Working

Frequency of communications about strategies and approach and about the team member's role in the overall success of the company is high. Input for change comes from all organization members. Change cascades down from the top. Top management acts as a catalyst for change, a champion and sponsor, and a model. "We are in this together" becomes the message. Databases serve as the collective memory for the group and are used to bring new members up to speed.

✗ When It Is Not Working

Top management delegates responsibility for change, rather than leading it. They say, "It's for them, not for us." Phrases like "Not invented here" or "We always do it this way" are often heard. Customers hear "We can't do that." Policies are followed and structures maintained, even when most people consider them to be inappropriate. The focus is on the past, not on how the present can create the future.

Implications for Executives

Key actions and implications for executives and leaders of manufacturing systems are provided below. These are key things executives and leaders can do to improve the effectiveness of their collaborative work systems in manufacturing settings:

1. *Involve key stakeholders.* The three most resistant groups to building effective collaborative work systems will be middle management, the union, and executives, in that order. Involve middle management in planning and decision making; include them as members of the steering and design teams; keep them well informed. In unionized plants, involve union members in planning and decision making, include them as members of the steering and design teams. Have executives meet the teams and hear their stories and go on benchmarking visits—both internally and externally.

2. *Lead from the top.* Top management leads development of the collaborative organization through strategically planning the evolution of the culture and structure so that it supports business goals and builds resources. Consider adoption of Alberto-Culver's new role of "growth development leader" to formalize culture change.

3. *Manage the information vacuum.* The grapevine will be active; information will not only be passed around quickly among the connected (sometimes leaving out the less connected), but it will also be created. When the reason for a decision is not communicated, the employees will speculate on their own and generate much less favorable reasons than the truth.

4. *Model the new way of working.* Walk the talk. Demonstrate collaborative practices in appropriate ways and times. Talk with people who are not

executives. Invite teams into meetings with your colleagues to share their accomplishments and needs. Publicly reward reduction in hurdles that impede collaboration.

5. *Use sponsorship to enable collaborative experiments.*

6. *Utilize collaborative work systems as a strategic change and management tool.*

7. *Lead, anticipate, and adapt*—Lead where you can, anticipate where possible, and adapt when you have to.

8. *Create environments that foster performance excellence.*

9. *Model collaboration.* Make eye contact, listen, respond in a timely fashion, ask questions, seek diverse viewpoints, and co-create the future with the other members of the organization.

10. *Sustain the commitment to building a collaborative organization over time.*

11. *Give up micromanagement for other forms of control.* These might include concerted control from team members, reward and recognition systems, measurement and feedback, clarity in goal setting, and modeling.

12. *Recognize there is intelligence on the shop floor and harness it.*

13. *Recognize that there are managers who must work within significant constraints and at a detailed level.* Either listen to them the way they now share or teach them to share in a different way so you can hear them better.

Collaboration occurs at all levels inside and outside the organization. In building collaborative capital, you can make choices about where to focus—inside or outside and micro or macro or a balance of both. Focusing on either extreme will limit development. For example, because of the tendency of manufacturing sites to focus on individual teams and their development, collaboration *between* teams has often been neglected. A significant increase in performance occurs when attention is paid to the processes that link teams together. However, that takes more resources in the beginning than just focusing on teams, or it takes shifting some of the team resources, such as time spent on a meeting agenda, training time, discussion time, assessment efforts, away from the within-team level to the between-team level. The same is true for attending to other collaborative opportunities, such as links between support systems and teams, between teams and customers, between vertical levels in the organization, between shifts, and so on. *Manage the betweens.* Invest in the whole organization.

Table 3.1 provides a review of the Ten Principles of Collaboration in manufacturing settings.

Table 3.1. The Ten Principles of Collaboration in Manufacturing Settings

Principle	Importance to Manufacturing Settings	When It Is Working	When It Is Not Working
1. Focus Collaboration on Achieving Business Results	Help to align business units Focus attention on goal of performance improvement Shared understanding by all organizational members	Joint discussions of problems/decisions Leaders support collaboration Customer results pivotal point	Line workers don't know mission/vision/goals/strategies Front-line workers have learned helplessness Private concerns block business results Decisions block collaborative process
2. Align Organizational Support Systems to Promote Ownership	Facilitates carrying out necessary processes Teams and groups are embedded in the infrastructure	Sense of "can do" and empowerment Line workers seen as customers by management Upward feedback welcomed	Lack of alignment with team needs Slower than expected results Both performance and morale undermined
3. Articulate and Enforce "a Few Strict Rules"	Gives principles to adhere to Sense of membership	People know how things work Shared values	No curiosity about possibilities Groups follow own rules Innovation stifled
4. Exploit the Rhythm of Convergence and Divergence	Gives strength to organization Knowledge creates value	Higher quality solutions More commitment to decisions Trust and openness promote sharing	Opportunities missed Creativity rare Discomfort with ambiguity
5. Manage Complex Tradeoffs on a Timely Basis	Balance the pros and cons Principles driving criteria are clear	Decisions not being remade Multiple perspectives on values	Unilateral decision making Authority over expertise Employee frustration
6. Create Higher Standards for Discussions, Dialogue, and Information Sharing	Input from multiple perspectives Open sharing of information	Transformational exchanges Knowledge sharing New perspectives	Discussions "stuck" Stilted, tense communication
7. Foster Personal Accountability	Each person feels responsible for end result Commitments are taken seriously	Clear path to rewards Few hidden agendas	Unknown expectations Destructive practices Fear and defensiveness WIIFM?

Table 3.1. The Ten Principles of Collaboration in Manufacturing Settings, Cont'd

Principle	Importance to Manufacturing Settings	When It Is Working	When It Is Not Working
8. Align Authority, Information, and Decision Making	Know who makes the decisions Both information and authority considered	People with expertise decide Clear principles for decision making	Many poor decisions Excessive delegation Blame placing
9. Treat Collaboration as a Disciplined Process	Ten Principles practiced Processes standardized	Roles clear Disciplined processes	Undependable products or services Practices vary
10. Design and Promote Flexible Organizations	Shared understanding of problems Flexible work group boundaries People themselves facilitate collaboration Change is planned/expected	Input from everyone Databases used by all	Top management delegates change management Rigid adherence to past ways

CHAPTER 4

Collaboration in New Product Development Settings

T HE NUMBER OF NEW PRODUCTS brought to market each year is mind-boggling. The speed at which products are conceived, designed, developed, and distributed seems to increase daily. New product development (NPD) organizations are in a constant search for more creative ideas and for shorter, less expensive design cycles. Collaborative activities represent a huge amount of time in the design cycle and are a significant determinant of success. Surprisingly, however, there is a huge gap between what is known about successful collaboration and what is applied in NPD settings. This chapter is about using the Ten Principles of Collaborative Organizations to help bridge that gap.

Definition of New Product Development

New product development organizations are exactly that: organizations whose core purpose is to design and develop new products. The term applies to organizations designing totally new products as well as those working on significant upgrades and adaptations of existing products. Most often, however, new product development (NPD) refers to organizations engaged in the design of relatively complex products, requiring the combined efforts of people with differing types of specialties and expertise and involving significant amounts of time and cost to bring them to market. New car models, new drugs, new computers, and new software are a few examples of the product categories typically developed in NPD organizations.

One of the more important characteristics of NPD organizations is the abstract, complex, and futuristic nature of the work. Different views of what should be done, new circumstances that change the validity of basic assumptions, and unforeseen problems and opportunities create real challenges. It is this level of complexity and uncertainty that makes collaboration so exciting and so challenging. As Wheelwright and Clark (1992) explain: "At a fundamental level, the development process creates the future, and that future is often several years away." Ultimately, those who collaborate in NPD are working both to predict and to design the future.

New product development in semi-conductors is typical of some of the complexity and excitement of this kind of work. Breakthrough designs are hugely profitable, but increased competition renders the old designs obsolete in record time; production requires "clean rooms," highly sophisticated robotics equipment, and very precise (and somewhat dangerous) chemical processes. In addition, advances in technology create customers who want products designed to meet their specific needs, often at unpredictable intervals. Anyone designing a new semi-conductor must work with these realities and with the people who fully understand their implications.

Historical Context

New product development organizations continue to evolve to meet the challenges produced by accelerating change rates, globalized competitive pressure, and ever-increasing levels of complexity. As they evolve, they continue to expand both the requirements and the scope of their collaborative activity.

In the early 1980s, more and more NPD organizations began recognizing the need for greater coordination and collaboration, especially across functional lines. This recognition began a transition from sequential design processes (commonly referred to as "over the wall design") to more collaborative and simultaneous processes. In the "over the wall" method, the design/development cycle took place linearly, in a series of phases. One group of workers took responsibility for a specific component or phase of the task and then "handed off" the work to the next group. The responsibility of one group ended when they handed their work product to the next group. This approach encouraged little identification with the whole task and seriously limited learning and improvement across the total process.

In the new approach, tasks were assigned to multidisciplinary teams. Designers were expected to collaborate with those whose work preceded theirs in the design cycle and with those whose work was to follow. As recognition of the need to manage the transition points of the design/development process became more apparent, NPD organizations changed attitudes, procedures, and design structures to address that need.

As important as the structural changes was the evolution of the culture and the tools of NPD organizations. As products themselves began to expand to include more and more components, successful integration of what had been traditionally separate disciplines became more important. The rise of "time to market" as an important competitive differentiator had a similar effect. These realities created collaboration requirements across groups that had traditionally ignored each other at best, and more often openly dismissed the expertise held by non-similar groups. Collaboration under these circumstances required integration of what had been totally separate databases, as well as major changes in relationships and attitudes about each other and about the work. This transition is still going on and represents a continuing challenge.

Developing a "collaborative organization" is a conscious, systematic continuation of this evolution. The organization itself uses the ten principles to develop a context, a culture, and a set of aligned support systems that enable collaboration across individuals, teams, projects, and organizations. This level and complexity of collaboration was not possible in the past and, more importantly, was not perceived to be of value.

Trends Affecting New Product Development

At the micro level, new product development faces pressures generated by three major trends: fierce international competition; fragmented, demanding markets; and complex, dynamic technologies (Wheelwright & Clark, 1992).

Competition has created an environment in which no established industry is safe. Sustainable competitive advantage is rarely embedded in the product or service itself. New and better products, often aimed at market that the product itself created, are a requirement for organizational survival, whatever the industry.

Not only are the number and variety of products and services increasing, but customers expect a product to perform better, cost less, be more reliable, and provide better overall value. Thus, NPD organizations are expected to produce products much faster, with ever more complex and dynamic technology. The average product lifecycle for all industries is now about three years. The lifecycle of products in the high-tech industries is estimated at six months— and shrinking (Gray & Larson, 2000).

Technological changes create new opportunities not only in the design of the product, but in the manufacturing and distribution processes as well. Designers have to ensure that their product makes optimum use of the most effective technology and that the product is compatible with the appropriate manufacturing and distribution tools.

These realities add complexity to what is already a highly complex and uncertain endeavor. New product development organizations are always struggling with ways to understand customers, be aware of emerging technologies, anticipate and outperform the competition, reduce time to market, and manage the complex integration of ideas, perspectives, and abilities required to design, develop, manufacture, and sell a new product.

Common Ways of Organizing

The design and management of creative and cohesive NPD organizations appears to be a work in progress. Generally, however, there are three major categories of organization: (1) primarily functional, (2) primarily product or project, and (3) primarily team-based. Each of these models can be characterized as a matrix organization.

In *functional* organizations, units are grouped by type of expertise, typically reporting to managers who also hold that expertise. Projects represent overlays to this system, with the primary rewards structure being in the hands of the functional manager. In a *project-based* organization, product or customer families are the dominant organizing structure. Here the business unit managers are in control of the reward structure. Projects also exist within this structure, but are generally made up of people who report to the same boss at much lower levels in the organization. In a *team-based* model, a series of hierarchical and integrating teams manages the simultaneous creation of the product by a cadre of subordinate teams. The hierarchical and integrating teams exist to ensure cohesive progress and to resolve a multitude of issues, including: (1) the management of scarce resources, (2) emerging high-level tradeoffs, and (3) new developments in competition, technology, and markets that may affect the project or organization (Mohrman, Cohen, & Mohrman, 1995).

A concurrent trend in NPD organizations—and in many other organizations as well—is the evolution of project management as a discipline and a way of work. Gray and Larson (2000), define a *project* as "a complex, non-routine, one-time effort limited by time, budget, resources, and performance specifications designed to meet customer needs." While projects that meet this definition have long been a staple in NPD organizations, attention to and formal training in project management has increased exponentially of late.

Regardless of the structure used, NPD organizations group people with relevant expertise and perspectives, assign tasks, and expect innovation and timely collaborative work. In some cases, the structure itself works against productive collaboration; in others it works to support it.

Questions about the ideal organizational design for NPD continue, and differing requirements will undoubtedly generate different solutions. There is much more clarity, however, on the need to abandon "command and control" in NPD organizations. The approach is consistently seen as having a negative effect on productive collaboration and on the level of creative problem solving necessary (Mohrman, Cohen, & Mohrman, 1995; Purser & Pasmore, 1992; Wheelwright & Clark, 1992).

Challenges with Respect to Collaboration

Forces that challenge or deter successful collaboration in NPD organizations are both varied and complex. Speed, complexity, inexperience, insecurity, and what Purser and Pasmore (1992) have referred to as "position centered thinking" appear to be the most significant. Each of these is discussed separately below.

Speed. Time has always been a significant factor in NPD, but the pressure seems to be increasing. The 25 percent profit advantage that often results from being the first to market is a factor, as well as the increasing number of competitors in any market. Regardless of the cause, NPD members are often not provided the time necessary to collaborate effectively.

Complexity. The complexity of the product, the technology involved, and the markets served also offer serious challenges to successful collaboration. Members often need training to apply the relevant criteria and to process the information that has to be integrated to make informed decisions. In addition, teams or projects are making decisions that impact on the decisions of each other. Successful collaboration requires that they have almost instant access to decisions that are being made by others and ways to influence them when necessary.

Insecurity. Lifelong employment is a thing of the past. Organization members are well aware of the temporal nature of their jobs, which affects collaboration in two ways. First, it makes people very careful about making enemies. Disagreeing with someone in power is much more dangerous in a world of frequent layoffs. Second, it's hard to care as much when you aren't sure you'll be around.

Position-Centered Thinking. "A related challenge to collaborative success is the structure and management orientation of the organization itself" (Purser & Pasmore, 1992). These authors use the term "position-centered thinking" to refer to those collaborative situations in which the participants are more concerned about who receives the "credit, reward, visibility, or praise" than about solving the problem itself. Purser and Pasmore contrast this with what they call "possibility-centered thinking" in which the collaborative participants are totally involved in the task at hand and "their commitment to truth, inquiry, and knowledge takes command and precedence over their needs for personal glory." They also suggest that "possibility-centered thinking" is not the prerogative of the individual, but happens only "when [the group agrees] the path to knowledge is appreciated as the goal" (p. 63).

These challenges to effective collaboration exist in all NPD organizations. The more effective (and more profitable) ones actively use their culture and their support systems to help address these challenges.

When to Collaborate

The question is usually: "Who is it most important to collaborate with, about what, using what method, and during what time frame." At the macro level, major collaboration tasks are addressed by the project design itself. Teams of members with differing, relevant expertise are created to accomplish a particular segment of the work. Coordination and review teams and other integration and control mechanisms are built into the project to ensure that the work stays on task and tradeoff decisions are identified and managed at the appropriate levels.

Even in the best-designed and managed NPD projects and organizations, individual teams and individual members still make many, if not most, of the decisions regarding collaboration. On a daily basis, they decide whom to collaborate with, about what, using what method, and in what time frame. They make these decisions based on what they need in order to do their individual tasks, who's available, who they like, whose expertise they trust, what they're interested in, who may help them advance their careers, and a variety of other factors.

Collaboration topics and methods are chosen with a similarly complex set of agendas. Many of these selection criteria generate choices that are consistent with the organization's goals, but many do not. Most NPD members do not understand the importance of their decisions around collaboration, and many more lack the expertise to make informed choices about how to manage it in the best way. Providing NPD members with the tools and the perspectives that enable them to make better choices about collaboration would be an excellent investment.

How the Guiding Principles Apply

On the following pages, we describe each of the Ten Principles of Collaborative Organizations as they apply in NPD organizations. Each principle is defined briefly, followed by an explanation of its importance, a description of the characteristics of organizations in which the principle is working well, and a similar description of organizations in which the principle is not working effectively. Table 4.2 on page 121 provides a summary of this information.

1. Focus Collaboration on Achieving Business Results

In new product development, most collaboration is focused on some form of business results. The challenge is to decide which business results deserve the most focus. Deliberations on technical and design matters are so frequent and so important that it may seem wise to discourage too much attention on larger or more immediate business concerns. On the other hand, NPD designers who ignore these issues make very costly mistakes.

A number of organizations are developing productive ways to answer this challenge. They empower their NPD team members with the knowledge and perspectives that make them full, and extremely valuable, partners in the organization. At the same time, they insulate them from the most immediate demands of the business, providing the necessary space for innovation and creativity. Members in these NPD organizations understand the competitive pressures facing their organizations. They also understand the business strategies that underlie the investment in their projects and in the projects with which they share resources.

✓ When It Is Working

New product development organizations that are able to develop a business perspective in their members garner significant advantages. Their members are better able to make decisions in support of strategic imperatives and established priorities. The same members are also better able to identify and to argue effectively for changes in those priorities. New product development organizations with a strong focus on business results have members and teams that:

- Are aware of what's going on in their industry and of their organization's role in that industry;

- Understand and use the perspectives of their customers;

- Are committed to the larger goals of the organization and can call on that commitment when faced with difficult situations;

- Understand the relationship between time and profitability for their companies;

- Understand the marketplace and competitive realities and are able to use that information when making decisions; and

- Understand that processes that optimize profit sometimes limit the choices members and teams are able to make.

✗ When It Is Not Working

It's very easy for NPD organization members to lose their focus on business results. Typically, these members love the work they do and would much rather spend their time thinking about new products and new ideas rather than the business aspects of their work. Symptoms of NPD organizations that fail to put business results in the forefront include:

- Repeated conflicts between individual teams or projects, with little evidence that either is committed to a larger, common goal;

- Little or no attention to the customer's perspective or concerns during deliberations;

- Deliberations or decisions that reflect lack of understanding of competitive realities or profitability; and

- Perceived tension between profitability concerns and technical goals.

2. Align Organizational Support Systems to Promote Ownership

A colleague once summarized the rules for being promoted in his former organization, a very successful snack food company. Promotions, he explained, were given to those people who successfully undercut [his language was a bit more colorful] their colleagues, while appearing to do exactly the opposite. When asked if it was difficult to work in that environment, he said, "Not really; it's kind of fun once you understand the rules."

Support systems are extremely powerful. They communicate the rules much more effectively than written policies or oral communication. In NPD organizations, they may even be more powerful, because the link between supervisors and subordinates is intentionally left loose. Below is a summary of the kind of support systems that tend to promote ownership and effective collaboration in NPD organizations.

The Leadership System. Leadership in NPD organizations needs to be both strong and distributed—strong because those with formal leadership roles have to question, explain, and redirect to keep the organization on a single track and distributed because the formal leaders don't have the expertise or the time to serve as leaders in the multiple situations where leadership is required. Leaders evolve as situations warrant, and members at all levels of the organization have to be willing to follow when appropriate.

Information and Communication System. In NPD organizations, there is a strong correlation between the effectiveness of the information technology system and the performance of NPD teams. These systems are needed to connect all members electronically and to allow them to share common databases and languages. Similar connections with key customers and vendors are also important. These systems not only inform collaborative decisions, but they help ensure that people have a sense of ownership about decisions.

Frequent use of formal and informal communication channels is also extremely important in NPD organizations. Because both the business and the technical information tend to change often, frequent communication keeps members informed and provides the sense of belonging that comes from knowing what's going on. The more successful approach seems to be to provide as much information as possible, to as many members as possible, in as many modes as possible.

Performance Management System. Performance management in complex NPD organizations is challenging. The goal is to leave as much of the performance management as possible within teams and then to manage the work of those teams, primarily through tracking objective achievement (Mohrman, Cohen, & Mohrman, 1995). The success of the performance management system then depends on how well the objectives are articulated and on how well member teams are working toward the most critical objectives. Table 4.1 illustrates several types of incentives used at the various levels in NPD organizations.

The Learning System. The learning system includes the organization's attitude about learning; the internal practices used to raise, capture, and transfer learning; and the formal training and knowledge management programs. Many NPD organizations demonstrate an almost religious faith in the power of learning and the value of new ideas. Many have developed useful processes around lessons learned, scenario planning, and other methods that pool and share the emerging collective knowledge of the company.

The Organization and Design System. The organization and design system creates the formal collaborative units in the organization. The challenge is creating the right groupings, with the right people, the right task, and the right coordinating and correction mechanisms.

✔ When It Is Working

New product development organizations typically have something of a leg up in developing the kind of ownership necessary for highly effective collaboration. The majority of NPD organization members already love the work and the collegiality of a common pursuit. The first requirement of effective support systems

Table 4.1. Incentives in NPD Organizations

	Financial			Other					
	Salary Increase	Targeted Bonus	401k Matching	Training	Books	Software	Pens Shirts, Hats etc. with the Company Logo	Parties & Celebrations	Meetings w/Senior Managers
Individual	X	X		X					X
Team		X		X	X	X	X	X	X
Project		X		X	X	X	X	X	X
Organization		X	X	X	X		X	X	X

is to make sure that they do not work against the natural propensity of NPD members to become intimately and passionately involved in their work.

New product development organizations with aligned support systems demonstrate many of the following characteristics:

- Members who are highly committed to their work, their projects, and the organization itself;

- Members who are proud of the contribution they are making to the organization and who feel valued by the organization;

- Members who are willing to raise and work to resolve difficult issues;

- Formal and informal communication networks that provide continual communication about the organization's goals, achievements, and challenges;

- Information technology systems that enable easy access to accurate technical information and current project management information; and

- Performance management systems that work at the individual, team, project, and organizational levels.

✗ When It Is Not Working

New product development organizations with support systems that fail to support or that even work against the development of ownership also have common characteristics. These include members and teams who:

- Seem uninvolved or uninterested at organization and team meetings;

- Fail to follow through on tasks for which there is little obvious personal advantage;

- Identify more with their professional groups than with their organization, projects, or teams;

- Do not fight for the resources they need to do their jobs; and

- Are unwilling to spend extra time or effort to finish the work.

3. Articulate and Enforce "a Few Strict Rules"

"A few strict rules" refers to a set of strong guiding principles that govern decision making within the organization (Brown & Eisenhardt, 1998). These rules define the overall values and competitive approach of the organization and allow organization members a great deal of leeway to accomplish goals within these parameters. These "strict rules" also provide a consistent direction for the organization and ensure the cohesion necessary for productive collaborative effort.

Articulation and enforcement of "a few strict rules" seems especially important in highly collaborative NPD organizations. The complexity, coupled with the dynamic nature of the business, makes a somewhat unpredictable environment, even when everything works well. Too many rules and the organization is unprepared to respond to important and relevant changes in technology, competition, and customer requirements. Too few rules and the organization has trouble working together to achieve common goals. These organizations miss deadlines, fail to respond to customers' needs, and pursue too many directions at one time.

✓ When It Is Working

When "strict rules" are in place, NPD organizations exemplify a sense of purposeful effort in a seemingly chaotic environment. Symptoms that "a few strict rules" are working include:

- Members and teams know what matters, which deadlines are real, what they will be held accountable for, and how decisions are made;

- Members and teams know what their project or product is expected to do for the organization, including how much money it's supposed to make and where it fits on the list of priorities;

- Members and teams are very clear about what behaviors are highly valued in the organization (for example, getting the job done, coming up with innovative ideas) and what behaviors have significant negative consequences (dropping the ball, making commitments you can't keep, ignoring a customer);

- Members and teams expect change and are able to deal with it with grace; and

- Members and teams have a sense of what it means to be a part of their projects and organization, and they can articulate roles and responsibilities that are seen as important.

✗ When It Is Not Working

When there are too many rules in an NPD organization, some common symptoms are:

- Teams or projects don't change fast enough and continue to work in the same direction long after it's clear that something is not working;

- Members or teams are unable or unwilling to act without permission or to voice opinions or perspectives that differ from those of the majority or high status members;

- Too much attention is paid to the way the world (competitors or customers) should be and not enough attention to the way the world is; and

- Members and teams are repeatedly surprised and upset by change.

When there are no "strict rules" in an NPD organization, common symptoms are:

- Members, teams, or even projects start down multiple paths, changing direction so often that little progress is made;

- Members and teams are slow to reach agreements and even slower to carry them out;

- People are unclear what to expect from each other and unwilling to make real commitments;

- There is some sense of "every person for himself" and alliances are generally of small groups, often temporary, with little sense of identity with the larger organization;

- Members are issued unreasonable requirements, with little expectation that those requirements can be met; and

- The organization is seen as creative, but unreliable.

4. Exploit the Rhythm of Convergence and Divergence

How divergence and convergence are managed often defines success in NPD organizations. The essence of NPD work is processing a complex array of information and deciding on a course of action that guides the members in a common direction (Mohrman, Cohen, & Mohrman, 1995). Work takes place in repeated cycles of divergence and convergence, each cycle producing a "product" that guides the individual work of the participating members until they meet again and produce a new set of guidelines. As the work is finished, experience provides new sources of divergence that must be addressed in the next session. These cycles are mirrored at the project level, as teams or their representatives meet to make plans to ensure that the work of all the teams is done in a way that it can ultimately "fit" together.

Divergence and convergence are core processes in NPD organizations. Project management, and the myriad tools designed to support it, are created primarily to cope with the challenge of managing the people and tasks in a way that ensures they converge in a common direction toward a mutual goal. While fewer tools exist to manage divergence, the project design typically puts together the people and external influences that raise multiple perspectives.

✓ When It Is Working

There are at least two indications of how well NPD organizations are managing convergence and divergence. The first is level of success. Organizations that are successful are so because they manage these processes at least well enough to get saleable products out the door. The second indicator is how much pain goes into putting products out the door. Too many NPD organizations do their work at the expense of the people and the relationships involved. This is not success, and it is likely to result in long-term challenges for the organization.

Characteristics of NPD organizations that are managing divergence and convergence well include:

- The organization is known both for its creativity and its dependability;
- There is rhythm to the work that members and teams share and understand;
- Members know when it is especially important to try to expand their thinking and when it's important to try to converge so that the task can be finished;
- Discussion continues until participants (either members or teams) come up with a plan that they can carry out;
- Members don't argue for their individual points of view at the expense of team consensus, nor do they acquiesce to plans they do not intend to carry out;
- Members are very skilled in project management, and people adhere to deadlines or announce in advance reasons why they cannot, so there are few surprises;

- Escalation paths (moving the question to a higher level or more experienced team or authority) are used to help manage important divergent ideas whose potential for positive effect may be great, but whose implementation may endanger deadlines or promises made;

- Formal and informal reward systems exist to recognize people with new ideas and perspectives; and

- Members are aware of and use a variety of processes both to raise perspectives and to reach agreement.

✗ When It Is Not Working

The management of convergence and divergence is complex because time and creativity are both critical. New product development organizations that are not doing well in managing convergence and divergence exhibit one or more of the following characteristics:

- Teams or projects don't surface the perspectives of all stakeholders, and members' opinions that are not consistent with the majority are ignored or ridiculed;

- Data from important sources is ignored;

- Teams, projects, or the organization fails to generate differing options or scenarios, for instance, plans for only one view of the future when it's clear that a number of options could realistically occur;

- Abstractions are left abstract and the level of detail necessary to fully understand the perspective being generated is not present;

- Deadlines are not taken seriously; and

- Data or options are considered without agreeing on criteria or approaches.

5. Manage Complex Tradeoffs on a Timely Basis

New product development teams often report two strong and distinct emotions when a major sale of an in-development product is announced: elation and fear. The elation is because sales are directly tied to profitability, to salary raises, and to stock values. The second emotion, fear, often follows almost immediately because the designers begin to wonder exactly how many additional features the salespeople promised the customer and when and how they're going to find the means to redesign the product to keep those promises.

The above is typical of the tradeoffs in the NPD world. Final tradeoff decisions relative to features, time, and budget have been made, but as the designers know from experience, new opportunities often force major reconsideration, for which designers have limited or only after-the-fact input. One could argue that correct application of this principle will limit such surprises—and it should—but the challenges are numerous. Among the most common are:

- The tradeoff decisions are abstract, subject to continual revisions and rarely to immediate testing;

- The tradeoff decisions are complex, involving data and perspectives that are not easily accessed by those who have to make the decisions;

- The correctness of one team's decision is affected by decisions being made by others inside and outside the organization;

- Tradeoff decisions have to be made on "unknowns." For instance, when a tradeoff must be made between including a completely new feature in a product or service and the additional cost and risk that including it will incur, the decision represents a well educated guess. No one knows how valuable the feature will be as perceived by the customer or exactly how much it will cost to produce; and

- Decisions are made by members who have very different levels of understanding about different aspects of the criteria for making tradeoff decisions. For example, the sales people know what it takes to make the sale to a customer, but not what it takes to add the new feature they promised. Whereas, the design team may not know the relationship profitability or market share related to adding those features.

Because of these types of challenges, it is extremely important that members understand the complexity and inherent risks involved in the tradeoff decisions and approach them with as much discipline as possible.

✓ When It Is Working

When NPD organizations are making informed, timely decisions around key tradeoffs, they exhibit the following characteristics:

- Members of decision-making groups have a shared understanding of the criteria to use or a shared understanding of the need to create those criteria;

- There are clear escalation paths for resolving tradeoff decisions when agreement cannot be reached;
- Members and teams are aware of the need to remake tradeoff decisions when conditions change; and
- Members are aware of the various weightings senior management has selected for specific situations.

✗ When It Is Not Working

Teams and projects make decisions that indicate they haven't recognized the true nature of the tradeoff. For instance, a project team may try simultaneously to meet customer expectations and to develop a much more technically sophisticated product. The needs are mutually exclusive. Trying to decide which one to pursue results in a failure to meet both goals. Other examples include:

- Teams continue to debate the efficacy of a project or product, creating major delays in the schedule and major damage to the relationships (and careers) of the team members;
- Members make decisions, but ignore important criteria, perhaps deciding to add additional features, although there is no evidence that the customer wants or will be willing to pay for them;
- Teams present decisions that indicate little or no consideration for key tradeoff criteria; or
- Functional or other groups within the organization make decisions without considering the perspectives of other key groups.

6. Create Higher Standards for Discussions, Dialogue, and Information Sharing

New product development organizations have to continually "raise the bar" on discussions, dialogue, and the sharing of information to remain competitive. The most outstanding organizations do this on a systematic basis, continually developing their capability to process more information and to make decisions that include a greater variety of perspectives.

✓ When It Is Working

New product development organizations committed to constantly "raising the bar" exhibit most of the following characteristics:

- Shared databases that include all relevant information about the project;
- Managers and team members who are skilled at asking complex and sophisticated questions;
- Little information that is shared only on a "need to know" basis;
- Good listeners at all levels of the organization; and
- Sophisticated and useable knowledge management systems.

✗ When It Is Not Working

New product development organizations that are not "raising the bar" also exhibit certain characteristics. These include:

- Members and teams are uninformed or unnecessarily delayed because decisions do not take key information or perspectives into consideration;
- Decisions are made using the criteria the team has used in the past, even though the complexity of the situation requires more sophisticated criteria;
- Knowledge management systems are so cumbersome that no one uses them;
- Members at all levels of the organization have inadequate listening skills; and
- Inadequate questioning (and listening) skills exist, especially at the top of the organization.

7. Foster Personal Accountability

A senior executive at Texas Instruments' defense group, after reviewing an innovative project design, expressed his opinion that the premise on which the design was founded was flawed and that, consequently, the project would fail. The project team, being equally confident that it would not fail, ignored the senior executive's advice, completed the project, and tested it with the customer. The test was a resounding success. The senior executive then invited all members of the project team to dinner and apologized.

This story is about an organization that both values and rewards personal accountability. The project team was willing to go against the advice of a very successful and very senior engineer, because they believed in their design. The executive was willing to allow the team to use the company's resources to pursue what he believed to be a flawed design. He did this because: (1) the team had done their homework and the rationale was defensible, if not compelling for the senior executive; and (2) he ultimately believed that the final decision, and final accountability, rested with the project team. Similarly, the dinner and apology demonstrated that making and publicly admitting mistakes was acceptable and that taking a risk and winning was rewarded.

On the other hand, had the project failed, the project team would have been expected, indeed required, to admit their mistake—and it wouldn't have been at a dinner meeting. Indeed, such a failure may well have resulted in a change in project leadership. The point is not that a team had permission to fail, or even to make mistakes, but that it was accountable. The executive would not mitigate that accountability by asking the team to substitute his judgment for theirs.

It's no accident that this kind of behavior takes place in NPD organizations. Personal accountability, that is, the desire and the ability to take responsibility for the ideas, the quality, the timing, and the completion of one's work, is a requirement. While managers work to improve the judgment and maintain the commitment of their members, they fail when they substitute their own judgment or commitment.

✓ When It Is Working

When organizations and teams are composed of members with high levels of personal accountability, the following characteristics are often found:

- Teams fight for the resources necessary to finish their tasks;
- Members and teams are actively involved in checking their own thinking and perceptions, asking for feedback and seeking additional information;
- Members and teams put in additional time and effort for which there are not obvious rewards;
- Managers are more concerned about follow-through and responsibility than they are about subservient behavior, so disagreeing with a senior manager is acceptable; and
- "Dropping the ball" happens rarely, but when it does happen, the member loses status in the organization.

✗ When It Is Not Working

When teams and members in NPD organizations do not assume personal accountability, the organization tends to exhibit the following characteristics:

- Teams and members seek direction instead of reactions, escalating issues that they should be able to address or resolve on their own;

- Teams and members do not defend their positions, but change their plans or assumptions with little resistance;

- Teams and members do not seem to fight for resources with each other or with management and there is little evidence that people are passionate about what they are doing; and

- Few ideas are presented for improving things, and few people volunteer for challenging tasks.

8. Align Authority, Information, and Decision Making

Aligning information and decision making in NPD organizations should be easy. Project designers typically divide the work into bounded subcomponents and create a team with the appropriate expertise to do the work. As long as the managers leave the decisions in the hands of the teams, the requirements are met, and the right processes are used, authority, information, and decision making are aligned well.

The real challenges to aligning authority, information, and decision making in new product development occur when (1) the work of the teams requires a great deal of cross-coordination or (2) what is known at the time the project is designed does not remain constant. Unfortunately, both of these situations occur more often than not. Consider the task of creating a new car model. The cost is overwhelming and the design must work for an international audience. The number of teams that are created and the points of coordination among potential customers, marketers, salespeople, vendors, and designers are overwhelming—and the alignment process very challenging. Similarly, regardless of how skilled the project designers are, so much is learned in the process of creating and producing a new car model that teams have to be formed and re-formed to meet the emerging needs of the project.

Clearly, it is critically important to align authority, information, and decision making. The problem is that the alignment often has taken place at higher levels and with the use of coordination teams to deal with the emerging plans.

Think about the new car model again. Suppose market research determines that a larger driver's seat would make the car more marketable. Who decides whether, in fact, it's worth it to make the seat larger? Who can figure out whether it's even feasible? Who knows how much it will cost? What will it do to other components of the car? Each of these decisions is based on information found at different levels and obtained from members and teams with different expertise. This means that, at some level, everyone has to understand the larger effort of which they are a part, and they have to have some control of that part of the operation for which they are most accountable.

✔ When It Is Working

New product development organizations that successfully align decision making with authority and information are characterized by the following:

- Management that functions as a team to make decisions and resolve conflicts at the management level;

- Members and teams that function effectively in coordinating with other teams;

- Team decisions that are rarely overturned by management and, when they are, the rationale is always fully explained;

- Team decisions that are made on the basis of all relevant information;

- Members and teams who believe they can do the job they are expected to do;

- Members and teams who believe they have (or can find) the resources necessary to do their jobs; and

- Members and teams who understand their role in relationship to the larger endeavor.

✗ When It Is Not Working

New product development organizations that have *not* succeeded in aligning authority, information, and decision making demonstrate one or more of the following characteristics:

- Teams become "bottlenecks" in the overall process because they are missing the expertise necessary to make key decisions or to perform key tasks;

- Teams are charged with making decisions that they don't have the information or authority to make; usually these are decisions that have been left with an individual team, when they should be made by a management team or by a higher level team charged with coordination;

- Decisions made by or requirements for teams are changed without input from the teams; and

- Members and teams believe they have no way either to renegotiate or to meet expectations.

9. Treat Collaboration as a Disciplined Process

The primary work process of NPD organizations is collaborative decision making, so it is surprising that relatively few treat collaboration as a disciplined process. Organizations that are diligent about financial management, project tracking, customer feedback, and a variety of other systems often tolerate, even model, collaborative processes that would put a Boy Scout troop to shame. They hold meetings without agendas, they assign tasks without recording dates or persons responsible, they argue for hours over a decision, make it, and then meet again in a week and make it all over again, often with a different outcome. The organization simply doesn't pay attention to processes they use to do work through collaborative action.

It's hard to overstate the importance of these processes in NPD. New product development members are expensive. Reducing time to market is a huge competitive advantage. Paying attention to the collaborative processes pays huge dividends in time saved and in quality of decisions made. These "processes" range from setting agendas and recording minutes to sophisticated decision-making processes that "specify the way an organization will make certain decisions, including the steps to be followed, and possibly, the people to be included" (Mohrman, Cohen, & Mohrman, 1995).

✓ When It Is Working

When an organization treats collaboration as a disciplined process, the following characteristics can usually be found:

- Team members can name one or more processes for making certain types of decisions;

- Team members can explain who should be involved in making which decisions;

- Members know what kinds of questions to expect from their management and from other teams and prepare for those questions;

- Members and teams are comfortable that they understand how decisions are made;

- Meetings routinely have agendas generated in advance and detailed minutes distributed afterward;

- Meetings are businesslike and productive, start on time and end on time;

- Decisions made remain made, unless a major rationale is provided to change them, and teams don't continually re-make the same decision; and

- There is a sense of order and discipline in collaborative activities.

✗ When It Is Not Working

When NPD organizations don't treat collaboration as a disciplined process, symptoms can include:

- There is a general feeling that no one really knows what is going on;

- Management doesn't question teams on the criteria or process for making a decision;

- Slow and/or poor decisions are made by teams;

- Teams are unable to make complex decisions; and

- Decisions are made on the basis of power or energy, as opposed to information and consideration of key tradeoffs.

10. Design and Promote Flexible Organizations

New product development organizations are pioneering, flexible organizations. In many ways, these organizations represent an evolutionary step. The limitations of dominant functional organizations and dominant business unit organizations are more or less apparent. The changing requirements for the design and development of new products demands a kaleidoscope of continuously forming and re-forming teams—all of whom have critical tasks that must be completed in record time. The natural next step is to design organizations that sanction rapid teaming and effective collaboration and that allow members at all levels to help decide when and with whom much of the collaboration takes place.

Flexible or self-organizing systems are very different from traditional NPD organizations. Historically, to whom an organization member reported was extremely important. It told something about his or her perspective and loyalties—and often the best ways to influence him or her. In flexible organizations, this information is much less important, since more of the control mechanisms for the organization are vested in systems and culture. In flexible organizations, the strong, dominant relationship between an organization member and his or her immediate supervisor has been intentionally weakened.

Flexible organizational structures allow members to respond to the uncertainty and complexity that characterize NPD. Because the members expect change and are privy to higher level information about strategies and priorities, they adapt quickly to shifting product features, technology trends, customer preferences, and competitive pressures. Because so much NPD work is dynamic, organizations that use this approach to structure are able to gain significant competitive advantage.

✓ When It Is Working

When the organization's structure and perspective are flexible, typical characteristics include:

- Team members are able to serve on several teams simultaneously and sequentially;

- There is little or no inappropriate competition between teams;

- Members understand when and why their team membership and/or project membership changes, or why their focus changes, and have learned to manage those changes effectively;

- There is a consistency in the way teams behave, for example, top level expectations, respect for all members, task orientation, meeting commitments, energy devoted to the search for understanding, and so on are understood and practiced across teams and across projects;

- The IT system supports communication and collaboration across all relevant projects and getting up to speed on a project is facilitated by the way information is stored and accessed; and

- There is strong sense of, and perceived value for, being a member of the organization.

✗ When It Is Not Working

Organizations that are too rigid tend to exhibit the following characteristics:

- Almost constant reorganizations;

- A lot of attention around finding the right "structure," rather than on building effective networks, working on real-time communication systems, or building responsive resource allocation systems;

- Members and teams more loyal to their supervisors than to the company or to their work;

- Members, including managers, who still believe things will settle down if they can just get it right; and

- Members and teams that don't collaborate unless they are specifically instructed to do so either by design or by a supervisor.

Implications for Executives

We recommend to executives in general, and new product development executives in particular, that they become actively involved in developing the collaborative capacity of the organization. Because collaboration is among the most frequent and the most critical processes in NPD, improvements offer immediate rewards as well as significant long-term benefits. Better collaboration offers more ideas, better decisions, and shorter cycle times. It builds the organization's capacity to produce work that is more creative and faster, with fewer resources.

Improving collaboration is like any other improvement effort. There will be some "quick fixes" and some changes that require larger and more long-term commitments. Below is a list of improvement ideas that have worked in NPD organizations:

1. *Start a conversation about the overall ability of the organization to collaborate.* Just raising collaboration and the processes used in it helps to focus attention. Find out how well the senior management team rates their ability to collaborate. Find out how well they rate their ability to model the process effectively for others.

2. *Find out what and where the organization is especially effective or ineffective in collaboration.* Which members and teams are especially skilled at collabo-

ration? At which processes does the organization excel and which are in serious need of improvement? (For example, some organizations are great at generating new ideas and terrible at weighing the tradeoffs necessary to agree on one direction in which to go.)

3. *Model effective collaboration.* Demonstrate collaborative practices in appropriate ways and times. Talk with members and teams who are not executives or managers. Invite representatives from one or two levels down to sit in on management or other senior-level meetings.

4. *Sponsor a "best practices' competition or conference around collaborative process.* Encourage adoption of a best practice when appropriate.

5. *Invest in the information systems that support collaboration.* Be sure that the people who will use the system have input into its design.

6. *Replace supervisor direction with other forms of direction setting and performance management,* such as peer control from team members, reward and recognition systems, measurement and feedback, clarity in goal setting, and modeling.

Table 4.2 provides a review of the Ten Principles of Collaboration in NPD organizations.

Table 4.2. The Ten Principles of Collaboration in NPD Organizations

Principle	Importance to NPD	When It Is Working	When It Is Not Working
1. Focus Collaboration on Achieving Business Results	Range of business results long-term or short-term, immediate profitability or market share, innovation or something else Technological arrogance a risk	Agreement on top-level priorities and on when and how priorities will be changed Deliberations reflect understanding of business realities Groups or teams subjugate goals to meet organizational goals	Frequent and nonproductive conflict between teams and projects Deliberations that suggest a lack of understanding of (or interest in) customer realities and concerns Deliberations that suggest a lack of understanding of competitive realities or profitability concerns

Table 4.2. The Ten Principles of Collaboration in NPD Organizations, Cont'd

Principle	Importance to NPD	When It Is Working	When It Is Not Working
2. Align Organizational Support Systems to Promote Ownership	Fosters commitment to the task and understanding of the overall goals of the organization, the team, and the individual	Members highly committed to the work they do, the product or project they support, and the organization Members love the work they do and feel proud of the contribution they are making Little conflict between personal goals (financial, career growth, and contribution to profession) and goals of teams and organization Members excited about what they're learning	People seem uninvolved or disinterested at team or organizational meetings Members fail to follow through on tasks for which there is little obvious personal advantage Members identify much more with their professional groups than with the organization Teams don't fight for the resources required to do their jobs Members unwilling to make commitments of extra time or effort
3. Articulate and Enforce "a Few Strict Rules"	Creates the necessary cohesion to foster goal-directed, cooperative effort while maintaining the flexibility to respond to changing demands and opportunities	Individuals and teams know what matters, which deadlines are real, and for what they will be held accountable Individuals know what their project or product is expected to do for the organization, including how much money it is supposed to make Members expect change and are able to deal with it well Members have a sense of what it means to be a part of the organization	Teams continue on the same path too long, even when it is clear that the path will not lead to success Members are unable and unwilling to act without permission Members fail to respond to new opportunities and demands and spend almost all of their time managing upward Individuals or teams start down multiple paths, but have to change direction so often they make little progress Small group and individual goals dominate; there is a sense that "no one is in charge"

Table 4.2. The Ten Principles of Collaboration in NPD Organizations, Cont'd

Principle	Importance to NPD	When It Is Working	When It Is Not Working
4. Exploit the Rhythm of Convergence and Divergence	Provides the necessary balance between generating new and exciting ideas and the discipline necessary to get the job done	Organization able to create new, shared ideas and to meet their commitments to customers, shareholders, and employees Members recognize when it's important to concentrate on "thinking outside the box" and when it's time to finish the product or deliver the service	With too much divergence, decisions are made and remade, products are not finished on time, and organizational goals are not met With too much convergence, new or creative ideas are limited; members move to a decision too quickly with little exploration of new ideas, different perspectives, or information from external sources
5. Manage Complex Tradeoffs on a Timely Basis	Provides the information and disciplined processes for making complex decisions in situations previously not encountered	Members know the difference between emerging and existing tradeoffs Members of decision-making groups have a shared understanding of the criteria to use in making decisions or of the need to make decisions as tradeoffs become clear Members are aware of the various weightings senior management has selected for tradeoffs in specific situations	Bad decisions are made No decisions are made Available expertise is ignored when making decisions Teams cannot articulate the issues or decision-making criteria used in making decisions

Table 4.2. The Ten Principles of Collaboration in NPD Organizations, Cont'd

Principle	Importance to NPD	When It Is Working	When It Is Not Working
6. Create Higher Standards for Discussions, Dialogue, and Information Sharing	Raising the standards for discussions and dialogue ensures that more information is considered and more potential consequences anticipated	People have the information they need, when they need it, in formats they can use Discussions indicate a level of understanding and sophistication that ensures that the right issues are being considered	Discussions do not involve key information or perspectives Decisions are made using the same criteria, even through the situation is more complex Decisions are made that undercut the goals of the total organization
7. Foster Personal Accountability	NPDs are dependent on every member's willingness and ability to meet his or her commitment to others and to the organization as a whole	Members are highly motivated to do the work Members identify what needs to be done and initiate actions to accomplish those things Members perform work that is of high quality and meet their commitments to their colleagues	People wait for direction before acting, place blame, and do not acknowledge their responsibility when a mistake is made Members are more committed to impressing the boss than to getting the job done Members frequently ignore their responsibilities to the team and/or the larger organization Managers overturn team decisions without explanations or considerations of the consequence

Table 4.2. The Ten Principles of Collaboration in NPD Organizations, Cont'd

Principle	Importance to NPD	When It Is Working	When It Is Not Working
8. Authority, Information, and Decision Making	Collaborative decision making is most effective when the team has the information necessary to make good decisions and the authority and accountability to implement those decisions	People are willing and able to make effective decisions in a timely manner and to be held accountable for those decisions People who have the information and authority make the decisions	Decisions are made at one level in the organization and then have to be remade as previously existing information is discovered Teams make decisions, but the decisions are not implemented Decisions are made at one level and the people who have to implement them are still wondering "Why are we doing this?" Teams do not make decisions
9. Treat Collaboration as a Disciplined Process	Ensures that the correct information is considered, the deliberations are focused and balanced, and the decisions are workable	Team members can explain how they make decisions Common forms exist for summarizing and reporting collaborative activities There is a sense of order and discipline in collaborative activities	Decisions are made without consideration of all relevant points of view People with power exert more influence then their information or accountability warrants Collaborative activities are characterized by chaos
10. Design and Promote Flexible Organizations	Flexible organizations allow for frequent changes in how members are grouped and tasks are assigned	People are able to work productively with members at other levels and with all functional groups within the organization Groups form and reform seamlessly to do the work	The organization is continually being redesigned Collaborative activities that involve people with different managers are nonproductive New groups take a long time to be productive

CHAPTER 5

Collaboration in Service Settings

COLLABORATIVE ORGANIZATIONS are effective at responding to the escalating demands of the marketplace. No longer are current assumptions about service standards acceptable. Rather, agile organizations that proactively address the complex market conditions and expectations of customers are most successful. This chapter describes collaborative principles that foster new levels of performance in service settings.

Definition of Collaboration in a Service Setting

Collaboration in a service setting is a group of people responsible for a non-tangible output who have common goals and shared metrics and who must pool their skills and knowledge to achieve their goals. Often in these settings, each person is expected to contribute his or her discretionary effort to exceed customers' expectations. Characteristics of effective service teams include: their ability to respond to customers' expectations, their willingness to challenge barriers, and their commitment to innovative solutions.

Lawler, Mohrman, and Benson (2001) found that "developing a strong customer focus" is the most popular strategy for employee involvement. As they point out, employee involvement, along with other participative practices, can contribute to the development of strategically important organizational capabilities. The degree of participation required for employee collaboration and the flexibility granted to the service team members to cross boundaries and challenge barriers depend on the organizational context. However, there are some common issues to consider, such as who should be on the team, how the teams should be measured, and how they connect with the business.

Historical Context

Workplace collaboration is not new. The frequency and duration of collaboration have been both high and low over the history of American business. Organizations have tried to increase collaboration through employee enrichment programs, job rotation, and teaming (Hackman & Oldham 1980). At other times organizations have attempted to minimize collaboration by segmenting work, increasing supervision, and building walls between functions (Lawler, 1986).

The frequency and forum for collaboration were often left for executives to decide. Executives had visions about the right time and place for collaboration, often limited to projects and to teams. Employees had their own perspective about collaboration. For them, the grapevine and unions filled the gaps for collaboration that executives deemed not necessary. Greco (1950) recognized the need for collaboration by stating that learning, influencing, and being influenced by conversation are intimate elements of the desire for belonging, perhaps the most human of needs.

To understand service settings in collaborative organizations today, it is necessary to look at some historical practices. There are three kinds of collaboration in service settings, exemplified by the following examples:

1. Manufacturing teams pulling support groups, such as engineering, planning, and control into their teams;

2. Paper-processing businesses, such as mortgage applications and claims processing; and

3. Service businesses, such as consulting and engineering practices, as well as retail businesses, such as Whole Foods and Domicile home/lifestyle stores.

Each phase of collaboration in service settings will be discussed briefly here.

Initially, most production teams excluded people from the service areas, then later realized that they needed to partner more closely with support areas. The service areas brought engineers, planning and control technicians, and other "service resources" to the teams, and all were expected to partner together. While these teams were told to "work better together," little more than the words changed as the service areas were called "teams." Some organizations recognized that stronger collaboration between line and manufacturing was necessary to improve business, but few invested the time to establish it.

A few examples of organizations investing in service teams and line teams working together include: Carter Mining, a division of Exxon, decided that they could be more effective if their mining and excavation teams were joined by engineers. Jointly, they identified opportunities for improved efficiencies and increased their safety standards. Otis Elevator Company, part of United Technologies Corporations, organized service and maintenance teams to serve escalating needs of the marketplace. Other pioneering efforts at collaboration between manufacturing teams and service teams include General Electric, Procter & Gamble, and Kimberly-Clark.

While organizations struggled to find the appropriate amount of collaboration between service and manufacturing teams, Klein (1991) found that up to 80 percent of the work completed by engineers could be done by teams. In many organizations, shifting this responsibility added to the tensions between engineering and manufacturing.

Many of these early adapters did not invest the time to define common metrics. As a result, early measures included number of meetings, action lists generated from meetings, and the number of training courses completed. These did not correlate to improving the business, nor did they help to improve the partnerships between service teams and manufacturing teams.

Besides poor measures, another problem was boundaries. Cross-functional teams lacked a common purpose and objectives. Robbins and Finley (1995) described many of the reasons these early teams disappointed their organizations:

- They do not believe in the outcome;
- They do not believe the outcome is reachable; and
- They cannot figure out what the boss really wants as an outcome. (p. 29)

Lack of clear outcomes made it tough for the teams to be successful and also made it difficult for them to cross their functional barriers and work together.

The second type of collaboration in service settings, found in paper-processing businesses, grew as the American economic base shifted to include more non-manufacturing businesses. Insurance, finance, and banking organizations focused on improving working relationships with customers. These non-manufacturing businesses struggled with efficiency and quality issues also. Some of them decided that teaming would foster the collaboration necessary to improve business results.

These organizations often had a very linear process that was highly predictable and stable. As Zuboff (1984) stated, "[The 1980s] were a time of transition from assembly-line paper factories of earlier decades to computer systems that allow clerks to accomplish similar processes online" (p. 126).

These organizations tended to have input from a client, such as an application for a mortgage, and output to the client (the mortgage check the applicant received). Some of the organizations that first implemented collaborative practices in a service setting were AAL Insurance in Appleton, Wisconsin, All-State Insurance, Prudential Insurance, and IDS American Express in Minneapolis. In the early 1990s, Aetna Health Plans in Dallas also moved to establish teams to "enable the service center to serve its customers more fully, so that servicing the customer became a competitive advantage" (McKinney, Childress, & Phipps, 1991, p. 17).

The third type of collaboration in service settings emerged in businesses that produced services with knowledge workers, such as in engineering firms and consulting firms. Tom Peters (1999) discussed the advantages of these highly collaborative service teams at McKinsey. He explained that these teams were able to complete the most complex projects, challenge the status quo, and find new ways to delight customers. Peters also discussed the satisfaction that team members had in working on a demanding project that allowed each person on the project to go outside of his or her comfort zone and bring the best to the project.

Regarding software engineering firms, Richards, Eddy, and Cabrales (1991) reported on a landmark MIT study that found "for optimal quality and productivity, the teams should be composed of system designers and users." This research pushed the boundaries of service environments to include users, not just the cross-functional groups that needed to work collaboratively to achieve their goals.

In the airline industry, SAS decided that increasing collaboration would improve customer satisfaction and their ability to set new standards. Their multiple rewards reflects that their collaborative strategy was highly effective and profitable for the business.

From the customers' point of view, increased collaboration allowed them to have one-stop service, instead of service workers being so highly segmented that customers had to speak to different people about different services.

While these pioneer organizations had impressive results, there were problems. First, organizations tended to use the teams in small pockets within the organization. All-State Insurance and Aetna Insurance are examples of effective service teams in a very limited part of the organization. One of the challenges these collaborative organizations have had is expanding the efforts.

A second challenge was quantifying the impact of the teams. As in manufacturing settings, tracking the output of the teams is important and fairly straightforward, so most service teams adapted metrics from manufacturing such as output, time to complete a defined segment of work, the number of people required to produce the service, and so on.

In the service-based economy, new standards of collaboration are essential. The survival of service organizations depends on the speed with which they understand the escalating market requirements and customer expectations. If service organizations continue to deliver at the level of today's service standards, they will soon be obsolete.

Three major trends are creating an urgent need for service organizations to become more effective at collaboration: (1) *segmentation of customers,* which has refined the needs of customers so that each customer wants a customized solution requiring significant amounts of information; (2) *information*—the rate and volume of information people need to synthesize and apply daily has increased exponentially; and (3) *competition in the marketplace,* which is constantly raising the bar on the minimal level of acceptable service. These trends have created a challenge to organizations to establish newer standards of service and broader ways to delight customers.

Common Ways of Organizing

Service environments can use collaboration full-time, as with permanent autonomous teams, or limit the frequency and breadth of collaboration. Or they may select a matrix structure that focuses on a project or a process that spans boundaries. There is no magic formula to determine whether the collaboration should be a full-time initiative or more limited in scope. Rather, the appropriate degree of collaboration depends on business objectives, leadership style, and organizational factors.

One common structure for collaboration is to organize around a customer group or geographical area. These teams pull together the functions that provide service to a common group. For example, all of the customer service people responsible for the Mid-Atlantic States would co-locate, share resources, and respond to the issues of the customers. Many of these types of teams use the formal collaboration tools available to them, such as meeting regularly, chartering their teams, assessing the team's performance, or using team-based reward and recognition.

Other service teams work remotely and depend on technology to foster collaboration. Tools such as databases and knowledge management systems are especially useful for service teams that require common information.

Challenges with Respect to Collaboration

While service organizations recognize the value of collaboration, it does come with a cost. Problems exist both for the individuals and for the organization. Some teams may not have the expertise to make effective decisions. Others may have individuals who lack the confidence to move outside of their comfort areas to work more broadly in the organization. Some of the common problems include (1) collaboration being less valued; (2) meetings and formal collaboration forums on a "need to share" basis; and (3) people who identify with their professional roles and are interested only in a narrow scope of work, rather than a broader collaborative set of behaviors.

Following are some guidelines about when to collaborate:

- When broader skills, knowledge, and expertise are needed;
- When the time to develop the skills is greater than the teams can spend;
- When tasks are interdependent and people must collaborate to complete them;
- When the work can be accomplished faster with more people working together;
- When both sharing and challenging ideas are valued;

- When the successful implementation depends on everyone's commitment;
- When multiple teams need to share resources to achieve alignment and coordination; and
- When innovation is dependent on a shared understanding of work and builds on multiple perspectives.

Organizations that have known effective collaboration are vibrant with energy and eager to share the power of their achievements. However, their exuberance can also foster "collaboration creep," the insidious expansion of collaboration into every nook and cranny of the organization. When this occurs, disaster is sure to follow. For organizations to flourish with collaboration, it's essential to recognize when NOT to collaborate.

Harnessing collaboration requires discipline. Here are a few guidelines for when to say no to collaboration:

- When customer needs do not require complex solutions;
- When management cannot share technical expertise and decision-making responsibility to fully empower the people collaborating;
- When the creativity of one individual is more important than the input of many people;
- When competitive practices are the dominant cultural norm, and when these practices would stifle honest dialogue;
- When individual incentives are the primary form of compensation and collaboration hurts the pocketbooks of the participants;
- When there is a dominant group process that is segmented and willing to accept only one right answer; and
- When time to develop a shared understanding is considered a luxury.

How the Guiding Principles Apply

The dynamics are complex in a collaborative service organization. At best, we can provide the reader with a cognitive understanding of these dimensions. The following section describes the Ten Principles of Collaborative Organizations laid out in Chapter 2 as they apply in a collaborative service environment. Table 5.1 on page 151 provides a summary of this information.

1. Focus Collaboration on Achieving Business Results

Members of a collaborative service organization realize how their work contributes to achieving the goals of the organization and the expectations of the customers.

Lawler, Mohrman, and Benson (2001) report that "Information about the performance of business is often the most important information for employees to have if they are to be involved in the business" (p. 33). While there was an increase in information sharing from 1987 to 1999, according to research reported by the Center for Effective Organizations, "Many organizations share only what the law requires them to share" (p. 33). Effective collaborate work systems move quickly, just like the marketplace.

For example, AT&T focused all employees on the business goals, recognizing that shared knowledge was important in preparing employees for their work. In 1992 AT&T Universal Card won the Baldrige award. Working collaboratively on business goals was essential for them to be successful. According to the AT&T's Baldrige report:

> "Achieving perfect quality, no errors, is not only doable, but it's a valuable strategy. For example, every month we took in eight million payments. If we had 1 percent error rate on those eight million payments, that would mean that 80,000 customers a month would be upset. They would be upset. They would be upset that their payments didn't get posted to their card, or that they got a late fee, or that interest was charged. That's an unacceptable number. Eighty thousand times twelve million customers a year who would get upset over one of our processes. We started at about a 99.8 percent error-free payment—processing rate and got to 99.9 percent."

Collaborative work systems often struggle with linking the business objectives to the group. Intangible products, the hallmark of service teams, are tough to track, and the contributions of many are essential for the multiple moments of truth present to the customer. Yet these moments of truth in which an external or an internal customer is impacted can be a "pause point." These "pause points" can encourage individuals to reflect on the impact of their contributions and on how they tie back to the business results.

✓ When It Is Working

Business requirements are clear, cascaded from the executive leaders to the people responsible for fulfilling the customers' service needs. This implies more than listing service standards and features or talking about earnings per share. Rather, people recognize the effort required to go outside of their comfort zones, seek new information, challenge old assumptions, and delight their customers.

✗ When It Is Not Working

Business results are not connected between levels in the organization. People do not understand their responsibilities and the expectations of the customers. When it is not working, people don't understand the internal and the external customer requirements, nor are they willing to challenge barriers to achieve their desired business results and delight their customers.

2. Align Organizational Support Systems to Promote Ownership

Modifying the support systems changes the culture of an organization. What systems to change? How to prioritize the system changes? When should the systems be changed? Well, it depends. There are few absolutes, but five critical systems must be pulled together. Descriptions of the five follow.

Leadership Systems. These systems include who is allowed or expected to lead; what criteria are used to decide who to follow in what situations; what the relationship of the leader is to accountability, expertise, and commitment; and what style of leadership is valued.

Clemmer (1992) identified different levels of commitment that executives can have in demonstrating support for customer-focused behaviors. According to Clemmer, leaders demonstrate five different types of leadership behaviors: permission, lip service, passionate lip service, involved leadership, and integration. Permission is passive support; integration is when leaders demonstrate a commitment to employees.

Performance Management Systems. These systems include what behaviors are important; how the organization monitors individual and collective action; and how it rewards these behaviors.

Lawler (1992) discussed the selection process in organizations with a commitment to having high involvement, thus fostering collaboration at all levels. Lawler offered the following guideline: acquaint the applicants with the nature of the jobs they are expected to fill and the nature of management style used in the organization. This emphasis, Lawler said, "allows the applicants to decide if they want to work in a participative environment" (p. 308).

The hiring process in a collaborative work system is extensive. Competencies are carefully assessed because each member of the service team must be fully capable of the technical parts of the work. Additionally, high-profile service environments select members with a passion for their customers. This deep concern motivates the individual to challenge the current workplace standards.

The selection process screens candidates to determine their desire to learn continuously and to take responsibility for that learning. New standards for learning are surfacing in these environments. Learning must take place on the person's own time. For this reason, motivation to learn independently is a critical screening requirement, even more significant than a candidate's technical proficiency.

Reward and recognition are key parts of a comprehensive performance management system. They maintain the desired behaviors and acknowledge individuals for their efforts to deliver stellar service. Entire books are devoted to this topic, so this section will just give a few highlights. Collaborative service work systems are relentless about recognizing superior sensitivity to customers. In service environments, employees are the differentiator, and when an employee makes a difference it's promptly noted.

Often customers are central to identifying teams or individuals who deserve recognition, so it is vital to solicit and apply customers' input.

Information and Communication Systems. These systems demonstrate what is communicated to different people and by what means. Broader communication allows people to understand the expectations of key partners in this collaborative system. Sharing customer information with the team members is essential. This information includes not only the conversations, but also concerns, issues, and preferences of the customers. By focusing on sharing information, the team can establish a common frame of reference that allows team members to interact with the customers in a seamless way. This fluid understanding of customers characterizes one-stop service.

Technical support teams have developed some effective approaches to working with customers. For example, when a person contacts Dell Computers for assistance, the customer service representative is able to retrieve records from all previous discussions, so customers do not have to repeat past information. Sybase is another example of a company that has invested in an extensive database to track all contacts with their customers.

Information systems are often integrated with the communication systems. For example, improving customer service was essential for Granite Rock, which used data to communicate crucial information about complaints. Granite Rock won the 1992 Malcolm Baldrige National Quality Award and the 1994 Governor's Golden State Quality Award. The company has twice been named one of the best places to work in America by *Fortune* magazine. Responding to customers' requests allowed them to analyze customer issues and address discrepancies.

According to Granite Rock's 1992 Baldrige Award Report:

> "Every complaint generates a product-service discrepancy report (PSD). The PSD helps Granite Rock management track trends in problems and identifies how much each one costs the company. The PSD also includes a 'root cause analysis' which provides an explanation of the problem and recommendations on what can be done to correct it."

Learning Systems. These refer to processes used to train and learn from experiences and the criteria and processes for making decisions.

Lawler, Mohrman, and Benson (2001) report on four of the skills identified by the 1990 Commission on the Skills of the American Workforce as necessary for effective employee involvement: "Two of these skills are interpersonal and group skills." The researchers explain that these skills are needed due to the number of meetings held, the requirement for group problem solving, and a need to influence others.

Another researcher, Frances Kennedy (2001) also identified meeting skills as critical, saying that meetings are the primary forums for collaborative exchanges in which there is an opportunity to exchange and challenge ideas while real work is being accomplished. Kennedy explained that there is a mental shift from seeing meetings as a "waste of time" to seeing them as places where real issues are addressed in real time. While not an easy shift to make, it is vital if the synergy of a collaborative work system is to achieve its potential.

Both formal and informal learning experiences are essential elements of the daily practices of collaborative organizations. Employees must be oriented to focus on "soft skills" such as listening, giving constructive feedback, requesting help, resolving issues with others, and seeking information. These foundational interpersonal skills establish a collaborative framework for working together.

However, Marsick and Volpe (1999) report that "organizations are regarding formal training programs as only one learning tool and are acknowledging that informal learning has always been the most pervasive type of learning in the workplace" (p. 3). According to Day (1998), "Seventy percent of team learning occurs informally." Informal learning moves the application of the knowledge closer to the work. Motorola's success with collaborative teams illustrates that informal learning enables team members to take responsibility for the quantity and timing of their own learning experiences.

Motorola includes informal learning as part of its development plan for team members. Stamps (1998) reports that Jim Fraiser, manager of learning, research, and evaluation at Motorola University, says that there is a rich interplay of formal and informal training back on the job. At Motorola, "Researchers have calculated that every hour of formal training yielded a four-hour spillover of informal learning" (Stamps, 1998, p. 2).

Motorola depends on informal learning as a significant part of its overall development plan. Additionally, Motorola realizes that the optimal development of team members is achieved when team members determine the learning they need and connect it to their work. Thus, informal learning fosters responsibility at a team level to develop the skills and knowledge required to perform additional tasks. Motorola, along with many other organizations, recognizes that informal learning is a significant dimension in developing today's workforce. While significant attention is being paid to understanding more about informal learning, Marsick and Volpe (1999) report, "We know little about how it can best be supported, encouraged, and developed" (p. 3).

With the increased realization that service teams will require a combination of formal and informal learning experiences, there is much more urgency to understand these workplace learning strategies. Marsick and Volpe (1999) reported that "formal and informal training and education as we have come to know them are now seen as insufficient" (p. 1). The increased pressure to learn faster is changing the standards for learning in the workplace. These changes place higher learning expectations on both employees and employers.

Besides formal and informal learning, learning systems examine the decision-making practices of collaborative organizations. Katzenbach and Smith (2001) suggest that effective teams "do not look to the leader to make key decisions." For example, Ritz-Carlton Hotels, a 1999 Malcolm Baldrige Award winner, have instilled in their seventeen thousand employees worldwide that the moments of truth with the customers are the times in which they need to make decisions. At Ritz-Carlton, there are no boundaries or departmental silos; rather, people work together to delight customers.

Organization and Design Systems. Here we mean attention and criteria used to create reporting and learning.

Goold and Campbell (2002) state that "for most companies organization design is neither a science nor an art; it's an oxymoron" (p. 117). Organizations that strive to foster collaboration need to follow the design principles of participative organizations.

There are few retail organizations that have collaboration as a central design principle. However, one example is Domicile, an upper end home/life store with locations in Chapel Hill, Raleigh, Charlotte, and Richmond, which fosters collaboration by focusing associates on the customers' issues. According to co-owners Seth McCutcheon and Adrian Brown, "Effective collaboration is the transference of ownership." Creating ownership among work associates is central to their organizational design principles. At Domicile, local store management is expected to build an effective customer-focused environment and the owners continually let go of responsibilities to transfer decisions to the local teams.

The owners believe collaboration is a dynamic process requiring ongoing examination of constraints preventing associates from contributing their best. The customer relationship managers, referred to as sales associates in other retail environments, are expected to manage the relationship with the customer to maximum lifetime value. They define two ways of examining the maximum lifetime value: first, securing maximum dollars and, second, ensuring that the customer receives maximum value for each dollar spent.

The strongest design principle that co-owner Seth McCutcheon operates with is that the business needs to make money, but the organization needs to be a place where people can find dignity and meaning from their work. When that is in place, McCutcheon believes, the details of the organizational design will be aligned with delighting the customer. By having meaning and dignity as the central design principles, the company fosters collaboration between associates, and each person finds value from the work. Additionally, the business will continue to grow with the amazing success it has known.

These five critical systems nurture a collaborative culture. Customers are delighted, employees feel challenged and supported, and information is available when it's needed. Most importantly, there is an atmosphere of trust and commitment to customer satisfaction.

✔ When It Is Working

Effective leadership systems have leaders who are present and available to employees at all levels of the organization. In highly effective service organizations, the leaders connect directly with customers, challenge the status quo, and reinforce practices that delight the customer.

Performance management systems are integrated, from the selection of service providers who are committed to delighting customers to reviewing, coaching, and promoting employees. In effective collaborative organizations, these systems are seamless to the employee and are observed by leaders in the organization. These systems require organizations to address individual as well as organizational needs.

As the teams become more proficient in their ability to delight customers, it indicates that they have knowledge of the recognition standards and practices. Some teams can also determine rewards that are meaningful to the team members and can be involved in establishing the criteria for recognition. The more closely involved the team members are in recognizing and rewarding one another, the more power the acknowledgement holds.

Information is available to the people responsible to use when they need it. In effective collaborative work systems, "I have to go and ask my supervisor for that information" is not heard. People go directly to the source of information. Also, the systems offer easy access for retrieving, sorting, and storing information.

Broad information about the customers, suppliers, and stakeholders is easily available. This information provides essential background for people to use in fulfilling service requests. Only the most sensitive information is kept restricted. Collaboration flourishes because people have what they need to make effective decisions.

Communication flows from a need to share rather than a need to know. Messages include not only the facts, but relevant background information and assumptions. Openness characterizes the communication exchange. People are encouraged to push back, ask clarifying questions, and examine underlying ideas about the information they receive. In these service teams, there is a broad discussion about information that is impacting not just the team, but multiple teams and even others outside of the organizational boundaries.

Decisions are trusted. Time is not wasted making then remaking decisions. Boundaries are clearly understood. If the decision needs to be made, it's clear who has the authority to make it. Decisions are not delegated; rather, people are prepared to make effective decisions because they have the skills, knowledge, and authority. Once people are ready to make a decision, their action is supported, not questioned.

✗ When It Is Not Working

Leadership systems are incongruent between what is said and what is done. Leaders focus on production matters more than on quality or customer service. These environments impact the behavior of employees, who learn to ignore the leader's messages.

People are hired and promoted on a subjective basis. Employees who are technically competent but ineffective in delivering service requirements are promoted and rewarded. Finally, employees can succeed even if they do not live and support the values of the organization.

Messages are mixed. What one is told to do differs from what one is reinforced for doing. Communication and information systems are not congruent. The information is restricted. Few have the passwords to unlock the essential information. For example, in the case of one state's department of transportation, information was most available to people who had personal email accounts or those with limited access to the company-wide system. As other restrictions were imposed, it was difficult for all employees to have equal access to essential information.

Formal learning is the only focus for the learning and development strategy. The formal learning experiences are limited to orientation sessions or to necessary technological training. Informal learning experiences are discouraged in their daily work practices.

Decisions are made, then debated, and then made a second time. This cycle of making and remaking decisions keeps the organization from having to implement any of its decisions and allows continual debating and undermining of the decisions that are made.

The organization design is micro-managed, and the employees have no sense of ownership of their work, except to collect a paycheck. This highly controlling environment is not satisfying for the employees, nor do the customers gain the benefit of outstanding service.

3. Articulate and Enforce "a Few Strict Rules"

"Strict rules" can bring us back to our elementary school days, but black and white parameters are rare in the complex world that characterizes business operations today. However, few areas are so dichotomous. As a result, team members value guidelines, with narrow parameters and set direction. So in service environments, "a few strict rules" set the tone and direction for the team members.

Effective service environments need simple rules. A few rules clearly stated allow all employees to understand the key tenants of the business. For example, Disney has engineered the guest's experience so that every moment is magical, from the entrance into the park to the long wait in the lines. Each Disney character knows his or her role is to create magical memories for the guests. What the guest needs must be delivered. By keeping the rules simple, employees understand what to do.

A few organizations are well-known for strict rules that guide employees. For example, Nordstrom's service culture is summarized with a one-sentence employee handbook that reads: "Do the right thing every time." When organizations have strict rules that are consistently enforced, employees follow them and customers understand their role in following the rules as well.

Focusing on customers is an example of a strict rule for organizations that have won the Malcolm Baldrige award. Texas Nameplate, 1998 winner, reported that:

> "It is key that we keep our customers satisfied. We know we have seven different kinds of customers. Each of those customer bases has different requirements. We have to identify those requirements to make sure we are satisfying them."

Other examples of companies that have won this prestigious award and kept strict rules around the customer include Merrill Lynch Credit Corporation, Xerox Business Services, and Los Alamos National Bank.

These organizations recognized that focusing on the customer was the strictest rule—and the one most important to follow so that they could work collaboratively to achieve their potential.

✓ When It Is Working

Meaningful strict rules are openly communicated and understood by associates. A few examples include business goals, project objectives, and customer expectations. Critical rules are determined by the business, yet it is the uncompromising implementation of the rules that defines the effective collaborative workplace.

✗ When It Is Not Working

Complicated standard operating procedures are written and employees are expected to consult the guides before action is taken. When customers demand exceptions from the operating guidelines, several levels of approval must be secured before the employee is able to respond to the request.

4. Exploit the Rhythm of Convergence and Divergence

A large medical center in the Northeast was recently crafting a new vision statement for their merged organizations. The room was full of loud voices, each putting a stake into the vision statement. After the group talked about their vision of the organization, they were asked to talk of their personal visions. Then the room was filled with hushed voices. This brief example conveys the sounds of divergent and convergent rhythms.

When discussing experiences with convergent and divergent rhythms of collaboration, people often talk about moments of tension, when individual agendas are replaced by a focus on a collaborative agenda.

In these moments of convergence and divergence, the members feel tension. However, effective collaboration requires tension characterized by open challenge of ideas, examination of assumptions, and questioning of what is known. Schein (2002) recognized that, in these moments of examining assumptions, transformational learning occurs. He stated that this examination of assumptions in transformative learning is essential for sustained change. Often, the moments are not fun. Schein (2002) talked of the anxiety people feel when they are engaged in this real level of discussion. Members feel that their comfort is threatened and ambiguity abounds. Young teams often need a facilitator, a person outside of the team, to direct the conversation through these points of divergence toward convergence. As the group matures, it determines how to move beyond individual agendas and how to support the group process—and becomes comfortable with that process.

For example, when a group needs to work through a customer issue, the team may need to first converge on a common understanding of the customer issue, then diverge to make sure all points of view are captured. As the group works through the problem-solving process, it alternates from converging on a point to diverging on alternative solutions. Most often groups use brainstorming and selecting solutions to draw from the multiple perspectives of the team.

However, as team members gain more experience with the rhythm of the group, they understand which part of the process is least effective. Again, teams may rely on an outside facilitator who is able to observe their process and determine their weaknesses. Effective teams "lean into their weaknesses" for their continual learning and growth. They draw inspiration from the collaborative process and know their breakthrough solutions are a result of this rhythm of convergence and divergence. However, it takes a long time before many people are comfortable in these moments.

✔ When It Is Working

Conversations are real, voices matter, and—whether in a large forum or one-on-one—each person contributes to the rhythm. Individuals can be uncomfortable in these moments when the collective rhythm is more important than the individual agenda. Yet it is this tension that signifies an effective rhythm. Individual agendas are brought into the organizational agenda so that the one voice of the organization is truly the voice of each member.

✗ When It Is Not Working

Paying attention to who says what is the most significant dynamic of the conversation. Participants are careful to agree with people who have more power, and they know that open disagreements are considered career-limiting. Also, there is more discussion after the meeting than during the meeting, when subgroups form coalitions to challenge ideas away from the public forum.

5. Manage Complex Tradeoffs on a Timely Basis

"The challenge of team management is not simply to execute existing processes efficiently. It's to implement new processes as quickly as possible" (Edmondson, Bohmer, & Pisano, 2001, p. 125). The fine line between complete analysis and efficient implementation is dependent on the context.

✓ When It Is Working

Processes are changed and programs are implemented to increase responsiveness to the customers. The tradeoffs are discussed briefly because there is a common understanding that allows people to fully know the expectations of customers and the expectations of the marketplace. It is working when it does not drain the organization of emotional and physical energy to make the changes required to balance the tradeoffs.

✗ When It Is Not Working

Timeliness is not characteristic of the organization. For example, one organization did not meet their client's expectations because they had to secure additional permission, decisions had to be remade, and the lapse from request to implementation was too long. When the tradeoffs cannot be made quickly, there is lack of agreement about the core operating principles, a lack of shared understanding, and people are not empowered to act at the moment of truth with the customer.

6. Create Higher Standards for Discussions, Dialogue, and Information Sharing

When people are able to gather for dialogue, there is organizational learning, defined as a sustained collective inquiry into the processes, assumptions, and certainties that compose everyday experiences (Isaccs, 1993).

Service work and knowledge work are based on an open exchange of issues and processing of information. Service groups bring a particular expertise, asking people for their opinions. Sometimes there is a service group mentality of feeling that they are the "experts." People need to have respect for experience and an understanding of the operation, and they must collaborate to understand the problems.

Effective dialogue provides a way to minimize defensiveness and reduce the feelings of anxiety about discussing real issues in the business, instead of avoiding them. As Argyris (1989) said, managers can reduce defensiveness by articulating underlying assumptions and reservations about the organization's practice.

✓ When It Is Working

Discussions are open, sacred cows are challenged, and meaningful dialogues are valued. These communication standards set the norm for new conversations. Some of the characteristics of these effective discussions are that (1) discussions are held across organizational lines; (2) mixed levels of the hierarchy solve problems jointly; and (3) people share information before others ask for it.

✗ When It Is Not Working

There is a limited sensitivity to other people's expertise. People maintain their own narrow views of the situation. Additionally, the conversations discourage examining diverse perspectives and do not challenge or explore ideas with an eye toward deeper understanding.

7. Foster Personal Accountability

Accountability in service environments means no one says, "It's not my job." Instead of bouncing the customer from department to department, one person takes responsibility to find the necessary information. Demonstrating personal accountability requires challenging organizational norms that block customer service.

Research indicates that excellent customer service is dependent on satisfied employees. Organizations must seek employees who consistently demonstrate personal accountability, provide the necessary support for them, and remove obstacles to their helping customers. Employee surveys are useful tools to solicit feedback on what might be interfering with customer service, such as multiple levels of approval required to make a decision. They can also be used to determine ways to foster ownership, such as easy access to information.

✓ When It Is Working

At a team level, multiple conversations are held with team members about their roles and about how they are meeting their responsibilities. Conflicts are resolved, gaps are identified, and trends are recognized. The level of discussion is complex and requires a high level of trust. Customers benefit from this personal account-ability because each time a problem is identified there is a relentless commitment to address it. The most appropriate way to address a concern depends on the competencies of the team members, as well as on the resources available.

✗ When It Is Not Working

Personal accountability is one of the areas that executives long to have present in their workplace, yet dread the time and patience required to implement it. Therefore, personal accountability is usually present only in pockets of the orga-nization and almost nonexistent in the rest of the organization.

8. Align Authority, Information and Decision Making

Organizations invest significant amounts of time segmenting work into very narrowly defined roles. People first consider whether or not it is their job to respond to a situation before investing time in understanding it. When clients make requests outside of the normal scope of work, they are told why the request will not be met and transferred to another part of the organization.

This principle requires that the people making the decisions have both the necessary authority and sufficient information. Frequently, collaborative decisions are not made because people do not have enough information to make them.

The Ritz-Carlton hotel chain, a Malcolm Baldrige winner, prides itself on the fact that employees are able to make the best decisions for customers. Too often organizations separate those with customer contact from those able to make decisions. An alignment of authority and information allows each moment of truth with the customer to be a successful interaction.

✓ When It Is Working

Employees are able to make key decisions and feel comfortable taking risks. For example, one organization has a monthly meeting to discuss poor decisions that were made and what could have been done differently. No one is pun-ished, and people are comfortable with taking risks.

Additionally, after-action reviews are usually part of this environment. Peo-ple can review projects to make sure that they were able to move as quickly as necessary because they had the appropriate levels of authority and information to make effective decisions. A book entitled *Hope Is Not Method* describes the after-action reviews that the U.S. Army conducts to examine projects and team activities. These reviews examine the alignment of the necessary authority, information, and decision making capability of the people involved.

✗ When It Is Not Working

The cartoon strip Dilbert has captured many moments when employees do not have the authority to make decisions or lack the necessary information. It is so common that authority is not aligned with information and decision making that readers readily resonate with the Dilbert moments. Usually, environments without this alignment have separated the employees who interact with customers from the employees able to make decisions. The multiple transfers of phone conversations and the amount of time that is necessary to reach a final decision for the customer are warnings that this principle is not in place.

9. Treat Collaboration as a Disciplined Process

Service organizations are now realizing that effective collaboration follows a well-defined process that is clearly communicated and consistently practiced. The outcomes are not dependent on individual skill and knowledge as much as on following the defined processes. Established norms allow the group to be agile and responsive to customer requirements. The disciplined processes focus the teams on their objectives and on their commitment to achieve them.

Peters (1999) discussed these processes with project teams, which are often challenging because people have to learn to work with professionals in different disciplines, but must collaborate in order to meet customer requirements. For example, Ernst and Young has invested significant time and capital to establish a knowledge management system. More and more organizations have realized that they need to create a common database and a well-defined process for working with customers.

For example, one large management-consulting firm has a stated value of collaboration. The actual collaboration process varies according to the maturity of the group, the experience of the managers, and the needs of the client. As one group works with a client, they realize that the commitment to the client means changing roles and remaining flexible. The team members and the team leaders understand the discipline of the collaborative process. Everyone recognizes the direction of the team leader and the common objectives that focus their attention. Completing the project does not depend on one person; rather, everyone follows the process.

✔ When It Is Working

Effective collaboration has rigor to ensure balanced participation of the team members and establishes an approach for addressing breakdowns that occur. The specific process is not an absolute; the entire team must establish and embrace it. Here are a few pointers about the ideal collaboration process:

1. It is designed to achieve the business goals in ways that allow each person to contribute.

2. The process changes as the objectives, timeframes, and individuals vary.

3. Effective collaboration is not a free flow of ideas, or a continuously open discussion. The discussion has boundaries determined by the limits of authority, information, and skills of the people in the group.

4. There are consequences for not supporting the collaborative processes.

5. At regular intervals the groups examine their process and make suggestions to improve its effectiveness.

✘ When It Is Not Working

Organizations cannot explain the process for achieving outcomes. These processes are not repeatable, and results are dependent on individuals. The knowledge that a team creates while completing the process is not shared with the other members.

Completing a task is similar to the children's game at an arcade, "whack a mole," in that whatever a person sees first is what he or she reacts to. The faster a person completes a task, the higher his or her status in the organization. Focus is on speed, hitting something, and getting on to the next "mole."

10. Design and Promote Flexible Organizations

Continually redesigning organizations requires a vigilant eye on the marketplace and customer requirements. This external focus provides the rationale for employees to leave their familiar collaborative relationships and branch out to other partnerships. By redesigning the organization, partnerships with customers can be improved while the white spaces in the business are minimized.

In this highly complex environment, few people have sufficient information. The charge to make a decision with less than adequate information is common. Yet for one to feel comfortable making decisions in this environment requires alignment. A rule of thumb is that collaborative decisions are possible when people have the information, skills, and authority to understand the issues and select the most appropriate course of action.

✓ When It Is Working

Information is sorted and analyzed to determine the emerging trends that provide the competitive differentiator for the business. As these patterns for emerging trends become known, the organization redesigns itself to configure the most able resources to capitalize on these trends. This ongoing organizational redesign challenges the individuals' need for stability and continuity, but it is essential.

✗ When It Is Not Working

Rigid structures are reinforced with past practices. The focus is on the way it has been done in the past. Territories are fiercely defended, and people understand that they are expected to defend the status quo.

Implications for Executives

Senior executives must encourage individual teams to cross boundaries, to collaborate with new groups in new settings. Steve Jones, from Middle Tennessee State, reports that 80 percent of the benefit of teams comes from cross-team interaction. Yet crossing team boundaries challenges organizational boundaries.

Executives in collaborative organizations are expected to shift in their understanding of the business and of how work is accomplished. Gone are the linear, simplistic frameworks of a manufacturing environment. Here are dynamic, concurrent paths that force meaningful conversations, question assumptions, and pull individuals into a new code of conduct unique to collaborative environments.

Sometimes, service teams fall short of their potential. Following are some indicators that this is likely to occur:

1. The team leader, often a former supervisor, has a very broad span of control and cannot provide the training or quality checks that ensure accuracy of the service.

2. Technical expertise is kept within the team, because team metrics penalize people working outside of the team structure.

3. Few employees deepen their understanding of the service or customer requirements.

4. Managers became concerned with the quality of team output, but are unable to address the team shortfalls or ineffective procedures and processes.

5. Layers are added to the hierarchy to have more checks and balances in the systems.

Collaborative organizations in service environments are still the exception. Yet collaborative organizations in service settings can be highly effective, because barriers are eliminated, communication is fostered, and there is clarity about the commitment to the customer. However, to achieve their potential, service environments must overcome some significant resistance.

While collaborative organization could be a significant tool to increase efficiency of output and reduce the time to achieve better results, the learning curve is steep and old patterns are tough to break.

For those reasons, collaboration remains an underutilized tool. As more people experience its benefit, they will find it less threatening and make the investment to foster collaborative organizations. This chapter serves as a guide for those pioneers who find it a little less frightening and who know that they have embarked on one of the most meaningful paths of their careers. It is not easy, but this chapter can be an opener for key conversations aimed at achieving the benefits of collaborative organizations. The following tabe provides a summary.

Table 5.1. The Ten Principles of Collaboration in Service Settings

Principle	Importance to Service Settings	When It Is Working	When It Is Not Working
1. Focus Collaboration on Achieving Business Results	Customer expectations are especially critical	Clear requirements	No connection between action and business results
2. Align Organizational Support Systems to Promote Ownership	Collaborative cultures exist to serve customers	Leaders available to workers and customers Integrated systems that address everyone's needs Meaningful rewards Available information on customers/suppliers Open communication Well-made decisions	Incongruence Subjective hiring and promotion Mixed messages Informal learning discouraged Decisions remade Micro-management

Table 5.1. The Ten Principles of Collaboration in Service Settings, Cont'd

Principle	Importance to Service Settings	When It Is Working	When It Is Not Working
3. Articulate and Enforce "a Few Strict Rules"	Few obstacles to serving the customers	Open communication of rules and expectations	Complicated procedures Too many levels for approval
4. Exploit the Rhythm of Convergence and Divergence	Individual agendas are replaced with a focus on serving customers	"Real" conversations Everyone counts Organization speaks for all members	People in power "win"
5. Manage Complex Tradeoffs on a Timely Basis	No need to add complexity to achieve end goals	Expectations are understood No energy drain	Decisions not timely Layers of decisions Lack of empowerment
6. Create Higher Standards for Discussions, Dialogue, and Information Sharing	Service work is based on an exchange of information	Open discussions Meaningful dialogue Problems solved across levels	Narrow views No diverse perspectives
7. Foster Personal Accountability	People feel responsible for providing service	Teams focus on how to do better Problems are addressed	No personal accountability Narrow role definitions
8. Align Authority, Information, and Decision Making	People need the authority and information to take action to benefit customers	Comfort with taking risks After-action review	Authority not aligned with information and decision making Shifting of responsibility/blame
9. Treat Collaboration as a Disciplined Process	Outcomes are dependant on good procedures, not on individual abilities	Balanced participation Everyone contributes to meeting business goals Process is flexible Bounded discussions Process is examined/improved	Process not clear or repeatable Results depend on individuals No information is shared
10. Design and Promote Flexible Organizations	The purpose of redesign should be to benefit customers	Results analyzed for patterns Ongoing organizational redesign	Rigid structure Territorial skirmishes

CHAPTER 6

Collaboration in Virtual Settings

O VER THE LAST TWENTY YEARS, companies have greatly expanded their use of virtual organizations. This chapter discusses how the ten basic principles of collaboration presented in Chapter 3 apply in the special situations of virtual organizations. Virtual organizations have some unique characteristics. They cross organizational (primarily company) boundaries. They can consist of larger numbers of people. For example, at Boeing a virtual organization of "teams of teams" consisting of thousands of interconnected teams collaborated virtually to design the 777. They may even represent whole organizations or inter-company ventures. The design and production of the international space station represents a virtual collaboration of many governments and private companies.

Virtual collaboration is broader than just teams. Virtual collaboration exists among individuals not considered part of a "team." People frequently come together to achieve tasks and then disband. They collaborate virtually, yet most people would not consider themselves a team.

This chapter provides guidance to those individuals who work virtually or leaders who are trying to improve collaboration in virtual settings. This chapter is organized around the following areas:

- Historical context—how virtual collaboration has evolved;

- Definition of the virtual collaborative organization;

- Trends affecting how we work;

- Common ways of organizing virtual collaborative organizations;

- Challenges virtual organizations face with respect to collaboration;

- When to collaborate in virtual settings;

- How the guiding principles apply in virtual settings, that is, the nuances of applying these principles specifically in virtual settings; and

- Implications for executives—what leaders can do to improve collaboration in virtual settings.

Historical Context

Historically, before the introduction of technology now available, conscientious efforts were made to physically co-locate groups of people who had to work together. Companies relocated people to the same city, physically moved people's offices within the same office complex, and routinely convened face-to-face meetings. Most people recognized the value of co-location. Co-location made groups of people who had to collaborate more effective. Similarly, the lack of technology now available precluded other forms of collaboration. Conducting business required face-to-face interactions, and the infrastructure was not available to permit electronic exchanges.

Before office automation (primarily word processing and email) revising documents was a labor-intensive effort. Once documents were revised, they traveled through the U.S. Postal Service ("snail mail"), often taking a week to reach their destination. Then the receiver revised it, added his or her comments or changes, and sent it back to the team. Some approaches, such as reviewing changes over the telephone or faxing edits, improved cycle time, but it was still cumbersome by today's standards. Even technology like the fax is relatively new. Even though the fax technology was developed in the World War II era, employees and managers did not start using it extensively until the 1980s and 1990s.

The lack of technology precluded companies from allowing groups of people to collaborate virtually. Conferencing technology was not well-developed or available until the 1990s. The "conference call" is a relatively new phenomenon. Prior to that, individuals had to make a series of one-on-one telephone calls to other individuals. Input from one individual was not readily available to other individuals due to the asynchronous nature of the telephone conversations between only two people. There were often repeated calls back and forth among different individuals as differing input was collected. Again, fruitful exchange of information and ideas required people to physically come together, and co-location expedited this.

While teleconferencing is now routine and a fairly refined technology, there exist a number of technology challenges with videoconferencing. Bandwidth is not available (or utilized) to permit images that are not grainy or jerky. The video feeds are slow and people continually "talk over" one another. Since the audio channels are limited, participants can hear only one voice. Participants cannot hear the other voices normally heard in live conversations. The visual range is generally limited. Scanning the participants requires a slow, manual process, using a joystick to move the camera. Quick glances with one's eyes to scan the group are not possible. Also, unless multiple cameras are available (hardly a common arrangement), participants are at the mercy of one individual who controls the camera shots. Revealing body language and many other visual cues escape participants.

Electronic storage and distribution of documents is a relatively new phenomenon. In the "old" days, hard copies had to be distributed to people. Storage was usually physical copies in filing cabinets. Compared to electronic storage, access to these documents was slow and cumbersome. Again, the sheer logistics of storing and distributing documents drove organizations to co-locate groups of people who had to collaborate.

Definition of Virtual Collaborative Organizations

But what exactly is a virtual collaborative organization? The working definition used here is

> "Groups of individuals working on shared tasks while distributed across space, time, and/or organizational boundaries."

This definition was derived from the work of many other authors and researchers addressing the topic of virtual organizations. Specifically, the primary sources included Fisher and Fisher (1998), Lipnack and Stamps (2000), and Lurey (1999).

The notion of working on shared tasks is the key determinant of when a group is a team. It is also a key criterion for when to collaborate. If the tasks are not shared or interdependent, collaboration may not be required. If the tasks are not interdependent, we have a group of individuals working on distinct and separate tasks. How one person performs a task has little direct impact on how others perform their tasks. While organizations and leaders often call these collections of individuals a team, the premise of this book is that a key characteristic of teams is that their members share interdependent tasks to achieve a common objective. Without interdependent tasks, a team does not exist. This parameter applies to collaborative organizations as well. There has to be a nominal amount of interdependency to warrant collaboration.

The notion of "distributed across space, time, or organizational boundaries" is a more critical discussion. A key attribute of virtual organizations is that their members are not physically co-located. While this generally is interpreted to mean geographically dispersed, the time and organizational boundaries are two other important dimensions for virtual groups. Examples below illustrate these three types of virtual organizations.

The most common understanding of virtual organizations consists of those groups *distributed across space* (that is, geographically dispersed). For example, Sybase maintained virtual organizations of developers located in New Hampshire, Colorado, and California. These groups of developers collaborated to develop suites of products that enabled individual desktop computers to access a network that linked them into corporate mainframe systems to access, extract, and update information. Using a variety of electronic tools, they developed product specifications, wrote and tested code, and packaged the final software for distribution. Similarly, Exxon Chemicals had chemists physically dispersed throughout the United States, Europe, and Japan. They shared information virtually on new catalyst systems to develop new products.

The second type of virtual organization consists of those groups whose individuals are *dispersed across temporal boundaries*. These organizations are less clear to most people. A good example is the design community for Hewlett-Packard. They have a disciplined process by which the design engineers in the United

States working on a product pass their work off at the end of the day to engineers in Japan who pick up where the U.S. engineers left off. They, in turn, at the end of their day, pass the work on to engineers in Europe. At the end of their work day, they pass it back to the engineers in the United States. In Hewlett-Packard's terms, their work "follows the sun." All the designers are members of a virtual organization. While dispersed geographically, the critical element is the time dimension. They intentionally use the difference in time zones to their advantage. Another example of a temporal virtual organization is that of a project team whose members work on different shifts. While separated by time, they accomplish their task by establishing processes to keep everyone apprised of individual progress and contributions to the task.

For example, one manufacturing company reorganized their shift teams (the traditional way of organizing) into what they call "vertical" teams. These act like process teams that cross all four shifts. This way of organizing presents some logistical challenges. The company managers only expect the team members to meet face-to-face once a quarter and to handle the rest of their business virtually. Even though they work in the same facility, they work like a virtual organization.

The third type of virtual organization is one separated by *specific organizational boundaries*. Members of these types of organizations belong to different organizations but collaborate on some set of tasks that furthers the purpose of both (or more) organizations. A merger integration team is one example. A task group of a trade association is another example. Technical representatives from different companies who form a standards committee represent a third example.

Agilent, a producer of electronic measurement and testing equipment, has a joint venture with its manufacturing partner. For each new product, a virtual product development organization is formed. It consists of technical representatives from Agilent and the manufacturing partner, design engineers, process engineers, and production-scheduling representatives. They collaborate to design and produce semiconductor chips that go in testing and measurement equipment.

Another key differentiator of virtual organizations is their communication mode. By necessity, virtual organizations communicate through electronic media to a greater extent than do other groups. They may occasionally come together face-to-face, but the predominant number of exchanges occur through email, telephone calls, teleconferences, and so forth. They establish websites to store and edit documents. They use groupware technology to facilitate their work processes.

The above discussion focused on formal, clearly established organizations of people. The term "virtual organization" also relates to informal collections of people. In the discussion that follows, many of the same principles apply to the informal virtual organizations as well as to the more formal virtual organizations.

Trends Affecting Virtual Collaborative Organizations

As technology evolved and business problems became more complex, companies expanded the use of virtual organizations. Additionally, numerous trends in the business environment are currently driving organizations to expand the use of virtual groups and develop means for individuals to collaborate "virtually." One of these trends is the dramatic increase in globalization. Expanding markets require companies to operate in different countries, consider differing national/cultural consumer preferences, and integrate managers and professionals of widely different cultures into their operational and leadership structures. Different people in different geographies have become the norm. For example, the auto industry maintains manufacturing facilities in different countries while designating two or three design centers in different parts of the world. Toyota manufactures some models in the United States, but uses parts from sixteen countries. This requires people in different parts of the world to develop new and different structures and processes to collaborate. Physically co-locating all individuals no longer makes business sense.

A second trend is that the nature of the problems that groups work on is becoming much more complex. This complexity forces organizations to pull people together with specific expertise to best solve problems and develop appropriate strategies. Often, these people are geographically dispersed. Furthermore, these specific issues change and therefore the expertise required changes as well. Logistically, it becomes impossible to co-locate people, forcing them to collaborate virtually. To be adaptable and flexible to changing market conditions, organizations must be able to pull together people of different backgrounds and expertise quickly. Creating virtual organizations is the strategy for doing this.

A third trend is that the products/services are becoming increasingly complex. In some cases this necessitates different organizations pooling their resources. The international space shuttle project is a prime example of this. The United States could no longer bear the expense of such a massive and complex project. International collaboration is driving the project forward. Each country provides the resources and expertise that best suits the project. But this requires a virtual organization to operate from all corners of the globe to achieve the objective.

A fourth trend is the increasing sophistication of economies in developing and "second tier" countries. For example, Korea now possesses sophisticated manufacturing capability. Malaysia developed manufacturing capability primarily in the technology areas. Computer programming has become a competency of India. Hong Kong remains a financial and commercial center. Companies are developing strategies and partnerships throughout the world to leverage this expertise. In the 1970s and 1980s, this type of expertise and capability tended to be located in the United States. Companies either had easy access to it or vertically integrated to retain that expertise within their organization. Today, companies are using the best expertise no matter where it is located, and it tends to be located in different regions of the world and outside their organizational boundaries. This drives organizations to utilize virtual organizations and collaboration models so that groups can work virtually around the globe.

There exist fundamental changes in how organizations design themselves and their value chains. Organizations are adopting more sophisticated organization structures characterized by alliances, partnerships, and networks. Organizations are recognizing what their core competencies are and outsourcing other functions. For example, Hewlett-Packard no longer manufactures most of their printed circuit boards. They outsourced that to Celestica, a Canadian firm that specializes in the manufacturing of circuit boards and other electronic products. Similarly, Agilent, a spin-off from Hewlett-Packard, retains the design and marketing functions for testing and measurement equipment, but through a joint venture, a Singapore company manufactures the chips for the equipment.

Microsoft maintains many alliances and partnerships with software developers. They work with these software developers to ensure that their products are compatible with Microsoft's products. But this requires collaboration across organizational boundaries, generally through virtual teams.

The electronic technology available today enables virtual organizations to operate more effectively. Earlier in this chapter, we described many of the technology impediments to virtual organizations that drove companies to co-locate people who needed to collaborate extensively. Many of those technology hurdles have been eliminated. Word processing and email allow professionals to quickly develop, distribute, edit, and finalize documents. Groupware technology enables distant collaborators to see the edits of other people and allows them to accept or reject those edits. What used to take weeks to accomplish with people in different locations now can be done in days. Electronic whiteboards enable groups to work on complex issues remotely and collaboratively. Internet technology permits widely dispersed individuals to conduct deep dialogues and meaningful discussions that previously could only have been achieved in face-to-face meetings.

Common Ways of Organizing

There are two predominant ways of organizing virtual collaborative organizations. The first model is around a specific task or objective. The product development teams mentioned earlier are examples of this framework. The merger integration team is another. These organizations have a defined objective and starting and ending points. Their duration is shorter versus longer and dictated by the defined objective.

These organizations tend to be more formalized. They have a defined objective and generally create a work plan with deliverables, milestones, and target dates. Specific individuals are named to the team, and membership tends to be more static than dynamic. Given that nature, specific roles can be defined and are stable. Often these organizations are cross-functional in nature. Last, they dissolve after completing their task or mission.

These organizations tend to go through similar processes during their lifecycle. First, there is some sort of chartering action. The objective of the organization is defined with scope, budget, goals, and so forth. After chartering, the group begins its work. Periodically, the members convene for progress reporting and planning. They discuss and resolve key issues. This may occur in a face-to-face setting, but more typically happens via teleconference. For specific issues or technical matters, they convene special "meetings." These meetings may be teleconferences, a series of email exchanges, or face-to-face meetings. Members of these virtual collaborative organizations perform a significant amount of independent work. During the progress meetings, the group comes together and determines individual tasks and activities that need action, and individuals go off and perform that work. They maintain communications with other members to exchange information, request information, solicit input, check direction, and so on.

The second model is that of an ongoing virtual collaborative organization. Under this model, individuals come together over a long period of time to address some sort of ongoing purpose. A board of directors exemplifies this model. The board provides an ongoing role of corporate governance. However, their members belong to different organizations. While boards do conduct formal meetings, much of their work is done via teleconferences. In one case, no member of the board had ever met another face-to-face. They performed almost all of their work via teleconferences.

Another example of this type of virtual organization comes from Exxon Chemicals. They maintain a team of chemists who are responsible for advancing their technology. They are located around the world and exchange information and ideas about developing technology. They are specifically chartered to advance Exxon's technology. They collect and distribute research. They sponsor internal research. They share results of experiments conducted internally.

These organizations differ from the first model in several ways. First, they are less formalized in many ways. They do not have well-defined outputs or tangible results. The purpose of boards of directors is to provide overall corporate governance, but what exactly does that look like? Contrast that with a product development team whose output is a new product design delivered by a specified date at a specified cost. Similarly, the technology development team for Exxon mentioned above has the general objective of advancing Exxon's technology base. However, it does not have any definitive, measurable goals. Communities of practice are other examples of this type of organization. In this case, their purpose is a general goal of further developing some body of knowledge. They generally do not have specific, measurable goals and outputs.

A second difference is that the membership of these organizations tends to be more fluid. New members join, and others leave. Roles evolve and shift from one person to another. For example, board members are elected on an established schedule. While many tend to be reelected, some turnover occurs. Officers are elected and may change in subsequent elections. Additionally, because of the ongoing nature of their work, different members will participate at different times, depending on the nature of the task or issue. Consider the case of a technical support group of a software development company. They are aligned with a product development team and form a virtual technical support organization. Different people from both the technical support areas and the development area are involved in resolving different customer questions. Who is assigned to the case depends on the nature of the technical support question and available expertise. Essentially, a shifting set of smaller virtual teams form and re-form continually within the context of the larger virtual organization.

The way these organizations operate differs from the first model. They do have some sort of overall purpose, but the chartering process is more a definition of what the general responsibilities of the organization are, versus the definition of a specific measurable, tangible output. Second, the communications tend to be more spontaneous and ad hoc. Members solicit information from others, provide input as needed. When decisions are made between different members, they communicate those in "real time" rather than waiting for some established progress meeting.

Challenges with Respect to Collaboration

The lack of face-to-face and other personal interactions poses significant challenges to virtual organizations. In their book, *Virtual Teams*, Lipnack and Stamps (2000) state: "Group formation was difficult across distances using electronic media alone." Social bonds and personal/professional relationships cannot be developed through a series of email exchanges. The normal group development processes accelerate with the personal interactions that co-location provides. A technical engineering manager at Agilent remarked that having people who knew each other was a key differentiator in the success of virtual organizations he had managed. They do not need to be "best of buddies," but having worked together in the past provides information about the other individuals that aids collaboration.

Assessment technology may assist in this area. Assessment tools like the Meyers-Briggs Type Inventory® can identify complementary and conflicting behavioral patterns of people, particularly in ways they pay attention to different types of information and make decisions. Making virtual organization members aware of others' preferences for information sharing and decision making holds potential for accelerating relationship building.

A second challenge is that informal information exchanges diminish when people collaborate virtually. Individuals must make conscious efforts to place a telephone call or write an email to exchange information. They must be intentional and take the energy to initiate conversations. Those conversations generally have a specific purpose or focus, crowding out the opportunities for random thoughts or conversations to emerge. Simple serendipitous interactions, such as hallway conversations, dining hall conversations, and so on, occur less frequently when people work virtually.

A third challenge is that the media for exchanging information are limited when people work virtually. Virtual organizations rely heavily on email, written documents, teleconferences, and other electronic communication modes. This significantly decreases the amount of visual and graphic modes that people can utilize to share their thoughts and generate creative dialogue. For example, people cannot gather around a whiteboard and draw pictures to describe their ideas for others to build on or modify. Graphic representation of thoughts and ideas is a powerful communications tool that people lose when working virtually.

Technology is emerging that facilitates virtual conferencing and communications. Microsoft provides "Net Meeting" as a feature of the Office products suite. Net Meeting allows people from different locations to view and edit documents virtually via the Internet and hold a telephone conversation at the same time. Other companies provide other more sophisticated groupware tools, but they are not always available to individuals working virtually. These products are expensive, so some companies may not have them available for all employees, or if they do, usually only in selected locations or at limited times.

These products are still fairly complex. The authors of this book worked as a virtual organization. They explored use of Net Meeting, but were unable to easily access or utilize it. Individuals working virtually experience a learning curve with the technology that may limit the true potential of these emerging virtual technologies. During the life of this book, these technologies will likely develop further and become as broadly used as other forms of electronic communications.

Differences in time zones significantly diminish the time available for personal, interactive communications. To pull together people around the world on a conference call usually requires some individuals taking the call very early in the morning or late at night. Even with electronic communications, one may not receive a response from someone overseas for twelve to twenty-four hours. Even in the United States, with only a three-hour time difference between the East Coast and the West Coast, the effective overlap time is roughly half what is available to those working in the same time zone.

Another challenge for people collaborating virtually is the degree of concentration that people maintain. As mentioned earlier, a significant amount of work performed virtually requires extensive telephone communications. People have different attention spans and concentration levels when working over the telephone. Many people will only be "half-listening" during these teleconferences. Distractions abound. When in a face-to-face meeting where people can see their peers, there is less tendency for people to be working on email, generating other correspondence, working on spreadsheets, and so forth. While people have differing capabilities to maintain concentration while multi-tasking, maintaining the full attention of collaborators can be a significant challenge when working virtually.

All of these challenges result in an even greater challenge for virtual organizations. Given the limitations in how and what is communicated, virtual organizations have a greater potential for misunderstanding and more difficulty creating shared understanding among their members. The significant decrease in the amount of time spent in communications is certainly a factor. The reduction in the modes of communications is equally significant. People may believe they have a shared understanding initially, only to find out later in the process that they were mistaken.

This lack of understanding is surely a factor in the degree of conflict that some virtual organizations experience and how they deal with it. The lack of adequate social and personal relationships among individuals inhibits constructive challenging of thoughts and ideas. Virtual organizations may remain in the "forming" stage of Tuckman's model of group development (Tuckman, 1965). Individuals remain polite with other group members, avoiding confrontation and challenging discussions. When conflict does emerge, if individuals have not had the opportunity to develop positive social relationships, it may remain argumentative, versus constructive and engaged dialogue.

When to Collaborate

The general, socially acceptable premise is that collaboration is a good and generally beneficial approach that companies and individuals should strive for in all situations. A more critical assessment reveals that there are situations in which collaboration is more appropriate than others. The situations that require collaboration are

- When different forms of expertise, experience, information, and knowledge are required;

- When the tasks to complete the objective are interdependent; and

- When implementation requires the support, expertise, or commitment of multiple parties.

There is tremendous pressure currently to create and maintain virtual organizations. For many of the reasons provided above, organizations utilize virtual collaboration extensively. However, a more critical review reveals some situations that are better suited for virtual collaboration and some that are not. In the discussion that follows, it is assumed that collaboration is appropriate given the above criteria, and the decision is "Can the group collaborate virtually or would they be more effective with the individuals co-located?" The situations in which virtual collaboration is justified versus co-location are described below.

One such situation that calls for virtual collaboration is when individuals are better suited closer to the customer than to their work partners. Being able to physically meet with customers and maintain relationships with them provides some competitive advantage by itself. This is frequently the case when marketing/sales representatives are involved in new product development. The design engineers typically will be located at one site (or multiple sites throughout the world), while the customer liaisons (sales or marketing representatives) will be dispersed closer to their customers. As new product ideas develop, the sales representatives can meet personally with the customers to ensure that they will satisfy their requirements.

Jay Galbraith (2000) proposes one way of organizing a company called the "front-back" organization. The front end of the organization is organized around customers and markets, thereby creating the capability to recognize and respond to market shifts. The back end is organized to manufacture products for the front end in a way that maximizes economy of scale and efficiency. In these and related situations, it does not make sense to co-locate the collaborators, but instead to establish them as a virtual organization.

Another situation suitable for virtual collaboration is when individuals are not fully dedicated to a particular project. In fact, they are probably involved with several projects, often in different locations. There are other simple, pragmatic considerations. For example, what is the term of the project and what would be the costs for relocation or commuting? Do the length and scope of the project justify relocating people or paying for them to commute to a specific site so they can be physically co-located during the normal working hours? In these situations, virtual collaboration may be the proper business decision.

The personal needs and circumstances of the individuals should also be considered when deciding if a virtual organization is appropriate. For any number of reasons, individuals may not want to relocate or would choose not to relocate. As labor markets change and individuals value better work-family balance, virtual collaboration provides an alternative to relocation. And as technology continues to evolve, virtual collaboration will become easier and more effective.

The sophistication of the technology is another consideration for developing virtual organizations. Does the company have reliable networking and electronic information systems to enable quick, easy storage and distribution of information? Are the right telecommunications systems in place to enable individuals to access those networks from their remote locations (whether from an office or from home)? Is groupware technology in place to facilitate geographically/temporally-dispersed people? To the degree that systems and technology are available, the argument for virtual collaboration is enhanced.

There is a situation where virtual collaboration is counterproductive. It has been discussed that many virtual organizations will include people from different geographies and widely differing cultures. The disparity in cultures can be so great that without significant investment in time and energy effective collaboration is difficult to achieve. In these situations, the involvement of the different parties may slow the process down to the degree that deadlines are missed or issues cannot be fully resolved. In these situations, it is more appropriate to designate a strong leader. He or she still collects inputs and advice from the different people, but retains strong decision-making authority.

How the Guiding Principles Apply

On the following pages, we describe the Ten Principles of Collaborative Organizations as they apply in virtual settings. Each principle is defined, followed by a description of the characteristics of organizations in which the principle is working well and a similar description of organizations in which the principle is not working effectively. Table 6.1 on page 189 provides a summary of this information.

1. Focus Collaboration on Achieving Business Results

As with other types of collaborative organizations, the focus of the collaboration in virtual organizations needs to be on the achievement of business results. While collaboration is a desirable social value, increasing the effectiveness of collaboration requires leaders to ensure that the collaborating parties clearly focus on outcomes that further the business objectives.

With virtual organizations, it becomes even more critical to develop clarity in the early stages as to what the goals and objectives of the group are. While co-located groups achieve this clarity through their informal interactions, virtual organizations require a more explicit process. Since virtual collaborators perform more work independently and complete larger pieces of work before formal or informal review with peers, it becomes more critical to ensure that all members develop a shared mental model of the goals, objectives, and outcomes. This shared mental model will guide them in a consistent fashion as they go about their independent work.

This clarity of goals and objectives and the shared mental model are best achieved face-to-face. While this is often resisted, it is critical to ensure that the virtual collaborators achieve the level of understanding that allows them to move forward with greater independence. A project manager from Agilent, who has served on several virtual projects and is currently leading one, remarked, "Clarity of the goals and objectives is one of the critical success factors for virtual collaboration."

Subsequent face-to-face interactions may be limited, so the initial kickoff of a virtual organization becomes even more critical. While reaching clarity on goals and objectives, the kickoff should also be structured to allow people to get to know one another better. This includes aspects such as:

- How people like to communicate best (email, voice, and so on);
- Whether people are basically introverted or extroverted (Knowing this can help people understand how people respond to data and/or process information); and
- Personal work habits and styles.

All of these provide a base on which future personal relationships and group bonds can be developed.

For example, Sybase utilizes virtual organizations to a significant degree for their product development processes. In one business unit, at the beginning of a project, the project team members come together and define the project objectives. They discuss product features to include scope of the project, intended customers, budget, delivery date, and other issues. The common theme is "We are going to develop this project with these features by X date with these resources." This becomes the simple mechanism for focusing the team on the business objectives. They understand what the customer requirements are and how the product will contribute to the success of the company. Specifically, they discuss the margin contribution of the particular product to the overall profitability.

Microsoft often physically co-locates members of a project team initially. Project team members come to Redmond, Washington, for one or two months at the start of a project. They collectively define the project and the key parameters. They clarify how the product supports the overall strategy. They develop a strategy for breaking the project up into logical components and then disperse. From then on, they operate as a virtual organization.

Conversely, a research and development team in a major chemical company continually struggled with the business objectives. Their primary business objective was to develop new catalyst systems that were more flexible and created compounds with broader physical characteristics. However, they tended to focus on the pure science of what they were doing. They focused on advancing the science of the catalyst systems rather than on the commercialization of those systems.

In the above cases, all the virtual work groups collaborated very effectively. However, effective collaboration should be clearly focused on developing outcomes that improve key business results.

✓ When It Is Working

When this principle is operationalized in virtual settings, the following are observed:

- Members and teams are aware of their industry and their company's role in it;

- Members and teams understand the perspective of their customers and use that information in making decisions; and

- Members and teams commit to the larger goals of the organization and call on that commitment to help deal with difficult situations.

✗ When It Is Not Working

When this principle is not operationalized well in virtual settings, the following are observed:

- Members and teams retain loyalty to their particular function/work group rather than focusing on overall business goals;

- Little or no attention is paid to the customer's perspective or concerns during deliberations;

- Deliberations or decisions reflect lack of understanding of competitive realities or profitability concerns; and

- There is a perceived conflict between profitability concerns and technical goals.

2. Align Organizational Support Systems to Promote Ownership

There are numerous organizational support systems that impact the effectiveness of collaboration. These systems include leadership, performance management, information and communications, learning, and organization and design. The discussion below will describe how each of these systems impacts the effectiveness of collaboration.

Leadership. As noted in Chapter 3 (Collaboration in Manufacturing Settings), leadership relates to all levels of the organization. In effective collaborative organizations, all members take initiative, articulate visions and goals, and suggest solutions or decisions. Executives, senior managers, middle managers, front-line managers, and team members can all contribute. Virtual settings require this broad type of personal leadership to a greater degree. Virtual organizations require individuals with a high degree of self-initiation and personal accountability. There is no manager down the hall to oversee day-to-day work.

But there exists a paradox. With individual members distributed so broadly, a greater degree of coordination is required. The leadership system for virtual organizations needs to clearly define who is accountable for different decisions, when to involve others, and what style will be used.

The leadership style for virtual settings tends to be more empowering. Micromanagement in virtual settings reduces the effectiveness of the virtual organization. The logistics of trying to review every decision in a centralized fashion precludes quick, smooth decision making. Instead, the leadership style in virtual settings focuses on establishing clear guidelines for decisions and actions, delivering agreed-on work products and results, raising issues for debate, and providing information and resources to all members of the organization. Leadership also involves continually monitoring the "few strict rules" (see discussion below) and ensuring adherence to these rules as well as to established guidelines.

Performance Management. The performance management system to support virtual collaboration takes a slightly different form. The criteria for effective performance emphasize the following to a greater degree:

- Independent (but coordinated) decision making,
- Self-initiation,
- Personal accountability, and
- Communications about decisions and work actions.

These criteria enable individuals and work groups to collaborate more effectively without being physically co-located and provide the basis for the reward system.

The traditional reward and recognition systems are certainly present, but may be adapted to support virtual collaboration. There are additional opportunities to reward people in virtual organizations. People should be brought together periodically to celebrate achievement of milestones. In virtual situations celebrating achievements is even more important than when people are co-located. Celebrations also provide opportunities to convene people face-to-face to further develop personal relationships and support the collaboration.

Since people have to travel anyway, holding these meetings in desirable locations can enhance the value of the reward. One company holds their review sessions in the Napa Valley, which provides a pleasant environment to enhance collaboration, as well as providing individuals with an additional perk. Additionally, it encourages people to attend the meetings. Travel is inherently burdensome, and conducting meetings in windowless conference rooms or drab hotel meeting rooms can create a negative tone that does not support collaboration. While this may be perceived as an extravagance in many traditional organizations, it can be an important tool for improving collaboration.

Information and Communications. A greater investment in technology is required to increase the effectiveness of virtual organizations. Since people are not co-located, technology is the lifeblood of their communications. Sophisticated groupware technology enables virtual group members to edit, revise, and update documents in real time from remote locations. Databases that store key data need to be carefully designed to permit easy access and transmission of information. While often expensive, information technology is a required investment.

Many companies are making these investments. Companies such as TRW and Ford Motors utilize sophisticated product development management systems. Designs, test results, parts specifications, and even bills of materials are stored in these systems. Designers working on new products access these designs to learn from them and develop better designs quickly.

Similarly, Procter & Gamble installed a system that links nine hundred factories and seventeen product development centers in seventy-three countries (Ante, 2001). The system allows designers to search a database of 200,000 product designs to see whether they exist in another part of the company, thereby eliminating duplicate efforts. This system reduced the product development time by 50 percent by allowing designers in different parts of the world to collaborate via the Web.

Information systems designers need to pay attention to the integration of different systems. Historically, different platforms (Mac versus PC, for example) have created difficulties in exchanging data. This remains a critical problem for virtual organizations, especially those that cross organizational/company boundaries (consortiums, for example). These platforms and systems need to be integrated or made consistent across the different groups. Common standards for hardware and software can greatly increase the effectiveness of collaboration.

Virtual organizations require extensive sharing of information, but information overload can become a problem. Virtual organizations should carefully examine the kind of information that different people need, both those within the core organization and outside stakeholders. Since informal communication is minimized in virtual organizations, it is even more critical that group members make deliberate choices about what information to share with whom and by what medium. This is an important topic for the initial kickoff. Individuals can discuss their preferences and agree to protocols.

Learning System. The learning system focuses on the organization's attitudes about training and the processes it uses to train members and enable them to learn from their work actions. Making changes to the training system can improve collaboration. Individuals should receive more training in the technology itself, as this is the key communication mode. Time should also be spent on how to best capture and distribute information. In addition to the mechanical aspects of using the technology itself, the training should also focus on how the group process is impacted by technology and the lack of face-to-face interactions. Soliciting input from others via electronic media is fundamentally different than talking in person. Similarly, holding constructive dialogue in cyberspace brings different challenges. Some individuals are prone to "flame" others more readily in cyberspace than in person. Others are insensitive to the fact that words written in ALL CAPS in emails connote shouting. Training people in appropriate ways to express themselves in cyberspace is an area just now receiving attention and is important for effective collaboration in virtual settings. This training extends also to simple mechanics regarding how to use a virtual meeting. For one project group for a U.S.-based software company, this took on significant importance. While the core product group was located in California, the other members of the team were distributed. The California group typically organized their meetings, but failed to fully organize the logistics. Some of the actions they took that minimized the collaboration among their group included:

- Forgetting about time zone differences, scheduling meetings outside the normal working hours of some of their colleagues;
- Failing to send overheads and other material that would be discussed;
- Not putting overheads up on the screen used in the groupware system; or
- "Talking with the hands" or pointing to items that all could not see.

Similarly, achieving resolution on difficult issues in cyberspace is uncomfortable for many individuals. The natural tendency is to wait until people can get together face-to-face. However, this skill will become ever more important to virtual collaborators who have limited face-to-face time.

Different cultures have different norms around this. Since virtual organizations have greater cultural diversity, cultural sensitivity and awareness is another focus for training.

Organization and Design. This system focuses on decisions about who is part of the virtual organization, how many members are in the group, how interdependent their work is, and how much self-management is practiced. As important as organization design may be for the individual work groups, an organization consists of teams and many other forms of work groups—formal and informal, temporary and permanent, functional and cross-functional, and so on. The design of the organization can enhance or stifle the ability of people to work together effectively. In virtual settings, attention must be paid to these points:

- Who the "core members" are;

- What additional resources are needed, how many, and what expertise they bring, and how often they are involved; and

- What the specific roles and responsibilities of each member are.

A more detailed discussion of these points can be found below under Principle 10.

✓ When It Is Working

When this principle is operationalized in virtual settings, the following points are observed:

- Members are highly committed to the work, the projects in which they are engaged, and the organization itself;

- Members are proud of the contribution they are making to, and feel valued by, the organization as a whole;

- Members are willing to raise, and work to resolve, difficult issues;

- Formal and informal communication networks are established and provide constant communication about the organization's goals, achievements, and challenges;

- Information technology systems provide easy access to accurate technical information and current business information;

- Performance management systems work effectively at the individual, team, and organizational level; and

- Performance criteria encourage collaboration.

✗ When It Is Not Working

When this principle is not operationalized well in virtual settings, the following behaviors are observed:

- Members seem uninvolved or uninterested at organization and team meetings;

- Members fail to follow through on tasks for which there is little obvious personal advantage;

- Members identify more with their professional groups than with their organization, projects, or teams;

- Members don't fight for the resources they need to do their jobs; and

- Members are unwilling to spend extra time or effort to do their work.

3. Articulate and Enforce "a Few Strict Rules"

For virtual organizations, this principle holds particular significance. Collaborators are dispersed, so there is less opportunity to supervise or manage people. By default they have more autonomy. To ensure alignment among all collaborators, it is critical that the few strict rules be clear. The best virtual organizations do this by clearly defining the goals and objectives of the particular project. Parameters such as cost, delivery date, product features, and so forth are clearly specified.

If anything is "out of bounds," that should be specified also. Co-located teams tend to clarify these boundaries by having informal conversations or discussions about a particular aspect. Then the leadership of the group will specify whether that aspect is acceptable or not. Again, most of this is done through informal, casual conversations. Virtual organizations do not have as many of these opportunities. Therefore, it becomes more critical to think through any boundaries and clearly articulate those. Once those are articulated, they provide the guidance to collaborators for making any independent decisions they may have to make. These rules enable the organization to operate very freely and self-manage itself.

✓ When It Is Working

When this principle is operationalized in virtual settings, the following is observed:

- Members and teams know what matters, which deadlines are real, for what they will be held accountable, and how decisions are made; and

- Members and teams are very clear about what level of authority they possess.

✗ When It Is Not Working

When this principle is not operationalized well in virtual settings, the following can be observed:

- Members or teams continually seek approval for decisions or direction from upper management;

- Members or teams feel that they are being "second-guessed" by upper management; and

- Different members or teams value things differently (cost versus technical excellence versus responsiveness to customer).

4. Exploit the Rhythm of Convergence and Divergence

The convergence/divergence rhythm for virtual organizations relates primarily to the process by which it manages its work. Groups of people collaborating virtually typically do come together periodically. This is done largely via teleconferences, and to a lesser degree in person. During these convenings, they will make decisions or chart a course of action. In other words, they converge.

Prior to this, they have a number of discussions that:

- Generate different options;

- Determine implications of various courses of action; and

- Delineate the pros and cons of different options.

This, essentially, is a convergent process, generating alternatives, thinking expansively and broadly. It is typically done "offline" through a series of email exchanges, phone conversations, or however. It tends to be asynchronous and occur over a period of days, or even months in some cases. It is the "staff/professional/technical" work that needs to be done to generate the right data and support the thinking processes to reach a decision.

Effective virtual organizations recognize this dynamic and utilize it. They utilize the limited time in the convenings to gain agreement on a course of action and proceed with it. But it is critical that the convenings provide clarity about the next steps. This gives the group a new set of boundaries to work within and initiate a new series of divergent activities. Without this process, the collaborators tend to go off in their own directions, lacking alignment and focus.

For example, Case Logic, the manufacturer of audio and video equipment storage accessories, utilized this rhythm effectively in the design of its new products. They had a virtual organization that included its manufacturers in Hong Kong and the product designers in the United States. In the early phases of the design of a new product, product managers would develop initial product specifications. These included features like numbers and composition of zippers, numbers of and sizes of pockets, fabric, and so on. They would then review these specifications with the manufacturer. During this review, conducted either on a personal trip to Hong Kong or via a conference call, they would check the specifications, price points to consumers, and other issues and determine whether they could manufacture the item at a proper margin. If not, they made adjustments to the design. For example, they might decide to eliminate one pocket or change the quality of the fabric to reduce manufacturing costs. The output of this deliberation was an agreement on the initial product design. The different parties could then go off and begin doing more detailed work around bills of materials, customer focus groups, and so on. This started another set of actions that were more divergent, but within a specified direction.

✓ When It Is Working

When this principle is operationalized in virtual settings, the following observations can be made:

- The organization is known both for its creativity and for its dependability;

- There is rhythm to the work that members and teams share and understand;

- Members know when it is especially important to try to expand their thinking and when it's important to try to converge so that the task can be finished;

- Discussion continues until participants (either members or teams, as the case may be) come up with a plan that they can carry out;

- Members don't argue for their individual points of view at the expense of team consensus, nor do they acquiesce to plans they do not intend to carry out;

- Escalation paths (moving the question to a higher level or more experienced team or authority) are used to help manage important divergent ideas whose potential for positive effect may be great, but whose implementation may endanger deadlines or promises made; and

- Members are aware of and use a variety of processes both to raise perspectives and to reach agreement.

✗ When It Is Not Working

When this principle is not operationalized well in virtual settings, the following can be observed:

- Teams or projects do not surface the perspectives of all stakeholders and members whose opinions are not consistent with the majority are ignored or ridiculed;

- Data from important sources is ignored;

- Teams, projects, or the organization fails to generate differing options or scenarios, for instance, they plan for only one view of the future when it's clear that a number of options could realistically occur;

- Abstractions are left abstract and teams or projects fail to provide the level of detail necessary to fully understand the perspective being generated;

- Teams or projects fail to agree on common values, goals, tasks, and criteria; and

- Data or options are considered without agreeing on criteria or approaches.

5. Manage Complex Tradeoffs on a Timely Basis

Virtual organizations must continually manage complex tradeoffs, as other collaborative systems do. The difference with virtual organizations is that the data and expertise for managing these tradeoffs is so widely dispersed. The discussions for resolving tradeoffs must be held virtually, and that generally is asynchronous. It is more difficult to convene people and have comprehensive dialogues regarding the issue and to develop the appropriate course of action.

Effective collaboration in these cases requires that collaborators have greater trust in their colleagues. If one cannot fully participate in a dialogue, he or she must trust colleagues with some of that decision making. Each person must provide the relevant data and allow others to synthesize it. In a number of consulting engagements the authors have been involved in, they were not available to the client's design team (or other internal consulting body) when certain decisions were discussed. In these cases, they provided the client with the best possible advice and allowed the client to integrate that advice with other information they possessed about the particular issue.

✓ When It Is Working

When this principle is operationalized in virtual settings, the following can be observed:

- Members of decision-making groups have a shared understanding of the criteria to use in making tradeoff decisions or a shared understanding of the need to create those criteria;

- There are clear escalation paths for resolving tradeoff decisions when agreement cannot be reached within a team or project;

- Members and teams are aware of the need to remake tradeoff decisions when conditions change; and

- Members are aware of the various weightings senior management has selected for tradeoffs in specific situations.

✗ When It Is Not Working

When this principle is not operationalized well in virtual settings, the following can be observed:

- Members or teams make decisions that indicate they have not recognized the true nature of the tradeoff;

- Members or teams make no decision regarding a tradeoff and continue to debate, creating major delays in the schedule and major damage to the relationships (and careers) of the team members; and

- Members do make tradeoff decisions, but ignore important criteria.

6. Create Higher Standards for Discussions, Dialogue, and Information Sharing

As we have said before, people in virtual organizations have limited time for personal conversations and need to use the opportunities they do have more effectively. The conversations of effective virtual collaborators are much richer, taking on the form of rich dialogue. They express assumptions, discuss implications, and develop shared mental models.

In addition to utilizing the time more effectively when they do convene, effective virtual organizations also develop the capability for richer electronic dialogues. They develop the skill to resolve issues through email conversations. They solicit input, synthesize suggestions, openly debate the merits of alternatives, and reach a conclusion, all through textual media. This may be supplemented by a teleconference or videoconference, but these are called only when the electronic exchanges are not leading to agreement.

Virtual collaborators need to build in feedback mechanisms for their online electronic dialogues. They cannot take for granted that they are meeting the needs of all members. They must actively fine-tune their electronic processes, just as co-located team should periodically review their face-to-face group dynamics.

Some of these same comments apply to phone exchanges. Virtual collaborators improve the quality of their exchanges if they develop and utilize a structure that explicitly builds relationships while efficiently accomplishing tasks. This structure must utilize meeting management techniques to accomplish tasks and other activities to develop relationships. These include:

- Greeting one another;
- Setting time aside at the beginning of the call for "small-talk" and making efforts to "connect" personally;
- Listening for concerns behind the words and making them explicit;
- Stating goals and clarifying them to form shared mental models;
- Sharing openly;
- Thanking one another; and
- Explicitly planning for follow-up.

Effective virtual collaborators become more disciplined around capturing and sharing of information. They are very deliberate about not only capturing an agreement on a decision, but also the rationale behind it. This provides a clear record for later, when that decision may come back to the group and the group is struggling to recall why they made it. They are intentional about who needs to receive the information and in what form.

For example, IBM chartered a virtual organization of transportation managers to develop the implementation plan for outsourcing their shipping and logistics function to a third party. During the process, they identified a plethora of issues about how to best execute this. They created a running "issues database." As they resolved an issue, they logged the resolution into the database with explanatory text. Often throughout the process, a resolved issue resurfaced. The group used the database as a tool: "We resolved the issue. Here's what we agreed to, and here's why." It helped keep the group on track and avoided wasted time repeating dialogues.

Virtual organizations need to be very precise and disciplined about what information they share, when to share it, and by what media. For example, BHP, a large international mining company, used a virtual organization in the construction of a new ore processing plant. They made conscious choices around what issues to share with the corporate group. If certain issues were shared prematurely, they could be taken out of context, which would damage the collaboration between the corporate staff group and the local engineering group. There was no opportunity to clarify situations, given the difference in time zones between the two groups. The project manager and the corporate staff manager came to clear agreement on what issues to raise and when.

At the local level, the project team defined clear standards on what issues to raise at the project review meetings. They clearly differentiated between "nice to have" and "need to have" as it related to design features for the new plant. They established clear norms around only discussing the "need to have" design features in their review meetings and were clear about why it was a "need to have."

✓ When It Is Working

When this principle is operationalized in virtual settings, the following can be observed:

- Shared databases that include all relevant information about the work for which the group is chartered;

- Relevant decisions are captured, documented, and stored for others to access;

- These databases are open to all members or teams;

- Managers and team members are skilled at asking questions that raise the complexity and sophistication at which issues are addressed;

- Little information is shared only on a "need to know" basis;

- Good listeners exist at all levels of the organization; and

- People focus on understanding the underlying assumptions of others' thinking.

✗ When It Is Not Working

When this principle is not operationalized well in virtual settings, the following can be observed:

- Members and teams are uninformed or unnecessarily delayed because decisions do not include key information or perspectives;

- Decisions are made using the same criteria each time, even through the situation is more complex;

- Knowledge management systems are so cumbersome that no one uses them;

- Members at all levels of the organization possess inadequate listening and dialogue skills; and

- People are punished for challenging current thinking or conventional wisdom.

7. Foster Personal Accountability

"Out of sight, out of mind." This phrase describes a lot of virtual organizations. Members lose many of the visual cues that co-located groups have. There is less direct supervision. There is less visibility regarding the tasks that others are doing. Virtual collaborators need to take greater responsibility for their own work and for delivering what their colleagues need.

Many of the coaching tools that people are familiar with aid in fostering personal accountability. Managers and leaders can still perform coaching, but this is generally now done via the telephone. Email and other electronic media provide other means, but may not be as effective. Many informal coaching opportunities are present with virtual collaborators. With co-located groups, it is not uncommon for a project leader to drop in on a project member and informally review what he or she is going to present at an upcoming meeting. This can still be done via the telephone, but it is more difficult.

Because there is limited opportunity for virtual organizations to come together, it becomes the personal responsibility of all members to ensure that they use that limited time to the fullest. Effective virtual groups establish clear norms around preparation and deliverables. They come to "meetings" (often in the form of teleconferences) prepared and able to concisely present their points. If the material is complex, they distribute it prior to the conversation.

Because individuals may not be able to communicate with others and receive the benefit of their expertise or experience, virtual collaborators may have to make decisions without the benefits of that information. They must be able to make decisions on their own. There is a tradeoff between waiting to obtain information and using one's best judgment to move forward. Virtual collaborators must:

- Clearly think through decisions;
- Take reasonable risks;
- Make decisions without all the desired information; and
- Clearly articulate their rationale to others.

If people wait for others to make decisions, the process can bog down.

✓ When It Is Working

When this principle is operationalized in virtual settings:

- Members and teams fight for the resources necessary to do their tasks;
- Members and teams actively check their own thinking and perceptions, ask for feedback, and seek additional information;
- Members and teams put in additional time and effort for which there are not obvious rewards;
- Managers are more concerned about follow-through and responsibility than they are about subservient behavior, that is, disagreeing with a senior manager is acceptable; and

- People complete tasks on time, are well-prepared for meetings, and distribute information without being asked.

✗ When It Is Not Working

When this principle is not operationalized well in virtual settings:

- Teams and members seek direction instead of reactions;

- Issues that they should be able to address or resolve on their own escalate;

- Teams and members don't defend their positions, but change their plans or assumptions with little resistance;

- Teams and members do not seem to fight for resources with each other or with management and there is little evidence that anyone is passionate about what he or she is doing; and

- There are few ideas for improving things and few volunteers for challenging tasks.

8. Align Authority, Information, and Decision Making

Closely related to the personal accountability principle is the principle of alignment of authority, information, and decision making. It is clear that in order for people to make the proper decisions, they must have the critical information related to that decision. Given that the information flow operates virtually, this becomes even more important. Effective virtual organizations clearly define what decisions can be made and by whom. Given the geographic and temporal dispersion, individuals in effective virtual organizations generally require more autonomy and authority for decision making. Associated with this autonomy is the responsibility for communicating decisions that are made to other team members, along with the rationale for those decisions.

✓ When It Is Working

When this principle is operationalized in virtual settings:

- Management functions as a team to assume joint responsibility for decisions that need to be resolved at the management level;

- Members and teams function effectively in coordinating with other teams;

- Management rarely overturns team decisions, and if they do the rationale is always fully explained;

- Team decisions are made on the basis of all relevant information; and

- Members and teams understand their roles in the larger endeavor and how that endeavor will affect what they do.

✗ When It Is Not Working

When this principle is not operationalized well in virtual settings, the following is true:

- Members or teams become "bottlenecks" in the overall process because they are missing the expertise necessary to make key decisions or to perform key tasks;

- Members or teams are charged with making decisions that they do not have the information or authority to make (Most often these are decisions have been left with an individual team, when they should be made by a management team or by a higher level team charged with coordination);

- Decisions made by or requirements for teams are changed without input from the teams; and

- Members and teams believe they have no way to either renegotiate or meet the expectations they've been given.

9. Treat Collaboration as a Disciplined Process

Virtual collaborators need to be more disciplined around how they use their limited personal interaction time. Effective virtual organizations clearly establish their work schedule and when they will convene. Weekly conference calls are usually the norm. The calls are used to review the progress of the project and to check how effectively the group is working together. The better groups utilize a standard agenda that they follow every week. They become explicit about when teleconferences are appropriate, when videoconferences are needed, and when face-to-face meetings are required. Much of this work is done during the chartering meeting, when virtual collaborators go through the process to establish protocols.

The discipline also includes clearly defining roles and communication patterns. If left undefined, over-communication may be as much of a problem as under-communication. For example, Agilent, when working with their overseas manufacturers of chips, learned this. In the spirit of openness, they wanted their design engineers to have open communications with the production and process engineers of the manufacturer. However, the design engineers began requesting numerous process changes to support their new designs. The manufacturer soon became overwhelmed with process changes that they could not accommodate. The project leader stepped in and established a new process by which all of those requests flowed through a single senior designer who prioritized the process changes and worked with the process engineers to determine a schedule for them. This example shows the importance of clearly determining the communications patterns and who needs to be involved in what decisions.

Effective virtual organizations utilize different process tools for establishing this discipline. A responsibility matrix/accountability chart is one useful tool. An issues tracking database helps groups track open issues and resolved issues. The discipline of defining what the resolution was AND the rationale can help groups not to rehash a decision that has already been discussed and resolved. Agendas and role charts are other tools to help establish an appropriate discipline.

The mere process of capturing key learnings and knowledge from a particular project or piece of work can be another effective tool. Most groups simply complete a project and move on. *Effective* collaboration requires more reflection and assessment of what helps collaboration and what impedes it. This post-completion review should include not only technical learnings, but process learnings. These learnings will be invaluable as new projects start up.

✓ When It Is Working

When this principle is operationalized in virtual settings:

- Individuals can explain the correct process for making certain types of decisions;
- Individuals can explain who should be involved in making which decisions;
- Individuals know what kind of questions to expect from management and from other teams;
- Members and teams clearly understand how decisions are made;
- The vast majority of meetings have agendas generated in advance and detailed minutes distributed afterward;

- Meetings are businesslike and productive;

- Decisions made remain made—unless a major rationale is provided to change them—and teams don't repeat decision-making processes; and

- There is a sense of order and discipline in collaborative activities.

✗ When It Is Not Working

When this principle is not operationalized well in virtual settings:

- A general feeling exists that "no one really knows what is going on";

- Management does not question a team on the criteria or process for making a decision;

- Slow and/or poor decisions are made by teams;

- Members and teams are unable to make complex decisions; and

- Decisions are made on the basis of power or energy as opposed to information and consideration of key tradeoffs.

10. Design and Promote Flexible Organizations

The application of this principle for virtual collaboration deals with the need to add or delete members of the group. With virtual organizations, one needs to be more selective about the core group. Natural selection defines the core group as those who tend to perform most of the governance processes. But one should be intentional about defining who the core group is. As the project progresses, additional people may be added. For specific issues, special expertise may be required. In an effective virtual organization, fluidity develops that enables the proper resources to be brought into the project at the proper time. The model becomes a core team with fluid extended members, including customers or stakeholders.

A product development team for Sybase exemplifies this type of fluidity. The product team was comprised of members from development, marketing, quality assurance, and technical support. Initially, marketing drove the project. They defined product features that would best serve the customer needs. They worked closely with development to ensure that the product features could be coded. As the product features became codified, the leadership shifted to development. They took the lead to ensure that the product was developed according to the cost and delivery schedule. As the delivery date approached, the technical support group became more prominent in the leadership role. They were the ones who would be helping customers support the new product, so they took the lead in the project.

New collaborative approaches are redefining the term "organization" itself. The emergence of e-marketplaces and trading networks brings customers, suppliers, and competitors together to optimize the flow of materials and goods throughout an entire industry. Ford uses digital conference rooms to manage the formation of the industry marketplace Covisent (Ante, 2001). Lawyers and automobile representatives share virtual rooms to negotiate contracts and supply agreements.

✓ When It Is Working

When this principle is operationalized in virtual settings:

- Members and teams understand when and why their membership changes—or changes focus—and they have learned to manage these changes effectively;
- New groups continue to form, disband, and re-form as business conditions dictate;
- The IT system supports communication and collaboration across all relevant groups;
- There is strong sense of, and perceived value for, being a member of the larger organization, regardless of what smaller group one belongs to;
- Members and teams trust the judgment of the senior managers in the organization; and
- There are frequent communications about strategies and approach and about team members' roles in the overall success of the company.

✗ When It Is Not Working

When this principle is not operationalized well in virtual settings:

- The organization is being redesigned to death;
- Lengthy, formal design processes are used and the resultant design is outdated before it is implemented;
- There is a lot of attention around finding the right "structure," but the organization fails to spend much energy on building effective networks, real-time communication systems, and responsive resource allocation systems;
- Members and teams are more loyal to their immediate management than to the company or to their work; and

- Members, including managers, still believe things will settle down if they can just get it right.

Implications for Executives

Key actions and implications for executives and leaders of virtual organizations are provided below. These are key things executives and leaders can do to improve the effectiveness of their virtual collaborative organizations.

1. *Carefully select members for virtual organizations.* Qualities of effective virtual collaborators include the ability to work in teams (versus individual contribution), more comfort with less structured environments, and greater self-initiative/self-monitoring.

2. *Relinquish control.* It becomes more difficult to manage virtually. Leaders must help the group clearly define goals and objectives, but then let the team operate freely within specified boundaries. The team will determine its own schedule, work processes, and outputs.

3. *Give sponsoring executives a means to work across cultural and geographic boundaries.* Provide support and resources from many different areas and give them different sources of power from which to influence and persuade.

4. *Become more competent in electronic communications and technology.* This is the core process for communicating and decision making for virtual collaborative organizations, so sponsoring executives will need to develop these skills the same way the group does.

5. *Be stronger advocates for the virtual organization to the rest of the organization.* It is hard to "see" virtual organizations. Without proper advocacy for their interests, they may be discounted. Sponsoring executives need to represent the interests of such teams and advocate strongly for things like travel budgets to enable the group to meet personally, budgets for groupware technology, rewards and recognition that may not fit the corporate systems, and so forth.

6. *Learn to deal with people outside of their direct control.* Many people participating on the group may not report directly to a sponsoring leader, so those leaders will need greater influencing skills/persuasive powers.

The following table sums up the Principles of Collaboration in virtual settings.

Table 6.1. The Ten Principles of Collaboration in Virtual Settings

Principle	Importance in Virtual Settings	When It Is Working	When It Is Not Working
1. Focus Collaboration on Achieving Business Results	Critical that members have shared mental model to move forward independently	Aware of company status within industry Understand customer perspectives Commitment to larger goals	Loyal to function, not to goals Little attention to customer perspective Lack of understanding for competitive realities Conflict between technical needs and profit
2. Align Organizational Support Systems to Promote Ownership	All levels of organization aligned through leadership	Highly committed members Pride in contributions and feeling valued Difficult issues raised Constant communication Easy access to information Strong performance management systems Collaboration encouraged	Lack of interest in meetings Poor follow-through No fights for resources Unwillingness to work extra
3. Articulate and Enforce "a Few Strict Rules"	Ensures alignment for dispersed employees	Members know what's happening and what's important Clarity about one's own authority for decision making	Upper management as decision makers Teams feel "second-guessed" No alignment on what is of value
4. Exploit the Rhythm of Convergence and Divergence	Need to come together and also work apart is strongest in virtual organizations	Organization known for creativity and dependability Rhythm to the work Both expanded thinking and convergent thinking Open discussion to a plan Agreement to work as a team Higher authorities decide if danger of deadlines not being met Variety of processes used in discussions	All perspectives not surfaced Some data ignored Lack of options Lack of details to make projects concrete No common values, goals, tasks, criteria Approaches to problems not thought out

Table 6.1. The Ten Principles of Collaboration in Virtual Settings, Cont'd

Principle	Importance in Virtual Settings	When It Is Working	When It Is Not Working
5. Manage Complex Tradeoffs on a Timely Basis	Data and expertise are widely dispersed and discussions are held virtually	Shared understanding of criteria for decision making Clear paths to resolve issues Awareness of when to remake decisions Awareness of values of senior management	Decisions are poor Decisions not made at all Some criteria ignored when making decisions
6. Create Higher Standards for Discussions, Dialogue, and Information Sharing	Time must be used more effectively in virtual teams	Shared databases with relevant information Decisions documented and stored in accessible format Questions get at depth of the issues Good listening skills Focus is on understanding	Lack of information Decisions made without all information Knowledge management systems too cumbersome to use Lack of listening and dialogue skills Punishment for challenging status quo
7. Foster Personal Accountability	Less visibility but added responsibility	Members fight for resources required Requests for feedback abound Additional time put into meeting goals Disagreements with senior management acceptable Tasks completed on time, information available to all	Members seek direction Issues escalate Few volunteers for challenging tasks
8. Align Authority, Information, and Decision Making	More autonomy and authority for decision making required	Management jointly responsible Much team coordination Few overturned decisions Relevant information used for decisions Role clarity	Bottlenecks No information or authority to make decisions Changes made without input of those involved Feelings of helplessness to meet expectations

Table 6.1. The Ten Principles of Collaboration in Virtual Settings, Cont'd

Principle	Importance in Virtual Settings	When It Is Working	When It Is Not Working
9. Treat Collaboration as a Disciplined Process	More discipline required to share information and work together	Processes are clear, as well as who should be involved and how decisions are made Meetings businesslike with good agendas Decisions are final Sense of order and discipline	Confusion and lack of understanding of processes Little communication with management Poor decisions or lack of ability to make a decision at all
10. Design and Promote Flexible Organizations	Need ways to add or delete group members	Membership changes are clear and well-orchestrated Strong sense of being a member of the larger organization Frequent communications among teams	Too much organizational redesign Processes of change take too long Search for structure overlooks natural networks Loyalty to immediate team rather than to organization Belief in ability to "get it right"

"In a world where a slight advantage easily turns into a leading position, think about the profits a company, correctly utilizing all its assets, might gain over a company that uses only 20 to 30 percent."

Johan Roos, Goran Roos, Nicola Carlo Dragonetti, Leif Edvinsson, Intellectual Capital: Navigating in the New Business Landscape, *1998.*

"Competition is subtle, and managers are prone to simplify. What we learn from looking at actual competition is that winning companies are anything but simple."

Michael Porter, Fast Company, *March 2001*

PART 3

STRATEGIES FOR IMPLEMENTATION

"Companies are realizing the power of collaborating. Collaboration is being forced by the connected economy. You have to collaborate to develop real power and potential within a value web."

McGehee, p. 52

CHAPTER 7

Moving Forward

THE PRINCIPLES DESCRIBED IN THIS BOOK provide guidance to leaders, consultants, and practitioners who wish to build collaborative organizations. These principles are the basis for developing and sustaining collaborative advantage by systematically creating and managing organizations to capitalize on collaborative opportunities. Today's business environment is so complex and changing so rapidly that collaboration is required. No one individual or small set of individuals can manage the complexity characteristic of today's organization. How well organizations operationalize the principles of collaboration will determine much of their effectiveness in the competitive arena.

The transformation to a collaborative organization is similar to the transformation to Six Sigma from total quality management. It requires time and sustained effort. An organization may, for a variety of sound reasons, choose to implement only a subset of the ten principles presented here. However, the number and effectiveness of principles operationalized will determined the degree to which collaboration improves. World-class collaborative organizations depend on the disciplined implementation of all the principles.

Each of the ten principles is probably already in practice to some extent in your organization. We recommend that you make that practice deliberate and systemic. Consider the difference between a junior high basketball team and the Chicago Bulls. The same principles for playing the game were in operation, but the Bulls were the masters at collaboration. Even the star played as a contributing team member when a win depended on it.

You can choose any of the ten principles as a starting point. Remember, however, that the main payoffs come from interweaving the principles into a net of disciplined practices.

None of these principles represents an absolute. Some readers may infer that the more each principle is applied the better. However, in some cases, more is not better; balance in application across principles will yield much better results. Those implementing the principles will need to apply sound business judgment in determining when and how to implement the principles. One should not, however, let pressure to maintain the status quo interfere with the application of these principles. Their studied application can move your organization forward into the 21st Century.

These principles are scalable at different levels of the organization. At the highest level, they describe how to improve the effectiveness across organizations. For example, joint ventures, alliances, or customer-supplier partnerships all require collaboration. Similarly, cross-functional groups working on a common task are examples of collaborative work systems within a company's boundaries. The principles also apply to individual teams and one-to-one interactions.

Whereas much of the previous writing on collaboration has focused on individual teams, the principles explicated here focus on larger systems and the integration of different groups. The scalability of the principles means that alignment across levels can be maintained so that investment in disciplined practices of collaboration can be leveraged.

The principles are highly interrelated. They are mutually reinforcing and synergistic. For example, aligning authority and decision making (Principle 8) is significantly enhanced by implementing personal accountability (Principle 7) and by creating higher standards for discussions, dialogue, and sharing relevant information (Principle 6). Therein lies some of the power of these ten principles. Operationalizing one or more creates significant positive impact on the others.

Applying the principles may challenge some of the behaviors that have helped leaders attain their current positions in an organization. To a large degree, the reward systems in traditional organizations remain individually based. They reinforce individual rather than collaborative achievement. Leaders must examine the context in which their organization is operating to determine what hurdles exist to building the collaborative organization. After lowering those hurdles, leaders should work together to determine the extent to which collaboration is required by the organization and then commit the resources needed for disciplined practice of the chosen principles.

Collaboration Diagnostic Tool: How to Move Forward

The authors have developed a Collaboration Diagnostic Tool to assist those who wish to initiate activities to improve the effectiveness of their organization's collaboration. It is a simple tool to assess how well each of the principles is currently in operation and to highlight what can be done to improve the application of that principle.

This tool provides the leaders of an organization with an initial assessment of the organization's current collaborative capacity and highlights strategies to begin improving that capacity. Use of the tool assumes that the leadership has identified collaboration as an important competency and wishes to assess its skill in that area.

How to Use the Tool

For each principle, consider the diagnostic questions. We recommend that you work with other members of your staff and/or other stakeholders when answering the questions. Depending on time available, you may choose to complete the tool over a period of several weeks or months. Do not rush the process. The dialogue you and your staff and/or stakeholders have around the questions is more important than specific answers. In fact, discussing the questions is consistent with the principles of collaboration.

We suggest that you capture key points of your discussion. This should provide ideas on practices you can use to improve as well as those you wish to continue or expand.

After discussing the questions, determine how well you execute that particular principle. Use a consensus approach (which generates a rich discussion) this discussion should guide you in prioritizing the steps to take now to begin to improving the organization's collaborative capacity.

Once you have completed the diagnostic tool, you will have a snapshot of your current collaborative capability. The next step will be to identify actions to increase that capability. Undoubtedly, you cannot work on all dimensions at once; you will need to prioritize. You may want to give the greatest attention initially to the dimensions with lowest scores. However, you will need to consider other factors as well. The level of resources you have available is surely a key consideration. Also, some of the principles are easier to operationalize than others. You likely have many other improvement initiatives underway in your organization. While some of these initiatives may be perceived as competing with improved collaboration, there often are opportunities for complementary, synergistic initiatives. First take the Collaboration Diagnostic Tool in Exhibit 7.1 and then continue reading below.

Exhibit 7.1. Collaboration Diagnostic Tool

1. Focus Collaboration on Achieving Business Results

This principle reflects the orientation that effective collaboration is focused on some sort of business outcome. The group's output is clearly aligned with the organization's higher level goals. Collaboration for collaboration's sake is not the objective, regardless of how desirable it may be as a social goal. Answer the following questions:

- To what degree do collaborative efforts in your organization focus on some sort of direct results that improve the business? Consider not only bottom-line hard results, but also other business results that lead to improved financial/business performance.

- What are the business results you are trying to achieve through collaboration?

Exhibit 7.1. Collaboration Diagnostic Tool, Cont'd

- How does the language you use focus on business results versus collaboration for collaboration's sake or as some socially acceptable value?

- Why do you need collaboration to achieve these results?

   Do you lack the necessary expertise?

   Do you lack the necessary resources (money, staff, technology, etc.)?

   Do you require others to execute your decisions and require their commitment?

- Overall, how well do you believe you and your collaborators practice this principle?

Very Poorly	1	2	3	4	5	Very Well

- What kind of impact do you believe you can affect in your organization by working on this principle?

Very Little	1	2	3	4	5	Very Great

2. Align Organizational Support Systems to Promote Ownership

The organizational support systems (leadership system, information and communication system, performance management system, learning system, and organization and decision system) are aligned to support collaboration and commitment.

- To what degree are people rewarded for individual problem solving and/or execution?

Exhibit 7.1. Collaboration Diagnostic Tool, Cont'd

- Do rewards include:

  Financial rewards (pay increases, stock options, bonuses)?

  Promotions?

  Public verbal recognition?

- To what degree do the norms of the organization promote broad participation in decision making?

- Is staff consulted for relevant decisions?

- Are other functions consulted?

- Are resident "experts" consulted?

- How are other stakeholders involved in the decision?

- How are decisions made?

Exhibit 7.1. Collaboration Diagnostic Tool, Cont'd

- Does the decision-making process encourage the solicitation and deliberate consideration of other stakeholders?

- Are the "right" people making the decisions?

- Do they have the power to make relevant decisions? Can they then execute their decisions?

- Are the information systems designed to distribute information broadly and quickly?

- To what degree are people "intentional" about whom they distribute information and data to?

- Do people possess the right values that predispose them to collaboration?

- To what degree have people been trained in skills to support collaboration (valuing differences, decision making, influence, setting standards)?

Exhibit 7.1. Collaboration Diagnostic Tool, Cont'd

- To what degree do people possess broad technical expertise that enables them to understand others' views? To what degree is this necessary?

- Can people easily access databases and other technology to find the right information to guide their decision making?

- Overall, how well do you believe you and your collaborators practice this principle?

  Very Poorly   1   2   3   4   5   Very Well

- What kind of impact do you believe you can affect in your organization by working on this principle?

  Very Little   1   2   3   4   5   Very Great

3. Articulate and Enforce "a Few Strict Rules"

Collaborating groups are given a minimum of boundaries, but these boundaries are clearly articulated and groups are accountable for abiding by them.

- To what degree is there clarity about "what's really important" across the whole organization (high technical standards, quality, cost)?

- To what degree are these same things important to the collaborating parties?

- To what degree are there sanctions for straying from these critical items?

Exhibit 7.1. Collaboration Diagnostic Tool, Cont'd

- What happens if people miss budget or milestone targets?

- To what degree are the goals and objectives clear to the collaborating parties?

- To what degree do the managers and leaders above the collaborating parties become involved? Is their involvement appropriate? To what degree is it "micromanagement"?

- Overall, how well do you believe you and your collaborators practice this principle?

  Very Poorly   1   2   3   4   5   Very Well

- What kind of impact do you believe you can affect in your organization by working on this principle?

  Very Little   1   2   3   4   5   Very Great

4. Exploit the Rhythm of Convergence and Divergence

This principle acknowledges that collaboration requires both divergent (creative and expansive) and convergent (narrowing, focusing) processes. During the collaborative process a certain amount of ambiguity remains that people must be comfortable with.

- To what degree is there open discussion that promotes creative thinking?

- To what degree are innovative suggestions prematurely dismissed?

Exhibit 7.1. Collaboration Diagnostic Tool, Cont'd

- To what degree are people open to exploring alternative suggestions even though they may be counter to the current thinking?

- To what degree can the group bounce back and forth between the "big picture" and high-level concepts and the operational details?

- To what degree can the collaborating parties reach closure on a decision or course of action after generating alternatives?

- Overall, how well do you believe you and your collaborators practice this principle?

  Very Poorly   1   2   3   4   5   Very Well

- What kind of impact do you believe you can affect in your organization by working on this principle?

  Very Little   1   2   3   4   5   Very Great

5. Manage Complex Tradeoffs on a Timely Basis

Effective collaboration requires that different parties must come together to balance competing objectives when making decisions (for example, balancing technical sophistication with cost). This must be done continually and in an expeditious fashion.

- To what degree are the collaborating parties able to consider multiple competing criteria when making decisions?

- How quickly can they make these tradeoff decisions?

Exhibit 7.1. Collaboration Diagnostic Tool, Cont'd

- How routinely are they faced with considering different tradeoffs?

- How often do they have to "kick a decision upstairs"?

- To what degree is upper management frustrated with the inability of their people to come to agreement?

- To what degree does upper management have difficulty coming to agreement?

- Overall, how well do you believe you and your collaborators practice this principle?

  Very Poorly   1   2   3   4   5   Very Well

- What kind of impact do you believe you can affect in your organization by working on this principle?

  Very Little   1   2   3   4   5   Very Great

6. Create Higher Standards for Discussions, Dialogue, and Information Sharing

This requires that everyone be clear about who needs what information and reflects the need to create systems that broadly distribute information and knowledge and allow people to have frank, open dialogues.

- To what degree do people openly express views and opinions?

Exhibit 7.1. Collaboration Diagnostic Tool, Cont'd

- To what degree is there open, candid dialogue about issues?

- To what degree do people consciously think about who needs what information? To what degree do they supply that information?

- To what degree do the information systems enable people to distribute and access information?

- To what degree are there systems by which people can engage in dialogue, share information, and create knowledge throughout the organization? How easy are these to use?

- Overall, how well do you believe you and your collaborators practice this principle?

  Very Poorly   1   2   3   4   5   Very Well

- What kind of impact do you believe you can affect in your organization by working on this principle?

  Very Little   1   2   3   4   5   Very Great

7. Foster Personal Accountability

This principle recognizes that effective collaboration requires individuals/parties who self-initiate, deliver on their commitments, and demonstrate personal leadership.

- To what degree do individuals and groups need direction?

Exhibit 7.1. Collaboration Diagnostic Tool, Cont'd

- To what degree do individuals determine a course of action and initiate it themselves?

- To what degree do collaborating parties deliver what they promise? To what degree is this within agreed-on timeframes and within acceptable quality guidelines?

- To what degree do individuals take it on themselves to influence others in an appropriate manner?

- To what degree does the organization promote independent thinking and action?

- To what degree do collaborating parties obtain the necessary resources by themselves with little assistance from others?

- Overall, how well do you believe you and your collaborators practice this principle?

  Very Poorly   1   2   3   4   5   Very Well

- What kind of impact do you believe you can affect in your organization by working on this principle?

  Very Little   1   2   3   4   5   Very Great

Exhibit 7.1. Collaboration Diagnostic Tool, Cont'd

8. Align Authority, Information, and Decision Making

Collaboration requires a redistribution of power and decision making. Leaders must provide the appropriate information to enable collaborating parties to make the proper decisions.

- To what degree are collaborating parties "empowered" to make and act on their decisions?

- To what degree is decision making aligned with expertise versus with position?

- To what degree do collaborating parties have the relevant information with which to make decisions?

- To what degree do collaborating parties feel they need to "check with their bosses" or other stakeholders?

- To what degree is this appropriate consultation versus lack of authority?

- Overall, how well do you believe you and your collaborators practice this principle?

  Very Poorly   1   2   3   4   5   Very Well

- What kind of impact do you believe you can affect in your organization by working on this principle?

  Very Little   1   2   3   4   5   Very Great

Exhibit 7.1. Collaboration Diagnostic Tool, Cont'd

9. Treat Collaboration as a Disciplined Process

There are deliberate, established practices that will make collaboration more effective. There is a need to identify these practices and reinforce them.

- To what degree do people view collaboration as a process versus a social interaction?

- What are the specific actions and procedures that define collaboration as a process?

- Is there a disciplined process for identifying key stakeholders and soliciting their input?

- Is there a disciplined process for defining goals and objectives and the decision-making authority the collaborating parties have?

- Is there a process for defining how decisions will be made?

- Does that process support collaboration? Does that process make it explicit who should be consulted and who has final authority for different decisions?

- To what degree is a process defined for when agreement cannot be reached among the collaborating parties?

Exhibit 7.1. Collaboration Diagnostic Tool, Cont'd

- To what degree is any escalation process over-used or under-used?

- Overall, how well do you believe you and your collaborators practice this principle?

  Very Poorly   1   2   3   4   5   Very Well

- What kind of impact do you believe you can affect in your organization by working on this principle?

  Very Little   1   2   3   4   5   Very Great

10. Design and Promote Flexible Organizations

Collaborating groups must be fluid and flexible. Different parties join the collaboration at different times. Leaders must continually adapt the design of their organization and the collaborating groups to reflect this.

- To what degree are new parties added to the collaborating group as their expertise/experience is needed?

- To what degree do parties drop off as they fulfill their purpose?

- Is there a right level of continuity of members throughout the process?

- To what degree does power and decision making shift during the course of the activity? To what degree does it shift to the parties who have the expertise/experience most relevant for the current activities?

Exhibit 7.1. Collaboration Diagnostic Tool, Cont'd

- To what degree does the organization's design shift to reflect changing priorities or market demands?

- Overall, how well do you believe you and your collaborators practice this principle?

  Very Poorly   1   2   3   4   5   Very Well

- What kind of impact do you believe you can affect in your organization by working on this principle?

  Very Little   1   2   3   4   5   Very Great

Strategies for Moving Forward

The results from the Collaboration Diagnostic Tool will provide you with a snapshot of the collaborative capability of your organization. You will need to determine which areas will produce the "most bang for the buck" and then pursue those. Listed below are some strategies for increasing the collaborative capability in each of the principles. Use these ideas for actions you can take, but please recognize that this is not an exhaustive. Other strategies and actions that may be more appropriate to your particular circumstances and business needs.

Principle 1.
Focus Collaboration on Achieving Business Results

Effective collaboration is focused on some sort of business outcome. The group's output must be clearly aligned with the organization's higher level goals. Collaboration for collaboration's sake is not the objective, regardless of how desirable it may be as a social goal, and must involve a specific organizational purpose.

Strategies

- Fully articulate the business goals for each major project or work group; track and publish information frequently about progress toward those goals;

- Stage periodic question-and-answer periods with senior managers; expose members at all levels of the organization to detailed information about the business and its status;

- Bring customers and customer representatives in to talk to project teams, work groups, and larger units of the organization; and

- Ensure that business results issues are raised in all progress review sessions.

Principle 2.
Align Organizational Support Systems to Promote Ownership

The organization's support systems (leadership, information and communication, performance management, learning, and organization and design) must be aligned to support collaboration and commitment.

Strategies

- Redesign reward systems to provide incentives at all the levels (individual, team, project, and so on) at which you expect performance;

- Base rewards on collaborative performance as well as individual contribution (See Table 7.1 for examples of incentives for collaborative organizations);

- Move as much of the performance management as possible to within teams and work groups; then manage the performance of those teams and work groups by tracking objective achievement;

- Encourage members to collect feedback from team members and/or key customers and provide that data to those responsible for evaluating performance;

- Provide as much information as possible to as many members as possible in as many modes as possible, thus eliminating the "need-to-know" mentality;

Table 7.1. Examples of Incentives

	Financial				Other				
	Salary Increase	Targeted Bonus	401k Matching	Training	Books	Software	Pens Shirts, Hats, etc., with the Company Logo	Parties & Celebrations	Meetings w/Senior Managers
Individual	X	X		X					X
Team		X		X	X	X	X	X	X
Project		X		X	X	X	X	X	X
Organization		X	X	X	X		X	X	X

- Connect all members electronically and allow them to share common databases and language; establish similar connections with key customers and vendors;

- Establish training and development processes to learn collaborative skills; and

- Establish "communities of practice" to promote information sharing and creation of collaborative knowledge.

Principle 3.
Articulate and Enforce "a Few Strict Rules"

Member of collaborative organizations understand and apply the "few strict rules" or strategic principles and practices of their organization.

Strategies

- Articulate the strategy, assumptions, and expectations for the organization and for individual projects and work groups;

- Ensure that management is clear about what they see as the "few strict rules" (Some good opening discussion questions are: "Aside from anything that is clearly illegal or would put us in legal jeopardy, what should you be fired for?" "What about your boss or subordinates?" This discussion helps managers articulate what they really believe is important for organizational success.); and

- Designate clear escalation paths for complex or difficult decisions.

Principle 4.
Exploit the Rhythm of Convergence and Divergence

This principle acknowledges that collaboration requires both divergent (creative and expansive) and convergent (narrowing, focusing) processes. Conscious attention to the management of these processes is critical.

Strategies

- Provide adequate time and emphasis on the creative, generative processes;
- Establish hard deadlines for each stage of the project or work group objective to encourage convergence;
- Use both formal and informal review sessions to question process and help groups or teams probe for information or perspectives missed;
- For complex projects and work group assignments, provide training in and the use of problem-solving approaches and project management;
- Require adherence to project management principles; and
- Establish clear escalation paths, ensuring that any team (or project) can get help for any decision on which they are "stuck."

Principle 5.
Manage Complex Tradeoffs on a Timely Basis

Effective collaboration requires that different parties come together to balance competing objectives when making decisions (for instance, balancing technical sophistication with cost) and do so continually and expeditiously.

Strategies

- Design teams that include members knowledgeable about the most critical tradeoff criteria, then document and train on criteria in other relevant areas;
- Provide easy access to experts who can help explain tradeoff criteria and issues for teams or projects, then ensure that members understand both what the criteria are and why they exist;
- Use senior technology or business people or functional heads to articulate and communicate tradeoff criteria;
- Use progress reviews or informal meetings to ask about what members and teams see as key tradeoffs;
- Require summaries of tradeoff decisions and discussions in minutes, oral reports, and documents submitted for approval; and
- List, celebrate, and distribute best practices regarding tradeoff decisions.

Principle 6.
Create Higher Standards for Discussions, Dialogue, and Information Sharing

This principle emphasizes the need to continue to raise the standards for discussion at all levels of the organization. It reflects the need to actively create systems that broadly distribute information and knowledge and encompass members to expand their level of understanding of complex issues.

Strategies

- Mix experienced and new people on teams;
- Provide and demand use of information regarding relevant emerging technologies, work of related teams, competitive pressures, and so forth;
- Use reviews and intervene directly with questions that raise the bar;
- Train team members in facilitation and dialogue skills;
- Focus people on identifying key assumptions in their discussions; and
- Select and train managers to ensure that they are skilled "questioners."

Principle 7.
Foster Personal Accountability

This principle emphasizes that effective collaboration requires individuals/ teams who self-initiate, deliver on commitments, and demonstrate personal leadership.

Strategies

- Make responsibilities clear;
- Create W3 charts (who is responsible for doing what, by when) in meetings, and then review them at the next meeting;
- When tasks are not completed on time, ask what the person needs to finish the task. If possible, leave responsibility with the member or team to whom it was originally assigned, that is, don't reward failure to complete a task;

- Create opportunities for members and teams to experience interdependence;

- Make sure that teams and members live with the consequences of their own decisions (see Principle 8); and

- Clarify the rules around escalating issues and decisions and then if a team escalates what seems to be a routine issue, try to find out why.

Principle 8.
Align Authority, Information, and Decision Making

Collaboration requires a redistribution of power and decision making. This requires providing the appropriate information to enable collaborating parties to make the proper decisions.

Strategies

- Reexamine the project and organization design to determine whether enough coordination mechanisms exist and whether they are working as planned;

- Make sure everyone who serves on a team as a representative of another team understands his or her role and responsibilities as a representative;

- Make sure the person responsible for another person's review understands the other person's responsibilities;

- Make sure everyone understands how critical coordination across teams is and work with the managers of the team members to ensure that the message is clear;

- Encourage teams to escalate decisions they do not think they have the authority or information to make;

- Reward members and teams who confront management and other teams when they are not consulted on decisions they have to implement; and

- Encourage and assist managers in explaining the rationale for overturning team decisions.

Principle 9.
Treat Collaboration as a Disciplined Process

Deliberate, established practices makes collaboration effective. There is a need to identify these practices and reinforce them.

Strategies

- Hold a "best practices" competition around collaborative processes, then reward the winners and distribute the results to all members;

- Provide electronic forms for all common collaboration tasks: agendas, minutes, common tradeoff discussion, and so forth;

- Hire or use company-provided facilitators to work with teams and then help define common collaboration tools;

- Develop recommended "best practices" for use with all technology-assisted collaboration tools (conference calls, Net meetings, videoconferences);

- Model disciplined collaborative processes in senior level meetings and invite representatives of lower level teams to sit in on these meetings; and

- Make designing and training others on systematic decision-making processes a responsibility of specific functional groups or teams.

Principle 10.
Design and Promote Flexible Organizations

Effective collaboration requires individuals and groups that are fluid and flexible. Different parties will join the collaboration at different times. Leaders must continually adapt the design of their organization and the collaborating groups to reflect this.

Strategies

- Expect teams and team members to get more involved in deciding when and with whom to collaborate;

- Explain the complexity of the work to the members who are doing it, including why it's important for them to be continually identifying who they need to collaborate with about what;

- Recognize and reward members when they take the initiative correctly;

- Stop formally reorganizing for at least a year and spend the energy on building new and better networks within and outside the organization; allow these networks to evolve and grow, adapting to the needs of the business;

- Make sure managers know they will be rewarded on how much responsibility they have successfully "pushed down";

- Ask the following questions of managers and team members:

  "What new relationships have you built this year?"

  "What self-organizing skills have members of your organization developed?"

  "How have you helped other organizations or teams understand when and how they should work with you?"

- Make sure managers understand that it is their responsibility to collaborate with each other, with members in any part of the organization, and with external stakeholders.

Table 7.2 is a summary of the work necessary for helping to build a collaborative organization. Each principle is followed by summary strategies designed to improve the organization's performance in that principle. The final column provides a means to evaluate the importance of making the improvement in your particular organization.

Table 7.2. Improvement Strategies for Collaborative Organizations

Principle	Improvement Strategies	Priority
1. Focus Collaboration on Achieving Business Results	Fully articulate the business goals for each major project or work group objective; track and publish frequently information about progress toward those goals.	H M L
	Stage periodic question-and-answer periods with senior managers; expose members at all levels of the organization to detailed information about the business and its status.	H M L
	Bring customers and customers representatives in to talk to project teams, work groups, or larger units of the organization.	H M L
	Ensure that business results issues are raised in all progress review session.	H M L

Table 7.2. **Improvement Strategies for Collaborative Organizations, Cont'd**

Principle	Improvement Strategies	Priority
2. Align Organizational Support Systems to Promote Ownership	Redesign reward systems to provide incentives to reward performance and to create a sense of ownership. Base rewards on collaborative performance as well as on individual contribution.	H M L
	Move as much of the performance management as possible to within teams and work groups. Manage the performance of those teams and work groups through tracking objective achievement.	H M L
	Encourage members to collect feedback from team members and/or key customers and provide that data to the business manager. When the system works correctly, decisions as to rating, ranking status, and salary increases are data-based, collaborative decisions.	H M L
	Provide as much information as possible to as many members as possible in as many modes as possible. Eliminate the "need-to-know" mentality.	H M L
	Connect all members electronically and allow them to share common databases and language. Establish similar connections with key customers and vendors.	H M L
	Establish training and development processes to develop collaborative skills.	H M L
	Establish "communities of practice" to promote information sharing and collaborative knowledge creation.	H M L
3. Articulate and Enforce "a Few Strict Rules"	Articulate the strategy, assumptions, and expectations for the organization, for works groups, and for individual projects.	H M L
	Ensure that management is clear about what they see as the "few strict rules."	H M L
	Identify those changes that you know need to happen on a regular basis.	H M L
	Design teams and work groups with a mix of experienced and new people, making sure members know they are expected to exploit the advantages of each group.	H M L
	Designate clear escalation paths for all rules sets.	H M L
4. Exploit the Rhythm of Convergence and Divergence	Establish adequate time and emphasis on the creative, generative processes.	H M L
	Establish hard deadlines for each stage of the project or work group objective to encourage convergence.	H M L
	Use both formal and informal review sessions to question processes and help teams probe for information or perspectives missed.	H M L

Table 7.2. Improvement Strategies for Collaborative Organizations, Cont'd

Principle	Improvement Strategies	Priority
	For complex projects and work group assignments, provide training in and require the use of problem-solving tools and project management.	H M L
	For all projects, require adherence to project management principles.	H M L
	Establish clear escalation paths, ensuring that any team (or project) can obtain help on any decision on which they are "stuck."	H M L
5. Manage Complex Tradeoffs on a Timely Basis	Design teams to include members knowledgeable about the most critical tradeoff criteria. Document and train on criteria in other areas.	H M L
	Provide easy access to experts who can help explain tradeoff criteria and issues for teams. Ensure that members understand both why the criteria exist and what they are.	H M L
	Use senior technology or business people or functional heads to articulate and communicate tradeoffs.	H M L
	Use progress reviews or informal meetings to ask about what members and teams see as key tradeoffs. Require summaries of tradeoff deliberations and discussions in minutes, oral reports, and documents submitted for approval.	H M L
	List, celebrate, and distribute best practices regarding tradeoff discussions.	H M L
6. Create Higher Standards for Discussion, Dialogue, and Information Sharing	Mix experienced and new people on teams.	H M L
	Provide and demand use of information regarding relevant emerging technologies, work of related teams, competitive pressures, and so forth.	H M L
	Use reviews/intervene directly with questions that raise the bar.	H M L
	Train team members in facilitation and dialogue skills.	H M L
	Focus people on identifying key assumptions in their discussions.	H M L
	Select and train managers to ensure that they are skilled questioners.	H M L
7. Foster Personal Accountability	Make responsibilities clear. Create W3 charts (Who is responsible for doing what, by when) in meetings, and then review them at the next meeting. When tasks are not completed on time, ask what the person needs to get the task done.	H M L
	If possible, leave a responsibility with the member or team to whom it was originally assigned. Do not reward failure to complete a task.	H M L

Table 7.2. Improvement Strategies for Collaborative Organizations, Cont'd

Principle	Improvement Strategies	Priority
	Create opportunities for members and teams to experience interdependence.	H M L
	Try to make sure that teams and members live with the consequences of their own decisions.	H M L
	Clarify the rules around escalating issues and decisions. If a team escalates what seems to be a routine issue, find out why.	H M L
8. Align Authority, Information, and Decision Making	Reexamine the project, team or organization design. Determine whether enough coordination mechanisms exist and whether they are working as planned.	H M L
	Make sure everyone who serves on a team as a representative of another team understands his or her role and responsibilities. Make sure the person responsible for that person's review also understands that responsibility.	H M L
	Make sure everyone understands how critical coordination across teams is. Work with the managers of the team members to ensure that the message is clear.	H M L
	Encourage teams to escalate decisions they don't think they have the authority or information to make.	H M L
	Reward members and teams who confront management and other teams when they are not consulted on decisions they have to implement.	H M L
	Encourage and assist managers in explaining the rationale for overturning team decisions.	H M L
9. Treat Collaboration as a Disciplined Process	Hold a "best practices" competition around collaborative processes. Reward and distribute the results to all project members.	H M L
	Provide electronic forms for all common collaborative tasks: agendas, minutes, common tradeoff discussion, and so on.	H M L
	Hire or use company facilitators to work with teams and then help define common collaboration tools.	H M L
	Develop recommended "best practices" for use with all technology-assisted collaboration tools (conference calls, Net meeting, video conferences).	H M L
	Model disciplined collaborative processes in senior level meetings. Invite representatives of lower level teams to sit in on these meetings.	H M L
	Make designing and training systematic decision-making processes a responsibility of specific functional groups or teams.	H M L

Table 7.2. Improvement Strategies for Collaborative Organizations, Cont'd

Principle	Improvement Strategies	Priority
10. Design and Promote Flexible Organizations	Expect more decision making from teams and team members.	H M L
	Explain the complexity of the work they are doing, why it's important for them to be continually identifying and acting on, and who they need to collaborate with about what. Recognize and reward them when they take the initiative correctly.	H M L
	Stop formally reorganizing for at least a year. Spend the energy on building new and better networks within and outside the organization.	H M L
	Make sure managers know they will be rewarded on how much responsibility they have successfully "pushed down" the organization. Ask: "What new relationships have you built this year?" "What self-organizing skills have members of your organization developed?" "How have you helped other organizations or teams understand when and how they should work with you."	H M L
	Make sure that the managers understand that it is their responsibility to discover and act on the need to collaborate with one another, with members in any part of the organization, and with external stakeholders.	H M L

Conclusion

The exercise of working through the questions in Exhibit 7.1 and the strategies in Table 7.2 with the right people will generate a useful initial picture of the strengths and developmental needs of your organization. Acting on that understanding requires remembering the goals that you wish to achieve.

Development of collaborative practices can be treated as a major initiative by itself; also, it can complement the other initiatives and processes already underway in the organization. For example, better information flow due to improved collaboration benefits a number of work processes. TQM or BPR or lean manufacturing works better when it is done with collaboration as a key facet. Effective collaboration is a foundation for making other things work better—you still need the other things, but the payoff from them increases with collaboration.

Expanding the Boundaries

Collaboration must occur outside the organization as well as inside. Executives must focus on a number of macro level relationships. For example, when Texas Instruments and Hitachi created the new Twinstar computer chip plant, collaboration was built into seven levels of relationships, ranging from members in teams to the relationship between the plant and the community. Rosabeth Moss Kanter wrote about community context and community concern when she said, "For small companies that can meet world standards, innovate ahead of their customer, and offer production flexibility, there are enormous advantages. And cities that contain a higher proportion of such suppliers are better positioned to attract and keep good jobs. Communities have a stake in encouraging local suppliers to think globally" (Hodgetts, 1995, p. 61).

Outside relationships concern all industries. The health of all sectors is intimately intertwined, each is the customer and supplier of the others. For example, Quinn (1983, p. 3) wrote that "about half of the benefit from manufacturing R&D accrues to the services sector. Conversely, lower-cost, higher-quality U.S. banking, utility, transportation, communication, and software services help lower U.S. manufacturers' costs in international competition." The ability to collaborate provides advantages in all arenas.

Leaders and change experts must pay attention to a whole range of collaborative levels in order to develop and sustain the relationships that create collaborative organizations. These organizations represent a new opportunity for achieving business excellence in a challenging environment.

REFERENCES

Anderson, G. (2001, July). John Chambers, after the deluge. *Fast Company.*

Ante, S. (2001, August 27). Simultaneous software. *Business Week,* pp. 46–47.

Argyris, C. (1989). Strategy implementation: An experience in learning. *Organizational Dynamics, 18*(2), 5–15.

Baskin, K. (2001, May 23). *What your body would tell you if it could talk.* Keynote presentation. Collaborative Work Systems Symposium, University of North Texas, Denton, Texas.

Beyerlein, M.M. (Ed.). (2000). *Work teams: Past, present and future.* Amsterdam: Kluwer Academic Publishers.

Brown, S.L., & Eisenhardt, K.M. (1998). *Competing on the edge: Strategy as structured chaos.* Boston, MA: Harvard Business School Press.

Cairncross, F. (1997). *The death of distance.* Boston, MA: Harvard Business School Press.

Chemical Processing. (1990, August). Self-managed work CWS increase plant productivity.

Child, J., & McGrath, R.G. (2001). Organizations unfettered: Organizational form in an information-intensive economy. *Academy of Management Journal, 44*(6), 1135–1149.

Clemmer, J. (1992). *Firing on all cylinders: The service/quality system for high-powered corporate performance.* New York: Irwin/McGraw-Hill.

Davies, S., & Meyer, C. (1998). *Blur: The speed of change in the connected economy.* Reading, MA: Addison-Wesley.

Day, N. (1998). Informal learning gets results. *Workforce, 77*(6), 30–35.

Delpizzo, L. (1999). Transforming the business before the technology. *Behavioral Health Management, 19*(2), 35–37.

Dyck, R., & Halpern, N. (September/October, 1999). CWS-based organization redesign at Celestia. *Journal for Quality and Participation.*

Edmondson, A., Bohmer, R., & Pisano, G. (2001) Speeding up team learning. *Harvard Business Review, 79*(9), 125–134.

Emery, M. (1993). *Participative design for participative democracy.* Canberra, Australia: Australian National University.

Emery, F.E., & Trist, E.L. (1969). Sociotechnical systems. In F.E. Emery (Ed.), *Systems thinking.* New York: Penguin.

Fisher, K. (1999). *Leading self-directed work teams.* New York: McGraw-Hill.

Fisher, K., & Fisher, M. (1998). *The distributed mind.* New York: AMACOM.

Ford, M.W. (2001, July). Baldrige assessment and organizational learning: The need for change management. *Quality Management Journal, 8*(3).

Foster, R. (1986). *Innovation: The attacker's advantage.* New York: Summit Books.

Galbraith, J.R. (1994). *Competing with flexible lateral organizations: Strategy as structured chaos.* Reading, MA: Addison-Wesley.

Galbraith, J.R. (2000). *Designing the global organization.* San Francisco: Jossey-Bass.

Goldberg, M. (1998, February). Cisco's most important meal of the day. *Fast Company.*

Goold, M., & Campbell, A. (2002). Do you have a well-designed organization? *Harvard Business Review, 80*(3), 117–124.

Gray, C.E., & Larson, E.W. (2000). *Project management: The managerial process.* New York: Irwin/McGraw-Hill.

Greco, M.C. (1950) *Group life.* New York: Philosophical Library.

Hackman, J.R., & Oldman, G.R. (1980). *Work redesign.* Reading, MA: Addison-Wesley.

Haeckel, S.H. (1999). *Adaptive enterprise. Creating and leading sense and respond organizations.* Boston, MA: Harvard Business School Press.

Hall, C. (1998). *Organizational support systems for team-based organizations: Employee collaboration through organizational structures.* Unpublished paper. Denton, TX: University of North Texas.

Hall, C.A., & Beyerlein, M.M. (2000). Support systems for teams: A taxonomy. In M. Beyerlein, D. Johnson, & S. Beyerlein (Eds.), *Advances in interdisciplinary studies of work teams: New product development teams.* Greenwich, CT: JAI Press.

Hammer, M. (2002). Process management and the future of six sigma. *Sloan Management Review, 43*(2), 26–33.

Hodgetts, R.M. (1995). A conversation with Rosabeth Moss Kanter. *Organizational Dynamics, 24*(1), 56-70.

Hoerr, J., Polluck, M.A., & Whitestone, D.E. (1986, September 29). Management discovers the human side of automation. *Business Week.*

Holman, P., & Devane, T. (1999). *The change handbook: Group methods for shaping the future.* San Francisco: Berrett-Koehler.

Isaccs, W.N. (1993). Taking flight: Dialogue, collective thinking and organizational learning. *Organizational Dynamics, 22*(2), 88–115.

Katz, D., & Kahn, R.L. (1978). *The social psychology of organizations.* New York: John Wiley & Sons.

Katzenbach, J.R., & Smith, D.K. (2001). *The discipline of teams: A mindbook-workbook for delivering small group performance.* New York: John Wiley & Sons.

Keil, M., & Mixon, R. (1994/1995). Understanding runaway information technology projects: Results from an international research program based on escalation theory. *Journal of Management Information Systems, 11*(3), 65–86.

Kennedy, F. (2001, September). *Designing effective support systems.* Presentation at the 12th Annual International Conference of Work Teams, Dallas, Texas.

Kennedy, F. (2001, September). *ROI financial measurement.* Presentation at the 12th Annual International Conference of Work Teams, Dallas, Texas.

Kerr, S. (1975). On the folly of rewarding A, while hoping for B. *Academy of Management Journal, 18,* 769–783.

Kets De Vries, M.F.R., & Balazs, K. (1999). Creating the 'authentizotic' organization. *Administration & Society, 31*(2), 275–295.

Klein, J.A. (1991). A reexamination of autonomy in light of new manufacturing practices. *Human Relations, 44,* 21–38.

Kravetz, D. (1988). *The human resources revolution: Implementing progressive management practices for bottom line success.* San Francisco: Jossey-Bass.

LaBarre, P. (1996, June). This organization is dis-organization. *Fast Company,* (3), 77.

Lawler, A. (2000, March 29). NASA rethinking Mars plans. *Science Now, 3.*

Lawler, E.E., III. (1986). *High involvement management: Participative strategies for improving organizational performance.* San Francisco: Jossey-Bass.

Lawler, E.E. (1992). *The ultimate advantage: Creating the high-involvement organization.* San Francisco: Jossey-Bass.

Lawler, E.E., III, Mohrman, S.A., & Benson, G. (2001). *Organizing for high performance: Employee involvement, TQM, reengineering, and knowledge management in the Fortune 1000.* San Francisco: Jossey-Bass.

Lebensold, K. (1995). *Dialogue.* http://www.co-intelligence.org/P-dialogue.html

Lipnack, J., & Stamps, J. (2000). *Virtual teams.* New York: John Wiley & Sons.

Lurey, J.S. (1999). Five key strategies to improve your virtual teams. *International Conference for Advances in Management: Conference proceedings.*

Maccoby, M. (1999, September/October). Rethinking empowerment. *Research Technology Management, 42*(4).

Macy, B.A., & Izumi, H. (1993). Organizational change, design, and work innovation. *Research in Organizational Change and Development, 7,* 235–313.

Marks, M. (2002, February 15). Inside the No. 1 tech outsourcer. *Business Week Online.* www.businessweek.com/index.html.

Marsick, V., & Volpe, M. (1999). *Informal learning on the job: Advances in human resources.* San Francisco: Berrett-Koehler.

McKinney, R., Childress, R., & Phipps, S.(1991). Moving toward self-directed work teams in a service environment. *International Conference on Work Teams: Proceedings: Anniversary collection the best of 1990–1994.* Denton, TX: University of North Texas.

Miles, R., & Snow, C. (1994). *Fit, failure, and the hall of fame: How companies succeed or fail.* New York: The Free Press.

Mohrman, S.A., Cohen, S.G., & Mohrman, A.M., Jr. (1995). *Designing team-based organizations: New forms for knowledge work.* San Francisco: Jossey-Bass.

Mohrman, S.A., Tenkasi, R.V., & Mohrman, A.M., Jr. (2000). Learning and knowledge management in team-based new product development organizations. *Advances in interdisciplinary studies of work teams, Vol. 5: Product development teams.* Greenwich, CN: JAI Press.

Myers, I., & McCaully, M. (1998). *MBTI manual: A guide to the development and use of Myers-Briggs Type Indicator* (3rd ed.). Palo Alto, CA: Consulting Psychologists Press, Inc.

Ogdin, C.A. *Community defined: What we know.* (www.it-consultancy.com/extern/sws/community.html)

Pacanowsky, M. (1995, Winter). Team tools for wicked problems. *Organizational Dynamics, 23*(3), 36–52.

Packard, D. (1996). *The HP way: How Bill Hewlett and I built our company.* New York: HarperBusiness.

Pasmore, W.A. (1994). *Creating strategic change: Designing the flexible, high performing organization.* New York: John Wiley & Sons.

Peters, T. (1999). *Reinventing work: Service projects.* New York: Alfred A. Knopf.

Pinchot, G. (1985). *Intrapreneuring.* New York: Harper & Row.

Purser, R., & Cabana, S. (1998). *The self-managing organization: How leading companies are transforming the work of teams for real impact.* New York: The Free Press.

Purser, R., & Pasmore, W.A. (1992). Organizing for learning. In W.A. Pasmore & R.W. Woodman (Eds.), *Research in organizational change and development.* Greenwich, CT: JAI Press.

Quinn, J.B. (1983). U.S. industrial strategy: What directions should it take? *Sloan Management Review, 24*(4), 3–22.

Reynolds, M. (1967). *The soul book.* www.sisterschoice.com/soul.html.

Rhea, J. (2000). In the wake of Mars failures, should NASA still pursue, faster, better, cheaper? *Military & Aerospace Electronics, 11*(1), 8.

Richards, T., Eddy, J., & Cabrales, E. (1991). Self-managed teams in software engineering. *International Conference on Work Teams Proceedings: Anniversary collection the best of 1990–1994.* Denton, TX: University of North Texas.

Robbins, H., & Finley, M. (1995). *Why teams don't work: What went wrong and how to make it right.* Princeton, NJ: Petersons/Pacesetter Books.

Ruggles, W.S. (1997, October). President's report. *PM Network,* p. 52.

Schein, E. (2002). The anxiety of learning. *Harvard Business Review, 80*(3), 100–108.

Stamps, D. (1998). Learning ecologies. *Training, 35*(7), 32–41.

Stata, R. (1994). *A conversation about conversations: Analog Devices CEO on building high performance organizations.* http://cqmextra.cqm.org/cqmjournal.nsf/reprints/rp06200

Tuckman, B.W. (1965). Development sequence in small groups. *Psychological Bulletin, 63,* 384–399.

Tudor, T.R., & Trumble, R.R. (1996). Work teams: Why do they often fail? S.A.M. *Advanced Management Journal, 61*(4), 31–41.

Wageman, R. (1997). Critical success factors for creating superb self-managing teams. *Organizational Dynamics, 26*(1), 49–61.

Wall Street Journal, December 26, 1996.

Wheelwright, S.C., & Clark, K.B. (1992). *Revolutionizing product development: Quantum leaps in speed, efficiency, and quality.* New York: The Free Press.

Zaleznick, A. (1992). Managers and leaders: Are they different? *Harvard Business Review, 70*(2), 126–136.

Zuboff, S. (1984). *In the age of the smart machine: The future of work and power.* New York: Basic Books.

M ICHAEL M. BEYERLEIN, PH.D., is director of the Center for the Study of Work Teams (www.workteams.unt.edu) and professor of industrial/organizational psychology at the University of North Texas. His research interests include all aspects of collaborative work systems, organization transformation, work stress, creativity/innovation, knowledge management and the learning organization, and complex adaptive systems. He has published in a number of research journals and has been a member of the editorial boards for *TEAM Magazine, Team Performance Management Journal,* and *Quality Management Journal.* Currently, he is senior editor of the JAI Press/Elsevier annual series of books, *Advances in Interdisciplinary Studies of Work Teams,* as well as this new series of books on collaborative work systems. In addition, he has been co-editor with Steve Jones on two ASTD case books about teams and edited a book on the global history of teams, *Work Teams: Past, Present and Future.* He has been involved in change projects at the Center for the Study of Work Teams with such companies as Boeing, Shell, NCH, Advanced Micro Devices, Westinghouse, and Xerox and with government agencies such as the Bureau of Veterans' Affairs, Defense

Contract Management Agency, the Environmental Protection Agency, and the City of Denton, Texas.

J AMES R. BARKER, PH.D., is director of research and professor of organizational theory and strategy in the Department of Management at the U.S. Air Force Academy. His research interests focus on the development and analysis of collaborative control practices in technological and knowledge-based organizations. His research projects include collaborations with scientists at the Los Alamos and Sandia National Laboratories and with scholars at the University of Melbourne and the University of Western Australia. Dr. Barker's work has appeared in a number of professional journals, including *Administrative Science Quarterly, Journal of Organizational and Occupational Psychology,* and *Communication Monographs.* His new book, *The Discipline of Teamwork,* is now available from Sage Publications. He won the 1993 Outstanding Publication in Organizational Behavior award from the Academy of Management and the 1999 *Administrative Science Quarterly* Scholarly Contribution Award for his research on self-managing teams. He has lectured on teamwork in organizations at many universities and organizations, including the Sloan School of Management at the Massachusetts Institute of Technology and the University of Western Australia. He served as associate editor of the *Western Journal of Communication* and on the editorial boards of *Administrative Science Quarterly, Journal of Organizational Change Management,* and *Management Communication Quarterly.*

S USAN TULL BEYERLEIN, PH.D., holds a B.A. in English from the University of Oregon, an M.S. in general psychology from Fort Hays State University, and a Ph.D. in organization theory and policy with a minor in education research from the University of North Texas, Denton. Since 1988, she has taught a variety of management courses as an adjunct faculty member at several universities in the Dallas metroplex, with a particular focus on strategic management at both the undergraduate and MBA levels. Dr. Beyerlein has served as a research scientist/project manager with the Center for the Study of Work Teams at the University of North Texas and has been a recipient of research grant awards from the Association for Quality and Participation, the National Science Foundation, and corporate donors. Since 1995, she has co-edited the Elsevier/JAI Imprint annual book series, entitled *Advances in Interdisciplinary Studies of Work Teams,* and during the same period has served as an *ad hoc* reviewer for *The Academy of Management Review.* She has published book reviews on contemporary business offerings in *Business and the Contemporary World*, and her work has also appeared in *Structural Equation Modeling: A Multidisciplinary Journal, Teams: The Magazine for High Performance Organizations* (UK), *Journal of Management Education, Empirical Studies of the Arts*, and *Multiple Linear Regression Viewpoints.* She is a member of the Academy of Management, Beta Gamma Sigma—the honor society for collegiate schools of business—and Phi Kappa Phi National Honor Society.

MICHAEL M. BEYERLEIN, PH.D., is director of the Center for the Study of Work Teams (www.workteams.unt.edu) and professor of industrial/organizational psychology at the University of North Texas. His research interests include all aspects of collaborative work systems, organization transformation, work stress, creativity/innovation, knowledge management and the learning organization, and complex adaptive systems. He has published in a number of research journals and has been a member of the editorial boards for *TEAM Magazine* and *Quality Management Journal.* Currently, he is senior editor of the JAI Press/Elsevier annual series of books, *Advances in Interdisciplinary Study of Work Teams.* He is also organizing the launch of a new series of books for Jossey-Bass/Pfeiffer on collaborative work systems. In addition, he has been co-editor with Steve Jones on two ASTD case books about teams and edited a book on the global history of teams, *Work Teams: Past, Present, and Future.* He has been involved in change projects at the Center for the Study of Work Teams with such companies as Boeing, Shell, NCH, Advanced Micro Devices, Westinghouse, and Xerox and with government agencies such

235

as Veterans Affairs, Defense Contract Management Agency, Environmental Protection Agency, and the City of Denton, Texas.

SUE FREEDMAN, PH.D., is founder of and president of Knowledge Work Associates (KWA). She has specialized in organizational change in the design and management of organizations and teams in technical environments. Dr. Freedman's work with new product development organizations began at Texas Instruments, where she led the effort to inform the introduction of self-organizing teams in that environment. Working with USC, she managed the coordination of the study and testing of the intervention strategies that ultimately led to *Designing Team-Based Organizations.* More recently, she has worked with Hitachi on the design and management of consulting teams.

Dr. Freedman recently completed "Changing Tires in the Middle of the Race," a primer for executives responsible for implementing major change. She is currently finalizing a tool assessing the organization's capacity to thrive in high velocity change environments.

Prior to founding KWA, Dr. Freedman served as manager of organizational effectiveness for Texas Instruments and as vice president of organizational development for a real estate investment trust.

CRAIG MCGEE, PH.D., has over twenty years' experience in organization design and change management, with extensive background in team-based organizations, process improvement, and organization transformation. He has designed and implemented collaborative work systems in a wide variety of organizations, including Exxon, Xerox, Sybase, and the Canadian Air Command. He works extensively in changing organizational cultures to support collaborative work systems. He has served as an internal consultant, line manager, and external consultant. He is president and past president of the Association for the Organization Design Forum.

LINDA MORAN, Ed.D., works for AchieveGlobal and has more than twenty years of experience in organizational performance improvement. She has extensive experience in multicultural organizational change; designing team-based organizations and measures; change management; work redesign; and executive coaching. She applies her knowledge in a wide range of industries and organizational levels.

Ms. Moran is the co-author of numerous articles and books, including *Self-Directed Work Teams: The New American Challenge* (1990); *Keeping Teams on Track: What to Do When the Going Gets Rough* (1996); *Self-Directed Work Teams: A Lot More Than Team Work* (3rd ed.; 1989). Most recently she co-authored *Self-Directed Work Teams: Mastering* the *Challenge* (2nd ed.; 2000). She is frequently quoted in *Quality Digest, Training, Training & Development,* and the *Journal of Quality and Participation* and has collaborated with AchieveGlobal on a number of essays.

Ms. Moran earned a B.S. degree from the Pennsylvania State University and a master's degree in organizational communication from the University of Maryland. She became certified in advanced organizational development through Columbia University in 1996 and received her doctorate in organizational leadership and adult education at Columbia University.

A

AAL Insurance, 130

Accountability. *See* Personal accountability

Aetna Health Plans (Dallas), 130, 131

Agilent, 159

Aid Association for Lutherans, 24

Aligning authority/information/decision making: Collaboration Diagnostic Tool used with, 208*e*; described, 46, 54*t*; importance of, 46–47; manufacturing collaboration and, 85–86; new product development collaboration and, 115–117; service setting collaboration and, 147–148; strategies for moving forward with, 217, 222*t*; virtual settings collaboration and, 183–184; when it's working/not working, 47–48

Aligning support system/promoting ownership: applied to manufacturing collaboration, 69–73; applied to new product development, 103–104, 106; applied to service setting collaboration, 135–142;

Collaboration Diagnostic Tool used with, 199*e*–202*e*; described, 36–37, 52*t*; importance of, 37; strategies for moving forward with, 212–214, 220*t*; virtual settings collaboration and, 169–174; when it's working/not working, 38–39

All-State Insurance, 130, 131

Analog Devices, 80, 83

Ante, S., 171, 187

Archimedes, 28

Argyris, C., 146

Asea Brown Boveri, 17

AT&T Baldrige report, 134

Authority: aligning decision making/information and, 46–48, 54*t*; manufacturing collaboration and, 85–86; new product development collaboration and, 115–117; service setting collaboration and, 147–148; strategies for aligning decision making/information and, 217, 222*t*; virtual settings collaboration and, 183–184

B

Balazs, K., 17
Baldrige National Quality Award (1992), 137
Baldrige National Quality Award (1998), 142
Baskin, K., 89
Baxter HealthCare Corporation, 24
Benson, G., 25, 27, 128, 134, 137
Beyerlein, M. M., 23
BHP, 180
Bohmer, R., 145
Borg-Warner Automative, 24
Boundaries: dispersed across temporal, 156–157; expanding collaboration, 224; specific organizational, 157
"Broad-banding" compensation, 71–72
Brown, A., 139
Brown, S. L., 73, 106
Build to order (BTO), 62–63
Burger King, 62
Business performance information, 134
Business results focus: applied to manufacturing collaboration, 68–69; applied to new product development, 101–103; Collaboration Diagnostic Tool used with, 198e–199e; described, 34–35, 52t; importance of, 35; service setting collaboration and, 134–135; strategies for moving forward with, 211–212, 219t; understanding meaning of, 68; virtual settings collaboration and, 167–169; when it's working/not working, 35–36

C

Cabana, S., 21
Cabrales, E., 130
Cairncross, F., 11
Campbell, A., 139
Carter Mining, 129
Case Logic, 176
Celestica, 27, 159
Child, J., 12
Childress, R., 130
Clark, K. B., 96, 97, 99
Clemmer, J., 135
Cohen, S. G., 23, 24, 41, 42, 48, 99, 108, 117
Collaboration: cross-functional, 66; decisions which undermine, 69; difficulties in achieving effective, 7; expanding boundaries of, 224; principles of effective, 7; scenario of the current reality, 1–7; teams and, 23–25; as transference of ownership, 139; treated as disciplined process, 48–50
"Collaboration creep," 133
Collaboration Diagnostic Tool: used with collaboration principles, 198e–211e; described, 197; how to use, 197–198
Collaboration as disciplined process: Collaboration Diagnostic Tool used with, 209e–210e; importance of, 48–49; manufacturing collaboration and, 86–88; new product development collaboration and, 117–118; service setting collaboration and, 148–149; strategies for moving forward with, 218, 222t; treating, 48, 54t; virtual settings collaboration and, 184–186; when it's working/not working, 49–50
Collaborative capacity, 15–17
Collaborative capital (CC), 21–23
Collaborative culture: characteristics of, 20; example of, 21; support systems nurturing, 140. *See also* Culture
Collaborative organization principles: aligning authority, information, decision making, 46–48; aligning support systems to promote ownership, 36–39; applied to manufacturing, 67, 92t–93t; applied to new product development, 101, 121t–125t; applied to service settings, 133, 151t–152t; applied to virtual settings, 166, 189t–191t; benefits of using the, 195–197; Collaboration Diagnostic Tool used with, 198e–211e; creating standards for discussions, dialogue, and information sharing, 43–44; designing/promoting flexible organizations, 50–52; exploiting convergence/divergence rhythm, 40–42; "a few strict rules," 39–40; focus on achieving business results, 34–36; fostering personal accountability, 45–46; listed, 34, 52t–55t; managing complex tradeoffs on timely basis, 42–43; strategies for implementing each, 211–223t; treating collaboration as disciplined process, 48–50. *See also specific principle*

Collaborative organizations: benefits reported by, 26–27; benefits to overall "bottom line" by, 27–28; using collaborative competencies, 14–15; community characteristics of, 29–30; competitive advantages of, 13–14; example of, 21; learning dialogue/knowledge sharing in, 29; levels of collaborative work systems in, 18–19*t*; leveraging the most out of, 28–29; long-term process of building, 33; overview of, 17–19; payoff from, 25–30; qualitative benefits of, 25–26
Collaborative work team practices, 16
Commission on the Skills of the American Workforce (1990), 137
Communication: creating higher standards for, 43–44, 54*t*; cyberspace, 172; manufacturing collaboration standards for, 80–83; new product development collaboration standards for, 115–117; service setting collaboration for, 145–146. *See also* Information/communications systems
Community characteristics, 29–30
Compensation: for aligning support systems to promote ownership, 213*t*; "broad-banding," 71–72; in NPD organizations, 105*t*; for personal accountability, 84–85
Competitive advantage: collaborative capacity as source of, 17; of collaborative organizations, 13–14
"Conference calls," 155
Convergence, 40. *See also* Divergence/ convergence rhythm
Conversation. *See* Standards for discussions/dialogue/information sharing
Core competences: assessing robust, 30–31; building, 31; which create capital, 30
Corning Glass, 24
Covey, S., 35–36, 57
Covisent, 187
Cross-functional collaboration, 66
Culture: collaborative, 20, 21; "HP Way," 74–75; Nordstrom's service, 142; support systems nurturing collaborative, 140; Texas Instruments, 74n.1, 113–114. *See also* Collaborative culture; "A few strict rules"

Customers: employee involvement and focus on, 128; flexible organizations's response to, 89–90; Nordstrom's service culture regarding, 142; "pause points" and, 134; segmentation of, 131; service setting collaboration focus around, 132; technical approach to working with, 137
CWS (collaborative work systems): basic values/structures/practices of ideal, 16; collaborative capacity of, 15–17; competitive advantage using, 13–14; TBOs as advanced form of, 23
Cyberspace communication, 172

D

Daimler-Chrysler AG, 62
Dana Corporation, 24
Day, N., 138
Decision making: aligning authority/ information and, 46–48, 54*t*; contribution of disciplined processes to good, 48; made with limited information, 82–83; manufacturing collaboration and, 85–86; new product information collaboration and, 115–117; service setting collaboration and, 147–148; strategies for aligning authority/information and, 217, 222*t*; virtual settings collaboration and, 183–184; which undermines collaborative practices, 69
Dell Computers, 62, 137
Delpizzo, L., 20
Devane, T., 88
Developing countries economies, 159
Dialogue: creating higher standards for, 43–44, 54*t*; manufacturing collaboration standards for, 80–83; new product development collaboration standards for, 115–117; service setting collaboration for, 145–146; strategies for creating higher standards for, 216, 221*t*; virtual settings collaboration standards for, 179–181
Dilbert cartoonstrip, 148
Discussions: creating higher standards for, 43–44, 54*t*; manufacturing collaboration standards for, 80–83; new product development collaboration standards for, 115–117; service setting collaboration

for, 145–146; strategies for creating higher standards for, 216, 221*t*; virtual settings collaboration standards for, 179–181

Dispersed across temporal boundaries concept, 156–157

Distributed across space concept, 156

Divergence/convergence rhythm: Collaboration Diagnostic Tool used with, 203*e*–204*e*; exploiting rhythm of, 40, 53*t*; importance of, 40–41; manufacturing collaboration and, 75–77; new product development collaboration and, 108–110; service setting collaboration and, 143–145; strategies for moving forward with, 214–215, 220*t*–221*t*; virtual settings collaboration and, 175–177; when it's working/not working, 41–42

Domicile home/lifestyle stores, 128, 139

Dyck, R., 27

E

Eastman Chemical, 64

Eddy, J., 130

Edmondson, A., 145

Eisenhardt, K. M., 73, 106

Emery, M., 66

Emery's Participative Design Workshop (PDW), 88–89

Employees: "broad-banding" compensation of, 71–72; customer focus and involvement by, 128; employment insecurity and, 100; information to fill vacuum created by, 81–82; "soft skills" focus by, 138. *See also* Managers; Personal accountability

Empowerment to lowest levels, 86

Enron, 64

Ernst and Young, 148

Exxon Chemicals, 129, 161

F

FedEX, 61

"A few strict rules": articulating/enforcing, 39, 53*t*; Collaboration Diagnostic Tool used with, 202*e*–203*e*; importance of, 39; manufacturing collaboration and, 73–75; new product development collabora-

tion and, 106–108; service setting collaboration and, 142–143; strategies for moving forward with, 214, 220*t*; virtual settings communications and, 174–175; when it's working/not working, 40. *See also* Culture

Finley, M., 129

Fisher, K., 24, 156

Fisher, M., 156

"Flaming" e-mails, 172

Flexible organizations: Collaboration Diagnostic Tool used with, 210*e*–211*e*; designing/promoting, 50–51, 55*t*; importance of, 51; manufacturing collaboration and, 88–90; new product development and, 118–120; service setting collaboration and, 149–150; strategies for moving forward with, 218–219, 223*t*; virtual settings collaboration and, 186–188; when it's working/not working, 51–52. *See also* Organizations

Ford Motors, 171

Fortune magazine, 137

"Front-back" organization, 165

G

Galbraith, J., 165

General Electric, 129

Glabraith, J. R., 51

Globalization, 61

Goold, M., 139

Governor's Golden State Quality Award (1994), 137

Granite Rock, 137

Gray, C. E., 98, 99

Greco, M. C., 128

Groupware technology, 160

H

Hackman, J. R., 128

Hall, C., 70, 72

Halliburton Energy Services Duncan Plant, 25

Halpern, N., 27

Hamel, G., 9

Hammer, M., 87

Hewlett-Packard, 74–75, 87, 156–157, 159

Hitachi, 224

Hodgetts, R. M., 224
Hoerr, J., 27
Holman, P., 88
Hong Kong, 159
Hope Is Not Method, 147–148
"HP Way" (Hewlett-Packard), 74–75

I

IBM, 180
IDS American Express, 130
Ill-defined situations, 31
Incentives: for aligning support systems to promote ownership, 213*t*; in NPD organizations, 105*t. See also* Compensation; Motivation
Information: aligning authority/decision making to, 46–48, 54*t*; business performance, 134; increasing rate of volume of, 131; manufacturing collaboration authority/decision making and, 85–86; NPD collaboration authority/decision making and, 115–117; opportunities for responsible acts and, 85; service setting collaboration authority/decision making and, 147–148; strategies for aligning decision making/authority and, 217, 222*t*; virtual settings collaboration authority/decision making and, 183–184
Information sharing: establishing high standards for, 43–44; manufacturing collaboration standards for, 80–83; new product development collaboration standards for, 115–117; new technology facilitating, 163; service setting collaboration for, 145–146; strategies for creating higher standards for, 216, 221*t*; virtual settings collaboration standards for, 179–181
Information/communications systems: manufacturing collaboration and, 71; new product development collaboration and, 103–104; promoting ownership through, 37, 38; service setting collaboration and, 136–137; virtual settings collaboration and, 171
Intellectual capital (IC), 21–23
Isaccs, W. N., 145
Izumi, H., 28

J

Japanese manufacturing industries, 61
Jazz metaphor, 76
Johnsonville Sausage, 17

K

Kaizen, 87
Kanter, R. M., 57
Keil, M., 66
Kennedy, F., 22, 137
Kets De Vries, M.F.R., 17
Kimberly-Clark, 129
Klein, J. A., 129
Knowledge sharing, 29
Korea, 159
Kravetz, D., 27

L

LaBarre, P., 21
Larson, E. W., 98, 99
Lawler, E. E., III, 25, 27, 35, 128, 134, 136, 137
Leadership systems: effective, 140; manufacturing collaboration and, 64, 70–71; new product development collaboration and, 103; promoting ownership through, 36, 37–38; service setting collaboration and, 135; virtual settings collaboration and, 169–170. *See also* Managers
Learning dialogue, 29
Learning systems: manufacturing collaboration and, 72; new product development collaboration and, 104; promoting ownership through, 37, 38; service setting collaboration and, 137–139; virtual settings collaboration and, 172
Lipnack, J., 156, 162
Lockheed Martin's Government Electronic Systems, 21
Los Alamos National Bank, 142
Lurey, J. S., 156

M

McCutcheon, S., 139
McGrath, R. G., 12
McKinney, R., 130
Macy, B., 28
Malaysia, 159

Malcolm Baldrige National Quality Award (1992), 137

Malcolm Baldrige National Quality Award (1998), 142

Managers: barrier removal by, 85; limited niche/price skimming/elitist strategies adopted by, 64; manufacturing collaboration and implications for, 90–91; using metrics to integrate organization parts, 68; new product development collaboration and implications for, 120–121; service setting collaboration and implications for, 150–151; types of problems faced by, 31–32; virtual settings collaboration and implications for, 188. *See also* Employees; Leadership systems; Personal accountability

Manufacturing: definition of, 60; mass customization of, 62–63; more risk/less security of, 63

Manufacturing collaboration: aligning authority/information/decision making, 85–86; aligning organizational support systems to promote ownership, 69–73; articulating/enforcing "a few strict rules," 73–75; challenges of, 65–66; creating higher standards for discussions/dialogue/and information sharing, 80–83; designing/promoting flexible organizations, 88–90; exploiting rhythm of convergence/divergence, 75–77; focus on achieving business results, 68–69; fostering personal accountability, 83–85; guiding principles applied to, 67, 92*t*–93*t*; implications for executives, 90–91; managing complex tradeoffs on timely basis, 78–79; treated as disciplined process, 86–88

Manufacturing organizations: challenges with respect to collaboration, 65–66; changing workforce/new technologies and, 62; common ways of organizing, 64–65; globalization and, 61; leadership of, 64, 70–71; market economy/spread of democracy and, 62; new forms/structures of, 59–60; supply chain management of, 63; when to collaborate, 67. *See also* Organizations

Market economy: globalization and, 61; spread of democracy and, 62

Marketplace competition, 131

Marks, M., 60

Mars Deep Space Microprobes 2 mission (1999), 78

Marsick, V., 138

Mass customization, 62–63

Merrill Lynch Credit Corporation, 142

Metrics, 68

Meyers-Briggs Type Inventory, 162

Microsoft, 159, 163, 168

Miles, R., 59

Mixon, R., 66

Mohrman, A. M., Jr., 23, 24, 41, 42, 48, 99, 108, 117

Mohrman, S. A., 23, 24, 25, 27, 41, 42, 48, 80, 99, 108, 117, 128, 134, 137

Monologue, 80

Monsanto, 26

Motivation: achieving business results focus and, 35; for aligning support systems to promote ownership, 213*t*; using "broad-banding" compensation, 71–172; in NPD organizations, 105*t*

Motorola, 138

N

Nested cultures, 20

Net Meeting (Microsoft), 163

New product development collaboration: achieving business results focus of, 101–103; aligning authority/information/decision making and, 115–117; aligning organizational support systems promoting ownership, 103–104, 106; articulation/enforcement of a few strict rules, 106–108; challenges with respect to, 99–100; creating standards for discussions/dialogue/information sharing, 112–113; designing/promoting flexible organizations, 118–120; exploiting rhythm of convergence/divergence, 108–110; guiding principles applied to, 101, 121*t*–125*t*; implications for executives, 120–121; managing tradeoffs on timely basis, 110–112; personal accountability and, 113–115; treated as disciplined process, 117–118; when to pursue, 100–101

New product development (NPD): common ways of organizing, 98–99; definition of, 95–96; historical context of, 96–97; trends affecting, 97–98. *See also* Products

New product development (NPD) organizations: divergence/convergence management characteristics of, 109–110; incentives in, 105*t*

Nordstrom, 142

O

Ogdin, C. A., 29

Oldham, G. R., 128

Ongoing virtual collaboration organization, 161

"Organizational software," 20

Organization/design systems: manufacturing collaboration and, 72; new product development collaboration and, 104; promoting ownership through, 37, 38; service setting collaboration and, 139–140; virtual settings communication and, 173–174

Organizations: characteristics of divergence/convergence managing NPD, 109–110; collaborative capacity of, 15–17; using collaborative competencies within, 14–15; collaborative culture of, 20–21; CWS as solution to challenges of, 13–14; differentiation between community and, 29–30; examples of successful team utilization by, 24–25; "front-back," 165; incentives in NPD, 105*t*; new and increasing demands on, 11–13; new trends in alliances/networks of, 159; "pick two" mentality applied to teams by, 46–47; TBO (team-based organization), 14, 16–17, 23; wicked problems faced by, 31–32. *See also* Flexible organizations; Manufacturing organizations

Oticon, 21

Otis Elevator Company, 129

"Over the wall" method, 97

Ownership: aligning support system to promote, 36–39, 52*t*; transferred by effective collaboration, 139

P

Pacale, R., 9

Pacanowsky, M., 21, 31

Paper-processing businesses, 130

Pasmore, W. A., 48, 99, 100

"Pause points," 134

Performance management systems: manufacturing collaboration and, 71–72; new product development collaboration and, 104; promoting ownership through, 37, 38; service setting collaboration and, 135–136; virtual settings collaboration and, 170

Personal accountability: Collaboration Diagnostic Tool used with, 206*e*–207*e*; fostering, 45, 54*t*; importance of, 45; manufacturing collaboration and, 83–85; new product development collaboration and, 113–115; responsibility vs., 83–84; rewards for, 84–85; service setting collaboration and, 146–147; strategies for moving forward with, 216–217, 221*t*–222*t*; virtual settings collaboration and, 181–183; when it's working/not working, 45–46. *See also* Employees; Managers

Peters, T., 130, 148

Phipps, S., 130

"Pick two" mentality, 46–47

Pinchot, G., 21

Pisano, G., 145

Polluck, M. a., 27

Porter, M., 193

Position-centered thinking, 100

Pratt and Whitney, 27, 79

Procter & Gamble, 129, 171

Products: complexity of, 100; defining, 99; speed of developing, 99–100. *See also* New product development (NPD)

Prudential Insurance, 130

PSD (product-service discrepancy report), 137

Purser, R., 21, 99, 100

Q

Quaker Oats Company, 24

Quinn, J. B., 64, 224

R

Responsibility, 83–84
Responsibility matrix/accountability
    chart, 185
Reynolds, M., 80
Rhea, J., 78
Richards, T., 130
Ritz-Carlton, 147
Robbins, H., 129
Roos, J., 193

S

SAS, 130–131
Saturn, 24
Schein, E., 143
Semco of Brazil, 17
Sequa Chemmicals, 21
Service setting collaboration: achieving
    business results focus of, 134–135; align-
    ing authority/information/decision
    making, 147–148; aligning organiza-
    tional support systems promoting own-
    ership, 135–142; articulating/enforcing
    "a few strict rules" in, 142–143; chal-
    lenges of, 132–133; common ways of
    organizing, 131–132; creating standards
    for discussions/dialogue/information
    setting, 145–146; definition of, 127–128;
    designing/promoting flexible organiza-
    tions and, 149–150; exploiting rhythm
    of convergence/divergence, 143–145;
    fostering personal accountability and,
    146–147; guiding principles applied
    to, 133, 151*t*–152*t*; historical context of,
    128–131; implications for executives,
    150–151; managing tradeoffs on timely
    basis, 145; treating collaboration as dis-
    ciplined process, 148–149; when not to
    proceed with, 133
Shenandoah Life Insurance, 24, 26–27
Simple, linear situations, 31
Snow, C., 59
"Soft skills," 138
Southwest Airlines, 17
Stamps, D., 138, 162
Stamps, J., 156
Standards for discussions/dialogue/
    information sharing: Collaboration
    Diagnostic Tool used with, 205*e*–206*e*;

creating higher, 43, 54*t*; creating manu-
    facturing collaboration, 80–83; creating
    new product development collabora-
    tion, 112–113; creating service setting
    collaboration, 145–146; creating virtual
    settings collaboration, 179–181; impor-
    tance of, 44; strategies for moving for-
    ward with, 216, 221*t*; when it's working/
    not working, 44
Stata, R., 80, 83
Strict rules. *See* "A few strict rules"
Supply chain management, 63
Support systems: manufacturing collabo-
    ration and, 69–70; reengineering, 70.
    See also Aligning support system/
    promoting ownership
Sybase, 137, 156, 167–168, 186
Syncrude Canada's Mine Mobile Mainte-
    nance Division, 21

T

TBO (team-based organization): as
    advanced CWS system, 23; character-
    istics of, 16–17; described, 14
Team-based model, 99
Teams: aligning authority/information/
    decision making by, 85–86; collabora-
    tion and the role of, 23–25; comparison
    of three levels of collaborative, 19*t*;
    learning experiences of service, 137–139;
    MIT study on software engineering,
    130; "pick two" mentality applied to,
    46–47; TBO (team-based organization)
    type of, 14, 16–17, 23; vertical, 157. *See
    also* Work teams
Technology: bias toward problem solu-
    tions using, 66; groupware, 160; manu-
    facturing and new, 62; new product
    development and, 98; virtual settings
    collaboration and new, 154–155, 159–
    160, 163, 166; used to work with cus-
    tomers, 137
Teleconferencing, 155, 163–164
Tenkasi, R. V., 80
Texas Instruments (TI): collaboration
    between Hitachi and, 224; culture of,
    74n.1, 113–114; experiments run by,
    59–60; manager barrier removal at, 85
Texas Nameplate, 142

Top management group (TMG), 81

Tradeoff management: Collaboration Diagnostic Tool used with, 204e–205e; importance of, 42; manufacturing collaboration and, 78–79; new product development collaboration and, 110–112; service setting collaboration and, 145; strategies for moving forward with, 215, 221t; timely management of, 42, 53t; virtual settings collaboration and, 177–179; when it's working/not working, 43

Trist, E. L., 66

Trumble, R. R., 25

TRW Company, 24, 171

Tuckman, B. W., 164

Tudor, T. R., 25

U

United Technologies Corporations, 129

UPS, 61

V

Vertical teams, 157

Virtual settings collaboration: achieving business results focus of, 167–169; aligning support systems promoting ownership, 169–174; articulating/enforcing "a few strict rules," 174–175; challenges with respect to, 162–164; common ways of organizing, 160–162; creating standards for discussions/dialogue/information sharing, 179–181; definition of, 155–158; described, 153–154; designing/promoting flexible organizations and, 186–188; exploiting rhythm of convergence/divergence, 175–177; fostering personal accountability and, 181–183; guiding principles applied to, 166, 189t–191t; historical context of, 154–155; implications for executives, 188; managing tradeoffs on timely basis, 177–178; technology and, 154–155, 159–160, 163, 166; treated as disciplined process, 184–186; trends affecting, 158–160; when to proceed with, 164–166

Virtual Teams (Lipnack and Stamps), 162

Volpe, M., 138

W

Wageman, R., 72

"Whack a mole" (arcade game), 149

Wheelwright, S. C., 96, 97, 99

Whitestone, D. E., 27

"Who, What, and When Action Charts," 87

Whole Foods, 128

Wicked problems, 31–32

WIIFM? (What's in it for me?), 85

W.L. Gore & Associates, Inc., 15, 17, 21

Work teams: collaborative practices of, 16; as collaborative work system level, 18–19t. *See also* Teams

Workforce, manufacturing and changing, 62

X

Xerox, 77

Xerox Business Services, 142

Z

Zaleznick, A., 69

Zuboff, S., 130

Breinigsville, PA USA
09 January 2010
230486BV00003B/31/A